HENRY STEDMAN wrote the first edition Hadrian's Wall Path and has rewalked and updated most of the subsequent editions including this seventh. Born in Chatham, Kent, he has been writing guide-books for over a quarter of a century and is the author or co-author of over a dozen Trailblazer titles including *Kilimanjaro, Inca Trail, Coast to Coast Path, Dales Way, London LOOP* and all three books in the *South-West Coast Path* series. On most walks he's accompanied by Daisy. Two parts trouble to one part Parson's Jack Russell, Daisy has now completed a dozen national trails as well as the Coast to Coast Path and Dales Way.

When not travelling or writing, Henry lives in Battle, maintaining his Kilimanjaro web-site and arranging climbs on the mountain through his company, Kilimanjaro Experts.

Author

Hadrian's Wall Path First edition: 2006; this seventh edition: 2023

Publisher Trailblazer Publications
The Old Manse, Tower Rd, Hindhead, Surrey, GU26 6SU, UK
info@trailblazer-guides.com, ☏ trailblazer-guides.com

British Library Cataloguing in Publication Data
A catalogue record for this book is available from the British Library

ISBN 978-1-912716-37-1

© **Trailblazer** 2006, 2008, 2011, 2014, 2017, 2020, 2023: Text and maps

Editing & Layout: Nicky Slade   **Proofreading**: Jane Thomas
Cartography & illustrations pp83-4: Nick Hill   **Index**: Jane Thomas
Photographs (flora): C4 middle right © Henry Stedman, all others © Bryn Thomas
All other photographs: © Henry Stedman (unless otherwise indicated)

The maps in this guide were prepared from out-of-Crown-
copyright Ordnance Survey maps amended and updated by Trailblazer.

Acknowledgements

I'd like thank those who made my research trip for this edition so enjoyable, in particular
Ray Purvis, Louise Foster at Coombe Crag, Lee Picker and Colin, Bala, and Malcolm at
Winshields Campsite. Plus, of course, all those people who took the time to chat to me
along the way, to tell me of their experience of walking the Wall, whose names I never
caught, but who made the walk so enjoyable, and so memorable. A big thank you to all the
readers who sent in suggestions for this new edition, in particular Tom Anderson, Lisa
Bates, Jared Bond, Hilary Bradt, David Bromley, Faith Darch, Jonathan Davies, Anne
Devecchi, Keith Dunbar, Ken, Rich & Sophie Eames, Don Edmonson, Keith Frayn, Andy
Harper, John Hersey, George & Julie Home, Dr John Higgs, Sharon Higginson, Dave Hyde,
Anna Jacomb-Hood, Murielle Jousseau, John Kersey, Pete and Sarah Marsden, Pete Mason
and son, Connie Meng, Antonio Mora-Blanco, Steve Nagle, John Nichols, Unni Oberhofer,
Kornelie Oostlander-Vos, Liz Opalka, Allan Ricketts, Cathy Rooke, Michael Scarlatos,
Philip Scriver, Jason Smith, Ingrid Strobl, Ursula Studer, Juliet Tese, Rick and Mel Toyer,
David Twine and Murray Turner, Pam & Stephen Turner, Doug Whitehead, Trevor Wilson
and Dr Ulrich Wolfhard. And, of course, thanks, as ever, to all at Trailblazer: Nicky Slade for
editing, Jane Thomas for the index and proof-reading and Nick Hill for the maps.

A request

The author and publisher have tried to ensure that this guide is as accurate and up to date
as possible. Nevertheless, things change. If you notice any changes or omissions, please
write to Trailblazer (address above) or email us at ☏ info@trailblazer-guides.com. A free
copy of the next edition will be sent to persons making a significant contribution.

Warning: long-distance walking can be dangerous

Please read the notes on when to go (pp13-16) and outdoor safety (pp72-75). Every effort
has been made by the author and publisher to ensure that the information contained herein
is as accurate and up to date as possible. However, they are unable to accept responsibility
for any inconvenience, loss or injury sustained by anyone as a result of the advice and information given in this guide.

Updated information will be available on: ☏ **trailblazer-guides.com**

Photos – Front cover: On a wonderful section of so-called 'Clayton Wall' (rebuilt by 19th-
century archaeologist John Clayton) towards Housesteads. **This page**: The Wall east of
Walton Crags, some of the most complete on the entire trail. **Previous page**: Walking east
towards Crag Lough. **Overleaf**: Passing fields of dazzling oilseed rape near Halton Shields.

Printed in China; print production by D'Print (☏ +65-6581 3832), Singapore

Hadrian's Wall
PATH

**Large-scale maps (1:20,000) for the entire route
& detailed guides to 30 towns and villages**

PLANNING – PLACES TO STAY – PLACES TO EAT

HENRY STEDMAN

TRAILBLAZER PUBLICATIONS

INTRODUCTION

PART 1: PLANNING YOUR WALK

PART 2: HADRIAN'S WALL

PART 3: MINIMUM IMPACT WALKING & OUTDOOR SAFETY

Contents

Contents

ABOUT THIS BOOK

This guidebook contains all the information you need. The hard work has been done for you so you can plan your trip without having to consult numerous websites and other books and maps. When you're all packed and ready to go, there's comprehensive public transport information to get you to and from the trail and detailed maps (1:20,000) to help you find your way along it. This guide includes:

● All standards of accommodation with reviews of campsites, bunk-houses, hostels, B&Bs, guesthouses and hotels
● Walking companies if you want an organised tour and baggage-transfer services if you just want your luggage carried
● Itineraries for all levels of walkers
● Answers to all your questions: when to go, degree of difficulty, what to pack, and how much the whole walking holiday will cost
● Walking times in both directions and GPS waypoints
● Cafés, pubs, tearooms, takeaways, restaurants and food shops
● Rail, bus and taxi information for all places along the path
● Street plans of the main towns both on and off the Wall
● Historical, cultural and geographical background information

POST COVID NOTE

This edition of the guide was research after the Covid pandemic but is liable to more change than usual. Some of the hotels, cafés, pubs, restaurants and tourist attractions may not survive the further hardships caused by rising fuel prices and inflation. Do forgive us where your experience on the ground contradicts what is written in the book; please email us – info@trailblazer-guides.com so we can add your information to the updates page on the website.

❑ MINIMUM IMPACT FOR MAXIMUM INSIGHT

Man has suffered in his separation from the soil and from other living creatures ... and as yet he must still, for security, look long at some portion of the earth as it was before he tampered with it.

Gavin Maxwell, *Ring of Bright Water*, 1960

Why is walking in wild and solitary places so satisfying? Partly it is the sheer physical pleasure: sometimes pitting one's strength against the elements and the lie of the land. The beauty and wonder of the natural world and the fresh air restore our sense of proportion and the stresses and strains of everyday life slip away. Whatever the character of the countryside, walking in it benefits us mentally and physically, inducing a sense of well-being, an enrichment of life and an enhanced awareness of what lies around us.

All this the countryside gives us and the least we can do is to safeguard it by supporting rural economies, local businesses, and low-impact methods of farming and land-management, and by using environmentally sensitive forms of transport – walking being pre-eminent.

INTRODUCTION

Just when you think you are at the world's end, you see a smoke from East to West as far as the eye can turn, and then under it as far as the eye can stretch, houses and temples, shops and theatres, barracks and granaries, trickling along like dice behind – always behind – one long, low, rising and falling, and hiding and showing line of towers. And that is the Wall!

Rudyard Kipling, *Puck of Pook's Hill*

On 23 May 2003, Britain's 13th National Trail, the Hadrian's Wall Path, was opened in the border country between England and Scotland. The trail (84 miles/135km from end to end) follows the course of northern Europe's largest-surviving Roman monument, a 2nd-century fortification built on the orders of Emperor Hadrian in AD122. The Wall marked the northern limits of Hadrian's empire – an empire that stretched for 3000 miles across Europe and the Mediterranean all the way to the Euphrates.

The trail follows the course of northern Europe's largest surviving Roman monument

To say that creating such a path was problematic would be something of an understatement. This was the first National Trail to follow the course of a UNESCO World Heritage Site. As such, every

The trig point at Green Slack (see p147), at 345m, is the highest point on the path.

time a fencepost, signpost or way-mark was driven into the ground, an archaeologist had to be present to ensure that the integrity of the Wall was not in any way compromised. To give you an indication of just how careful they had to be, it took *ten years* before the Hadrian's Wall Path was finally opened to the public. By comparison, it took the 2nd and 6th legions of the Roman army only six years to build the actual Wall!

Since its opening many have walked the trail and all seem to agree that the difficulties involved in its creation were well worth it, allowing the walker to follow in the sandal-steps of those who built it with the trail itself rarely diverting from the course of the Romans' barrier by more than a few hundred metres. And, though there's only about ten miles of the Wall left and it hardly ever rises to more than half its original height, it – or at least the route it would have taken – makes for a fascinating hiking companion. Punctuated by forts, milecastles

The western end is at Bowness-on-Solway, a day's walk from Carlisle. A small shelter and a little garden mark the spot on Banks Promenade. A sign on one side of the shelter reads *Fortuna vobis adsit* for those just setting off and on the other side is a sign to welcome those who've just arrived from Wallsend.

and turrets spaced evenly along its length, the Wall snaked over moor and down dale through Northumberland and Cumbria, between the mouth of the Solway

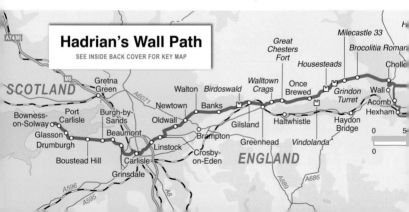

The eastern end is at Wallsend and Segedunum Roman Fort, in the suburbs of Newcastle. *Sentius Tectonicus* (**above**) is a commanding steel statue of a centurion by John O'Rourke.

River in the west and Roman fort of Segedunum (at the appropriately named Newcastle suburb of Wallsend) in the east. It's an incredible feat of engineering, best appreciated in the section from Housesteads to Cawfield Quarry where the landscape is so bleak and wild that human habitation and farming never really took a hold. It is here that the Wall stands most intact, following the bumps and hollows of the undulating countryside – as integral a part of the scenery now as the whinstone cliffs on which it is built. Here, too, are some of the best-preserved fortresses, from the vast archaeological trove at Vindolanda, set just off the Wall to the south, to the subtle charms at Birdoswald and the beautifully situated Housesteads itself.

After the Romans withdrew the Wall fell into disrepair. What we see as a unique and awe-inspiring work of military architecture was to the local landown-

ers a convenient source of ready-worked stones for their own building projects. The Wall is part of the fabric of many of the major constructions built after the Romans left: the churches, priories and abbeys that lie just off the Wall, such as those at Hexham and Lanercost; the Norman castles at Carlisle and Newcastle; the Military Road which you follow for part of the walk; the stronghouses at Thirlwall and Drumburgh – all beautiful, historically important buildings. And all of them incorporate stones from the Wall. Yet even in those places where its destruction was

❑ **Hadrian's Wall – the inspiration for a twenty-first century blockbuster!**

George RR Martin, the American author of the epic fantasy series, *A Song of Ice and Fire*, on which the all-conquering TV blockbuster *A Game of Thrones* is based, has acknowledged that Hadrian's Wall was the inspiration for the Wall in the book. He couldn't really deny it, for the similarities are clear. Indeed, the more one delves into his novels, the more you realise that Mr Martin, while a magnificent story teller, is also a bit of a historian too.

To give you a few examples of the similarities between the historical Hadrian's Wall and George's fictional version: the Wall in *A Song of Ice and Fire* stretches from coast to coast and is in the north of the country – just like Hadrian's Wall. The soldiers who man it are also drawn from all over the realm – just like the auxiliaries who manned the Wall for Hadrian, who came from Spain, Syria, Iraq, Belgium and the Netherlands. The soldiers who manned the fictional Wall took an oath that forbade them from marrying – just like those on Hadrian's Wall.

Even the design of the two walls is similar. Like Mr Martin's version, Hadrian's Wall is believed to have had a walkway running along the top for the soldiers' use; they also built milecastles and watchtowers (turrets), of which you'll see the remains of both on the trail. In the book, the Wall is actually falling into disrepair, and as you'll discover later in this book it wasn't long before Hadrian's Wall, too, began to be neglected, and some of the towers and milecastles were later used as shielings and even houses for the local farmers.

Of course, George's Wall is considerably larger than Hadrian's Wall. As anybody who has tried both methods will tell you, it's always so much easier building a fictional wall than a real one; indeed, you can pretty much invent whatever dimensions you want for your fictional Wall without having to worry about the cost, or whether it's actually feasible to build a wall so huge. And besides, the Wall in the novels was designed to protect the Kingdom of the North from zombie dragons and the Army of the Dead, whereas Hadrian's version only had a few 'wretched Britons' to deal with (not my description, you understand, but a translation of the word *Britunculli*, as found on one of the Vindolanda tablets – see p149).

George RR Martin has said that he visited the Wall prior to writing his novels, and I suppose there will be those who will accuse him of a lack of imagination for drawing so heavily on the history of Hadrian's Wall for his own novels. But as one who has visited the Wall many times now, and never (yet) managed to write an international bestseller and TV blockbuster based on what I have learnt whilst there, I think he still deserves a colossal amount of credit.

total, the Wall's legacy continues to echo through the ages in the names of the villages that lie along the route: Wallsend, Wallend, Wallhouses, Walton, Wall village and Oldwall are just some of the place names that celebrate the Wall. The past, it seems, is inseparable from the present.

Quite apart from the architectural and historical interest, all around the Wall is scenery of breathtaking beauty, from the serenity of Bowness-on-Solway, an Area of Outstanding Natural Beauty and a haven for birdwatchers and those seeking peaceful solitude, via the pastoral delights of Cumbria and the wild, wind-blasted moors of Northumberland, to the sophisticated cityscape of Newcastle. After all, what other national trail can boast that it passes through Paradise (a suburb of Newcastle), Eden (the river flowing through Carlisle) and the site of the Battle of Heavenfield (near Chollerford)?

You can see the impact the Wall has had on popular culture, too. Occasionally in the book you'll find quotes by such literary giants as WH Auden and Rudyard Kipling. And to bring it right up to today, it's hard to watch the blockbuster box set *A Game of Thrones* (see left) and *not* be struck by the similarities between the soldiers of the Night Watch keeping guard over a north-

Quite apart from the architectural and historical interest, all around the Wall is scenery of breathtaking beauty

ern Wall – soldiers who are described in the series as 'the only thing standing between the realm and what lies beyond' – and the Roman auxiliary legions who manned the Wall for Hadrian!

Yet perhaps the best feature of the Wall is that all its treasures are accessible to anyone with enough get-up-and-go to leave their armchair. The path itself is regarded as one of the easiest National Trails, a week-long romp on a grassy path through rolling countryside with the highest point, Green Slack, just 345m above sea level. The waymarking is clear and, with the Wall on one side and a road a little distance away on the other, it's very difficult to lose one's way. There are good facilities, from lively pubs to cosy B&Bs, friendly, well-equipped bunkhouses and idyllic little tearooms. And for those for whom completing the entire trail is over-ambitious, there are good transport connections, including a special Hadrian's Wall Country bus (the AD122). With a little planning, you can arrange a simple stroll along a short section of the trail, maybe take in a fort or museum on the way, then catch a bus back to 'civilisation'. While for those who prefer not to follow any officially recognised National Trail, the path also connects to 43 other walks, details of which are readily available from one of the tourist information offices serving the trail.

So, while the Wall no longer defines the border between Scotland and England (90% of Northumberland, an English county, lies to the north of the Wall, and at no point does the Wall actually coincide with the modern Anglo-Scottish border), it nevertheless remains an inspiring place and a monument to the breathtaking ambition of both Hadrian, the youthful dynamic emperor, and of Roman civilisation itself. And there can be few greater ways to appreciate it than by walking along this trail.

How difficult is the Hadrian's Wall Path?

The Hadrian's Wall Path is, for experienced hikers, just a long walk. Indeed, some rate this as possibly the easiest of the national trails in the UK. It only takes about a week to complete it, and for some no more than four days. Indeed, there's a guy called Elvis from Haltwhistle who completed it in one 30-hour stretch for charity.

> **The path itself is regarded as one of the easiest National Trails, a week-long romp on a grassy path through rolling countryside**

Age seems to be no barrier to completing the walk either. While updating the third edition of this book I walked with my friend, Peter Fenner, who was just a month shy of his 78th birthday. And while updating the fifth edition, Daniel McCrohan was joined by his whole family, including his six-year-old daughter Yoyo. So there's no need for crampons, ropes, ice axes, oxygen bottles or any other climbing paraphernalia, because there's no climbing involved. All you need to complete the walk is some suitable clothing, a bit of money, a rucksack full of determination and a half-decent pair of calf muscles.

The route is well marked with the familiar National Trail 'acorn' signposts, arrows and other waymarks, so keeping to the trail shouldn't really be a problem. That said, it is a fairly wild walk in places. Regarding safety, there are few places on the regular trail where it would be possible to fall from a great height, unless you stray from the path near the crags; and with the Wall on one side and a road on the other, it's difficult to get lost, too. Nevertheless, you may find a compass or GPS unit (see p17) useful. Your greatest danger will likely come from those sections where the trail follows or crosses a main road. These points are few and far between, but care should be taken on them nonetheless. (Sadly you will pass one roadside memorial to a hiker who was hit and killed by a vehicle while walking by a stretch of the B6318 at East Wallhouses.)

Your greatest inconvenience will no doubt come from the weather, which can also be hazardous at times. It is very important that you dress for inclement conditions and always carry a set of dry clothes with you. Not pushing yourself too hard is important too, as over-exertion leads to exhaustion and all its inherent dangers; see pp72-5. But really, while it is no mean achievement to complete this walk, it is nevertheless a straightforward but fairly exhausting stroll by the standards of other hikes in northern Britain and should be enjoyed and appreciated as such.

Below: This is farming country and you'll meet a lot of sheep and cows on your walk.

❏ **HADRIAN'S WALL HIGHLIGHTS**

Trying to pick one particular section that is representative of the entire trail is impossible because each is very different. Undoubtedly if I had to recommend one highlight it would be from **Steel Rigg to Chollerford** (see pp150-66), with its excellently preserved Wall, its milecastles and Wall forts. The landscape is the most dramatic here, too, as you ride the crests and bumps of the various crags. Others prefer the **Walltown section** of the Wall (see p140), the forts of **Housesteads** and **Vindolanda** (the former for its excellent state of preservation, the latter for the treasures of its museum), and the **Solway Estuary** (see pp90-3) because of its birdlife.

But just because these sections are our favourites does not mean that the others should be dismissed. The cityscape and suburbs of Newcastle, the absorbing roadside tramp from Heddon-on-the-Wall to Chollerford, the gentle rolling countryside of Cumbria, and 'The Land that Time Forgot' near Bowness are all worth experiencing.

Henry Stedman

How long do you need?

Most people take around six days to complete the walk, making it one of the shorter national trails. Of course, if you're fit there's no reason why you can't go a little faster, if that's what you want to do, and finish the walk in five days (or even less), though you will end up having a different sort of hike to most of the other people on the trail. For where theirs is a fairly relaxing holiday, yours will be more of a sport. What's more, you won't have as much time to enjoy the forts and other attrac-

Most people take around six days to complete the walk

INTRODUCTION

tions – one of the main reasons for visiting the Wall in the first place.

When deciding how long to allow for the walk, those intending to camp and carry their own luggage shouldn't underestimate just how much a heavy pack

See pp35 for some suggested itineraries covering different walking speeds

can slow them down; bank on taking more like seven or eight days if carrying all your luggage. On p35 there are suggested itineraries covering different walking speeds. If you have only a few days, perhaps don't try to walk it all; consider concentrating instead on one particular area, such as the popular central section, or the quieter Cumbrian section from Bowness to Carlisle.

When to go

SEASONS

Britain is a notoriously wet country and the north of England is an infamously damp part of it; '*Hadrain*', as one witty souvenir T-shirt puts it. It's fair to say that few hikers manage to complete the walk without suffering at least one downpour; two or three per trip are more likely, even in summer. That said, it's equally unlikely that you'll spend a week in the area and not see any sun at all, and even the most cynical of hikers will have to admit that, during the hiking

The hiking season runs from April to September

season at least, there are more sunny days than showery ones. The **hiking season** starts at Easter and builds to

a crescendo in August, before steadily tailing off in September. By September's end, few indeed are the hikers who attempt the whole trail, although there are plenty of people on day walks, and by the end of October many places close down for the winter.

Unusually, the authorities in charge of maintaining the path request that walkers do **not attempt the trail in winter** (which they define as October to April), when the path is at its most fragile; they do not, however, rule out walking in Wall country altogether; see the box on pp68-9.

❏ **FESTIVALS AND ANNUAL EVENTS**
As one of the emptiest parts of England, it is perhaps not surprising that there is a dearth of traditional annual festivals, at least when compared to other parts of the country. That's not to say that events don't happen, it's just that the many fairs, festivals and other happenings do not have the weight of tradition or history behind them. Though many of the activities do take place annually, it's not necessarily at the same time each year. Nevertheless, a look at the official Hadrian's Wall website does give a reasonable list of things going on, from lectures to Easter-egg hunts, guided tours to Roman re-enactments and bat walks to falconry displays. It's very possible that your trip will coincide with at least one event.

For more details and a complete list of what's on throughout the year, see
🖥 hadrianswallcountry.co.uk/events.

INTRODUCTION

There are two further points to consider when planning your trip. Firstly, remember that most people set off on the trail at a weekend. This means that you'll find the trail quieter **during the week** and as a consequence you may find it easier to book accommodation. (Furthermore, the bus to Bowness doesn't run at weekends, so you'll save yourself a taxi fare by starting during the week.) Secondly, Carlisle and the western end of the walk through the Solway Marshes can be prone to flooding, so you do need to be aware of the time of the high tides and plan your walk through the marshes so that you are not there during particularly high-level tides; the box on p87 gives advice on how to do this.

Spring

Find a dry week in springtime (around the end of March to mid June) and you're in for a treat. The wild flowers are coming into bloom, lambs are skipping in the meadows, the grass is green and lush and the path is not yet badly eroded. Of course, finding a dry week in spring is not easy but occasionally there's a mini-heatwave. Another advantage with walking at this time is that there will be fewer hikers and finding accommodation is relatively easy, though do check that the hostels/B&Bs have opened. Easter is the exception; the first major holiday in the year when people flock to the Wall.

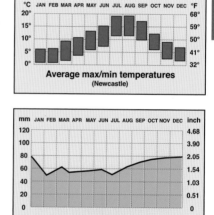

Average max/min temperatures
(Newcastle)

Average rainfall
(Newcastle)

Summer

Summer, on the other hand, can be a bit *too* busy but even over the most hectic weekend in August it's rarely insufferable. Still, the chances of a prolonged period of sunshine are of course higher at this time of year than any other, the days are much longer, all the facilities and public transport are operating and the heather is in bloom, turning some of the hills around the crags a fragrant purple. If you're flexible and want to avoid seeing too many people on the trail, avoid the school holidays,

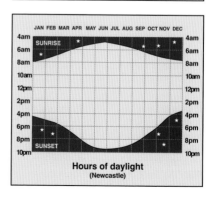

Hours of daylight
(Newcastle)

Believe it or not, this arch, in St Andrews Church, Corbridge, is in fact Roman and dates from the 2nd century AD. It originally stood in Corbridge Roman Town before being brought in its entirety to the village during the church's construction.

which basically means ruling out the tail end of July, all of August and the first few days of September. Alternatively, if you crave the company of other hikers, summer will provide you with the opportunity of meeting plenty of them. **Book your accommodation in advance**, especially if staying in B&Bs.

Despite the higher than average chance of sunshine, take clothes for any eventuality – it will probably still rain at some point.

Autumn

September is a wonderful time to hike, when many of the tourists have returned home, the path is clear and blackberries provide sustenance for the weary walker along the trail. The weather is usually fairly good too, at least at the beginning of September. The B&Bs and hostels will probably be open until the end of the month. By then the weather will begin to get a little wilder and the nights will start to draw in.

Winter

The National Trail authorities ask that you do not walk the trail during the winter, to give the path a rest and prevent damage. It is also a little more dangerous to walk it at this time, with few people around, a cold climate and a slippery trail. But while the advice discourages walking the actual trail, there is nothing to stop you trying one of the circular winter trails near the Wall. For leaflets with suggestions for walks you can take in Wall country that don't actually encroach on the main trail see 🖳 national trail.co.uk/hadrians-wall-path/leaflets.

RAINFALL

At some point on your walk it will rain; if it doesn't, it's fair to say that you haven't really lived the full Hadrian's Wall experience properly. The question, therefore, is not whether you will be rained on but how often. Dress accordingly, take note of the safety advice given on pp72-5 and this shouldn't be a problem.

DAYLIGHT HOURS

If walking in autumn or early spring, you must take account of how far you can walk in the available light (see table on p15). It won't be possible to cover as many miles as you would in summer. Remember, too, that you will get a further 30-45 minutes of usable light before sunrise and after sunset depending on the weather. In June, because the path is in the far north of England, those coming from the south may be surprised that there's enough available light for walking until at least 10pm. Conversely, in winter the nights draw in quickly. Bear this in mind if walking outside the summer season.

Above: While hikers are asked not to walk on the Wall itself, this moggy, at Irthing Bridge, clearly didn't get the memo. **Below**: Even the bits of the Wall that aren't Roman are still interesting, such as here on the Acomb-Hexham-Corbidge Alternative Route (see p213-224).

There's a great variety of scenery on this walk: it's not just about the Wall. On some stretches, such as between Carlisle and Bowness-on-Solway (shown here), almost all evidence of the Wall has disappeared.

Above: Statue of Hadrian, Brampton (see p119).
Left – Top: The Vallum (see p56) can be difficult to discern amongst all the bumps and contours in the fields but it is fairly clear here, east of Banks. **Inset**: The 'Cock of the Walk'. This phallic symbol is one of several inscribed on the Wall for good luck. It's just to the east of Birdoswald (see p129).
Bottom: The foundations of several defensive turrets appear along the Wall as lookouts at intervals between the milecastles. Turret 49b, here, was abandoned when nearby Birdoswald Fort was built.

A fine view on a summer's day: looking east towards Housesteads Fort and beyond.

This page – Vindolanda (p148) and one of the tablets (this one a sales receipt for bacon, lard and beer and now in the British Museum) and a glass decorated with gladiatorial scenes (**below**) – in the excellent museum at Vindolanda.

Opposite – Top: The unique arched gateway of Milecastle 37 (p152). **Middle**: The granary at Housesteads Fort (p154). **Bottom:** The splendid remains of Milecastle 39 (p151) displaying the classic playing card shape, with Crag Lough in the distance.

Above: Arbeia (see p212), four miles further east of Wallsend in South Shields, is one of several forts that served the Wall but aren't actually located on it. The reconstructed West Gate is impressive. **Below**: George Stephenson, the Father of the Railways, grew up in this cottage near Wylam (see p181).

Above – Newcastle: Your walk will take you past the city's many photogenic bridges and buildings including the 'Winking Eye' (p207), the BALTIC gallery and Norman Foster's Sage building. **Below**: On the Acomb–Hexham–Corbridge alternative trail (pp213-24) you can visit the ruins of Corbridge Roman Town (see p223).

❏ **DON'T WALK ON THE WALL**
There are plenty of ways in which hikers can help protect the Wall for future generations to enjoy (see pp68-9, **The Hadrian's Wall Code of Respect**), but the most important one is never, ever walk along, or climb onto the Wall, even if it's just to get a better angle for a photo.

Below: Sycamore Gap (see p153)

PLANNING YOUR WALK

Practical information for the walker

ROUTE FINDING

With the Wall to follow, it's difficult to get lost on this walk. The route is well marked with the familiar National Trail 'acorn' signposts, arrows and other waymarks, so keeping to the trail shouldn't really be a problem. Nevertheless, you may find a compass or GPS unit (see below) useful.

ACCOMMODATION

The route guide (Part 5) lists a detailed selection of the most convenient places to stay along the length of the trail. You have three main options: camping, staying in hostels/bunkhouses/camping barns, or using B&Bs/pubs/guesthouses/hotels. Few people stick to just one of these options the whole way, preferring, for example, to camp most

---

❏ **USING GPS WITH THIS BOOK**

I never carried a compass, preferring to rely on a good sense of direction ... I never bothered to understand how a compass works or what it is supposed to do ... To me a compass is a gadget, and I don't get on well with gadgets of any sort. **Alfred Wainwright**

While Wainwright's acolytes may scoff, other walkers will accept GPS technology as an inexpensive, well-established if non-essential, navigational aid, particularly since most people use sat-nav in a car. With a clear view of the sky, a **GPS receiver** will establish your position as well as elevation in a variety of formats, including the British OS grid system, anywhere on earth to an accuracy of within a few metres.

These days most **smartphones** have a GPS receiver built in and mapping software available to run on it (see box p41). Dedicated gadget-buyers can invest in a separate **GPS unit** such as a Garmin.

The maps in the route guide include numbered waypoints; these correlate to the list on pp226-9, which gives the grid reference as well as a description. You can download the complete list of these waypoints for free as a GPS-readable file (that doesn't include the text descriptions) from the Trailblazer website: 🖳 trailblazer-guides.com.

Bear in mind that most people who tackle the Hadrian's Wall Path do so perfectly successfully without using GPS.

of the time but spend every third night in a hostel, or perhaps to use hostels where possible but splash out on a B&B every once in a while.

When booking accommodation, remember to ask if a pick-up and drop-off service is available (usually only B&Bs provide this service). Few of the B&Bs actually lie on the Wall, and at the end of a tiring day it's nice to know a lift is available to take you to your accommodation rather than having to traipse another two or three miles off the path to get to your bed for the night.

The facilities' table on pp32-3 provides a quick snapshot of what type of accommodation is available in each of the towns and villages along the way, while the tables on pp34-5 provide some suggested itineraries. The following is a brief introduction to what to expect from each type of accommodation.

Camping

There are campsites most of the way along the Hadrian's Wall Path, though none in Newcastle or Carlisle, and fewer at the eastern end of the trail than elsewhere. Some sections between campsites can be quite long, especially if you're hiking with a heavy rucksack, tent and cooking equipment, so although there's usually no need to book campsites in advance, some advance planning is advisable, especially given that **wild camping is not allowed**. To help plot your route, see the Camping itinerary table on pp34-5.

A lot of people choose to camp some nights, rather than every night on the trail. You're quite likely to get at least one night where the rain falls relentlessly, soaking equipment and sapping morale, and it is then that many campers opt to spend the next night drying out in a hostel or B&B. There are, however, many advantages with camping the whole way. It's much more economical, for a start, with most campsites charging £5-10pp and one place, Wall, offering up its village green for free. And, although it's wise to phone ahead in the morning to check your planned campsite has space for that night, there's rarely any need to actually book a pitch at a campsite, unless perhaps you're hiking in a large group with a number of tents.

Campsites vary; some are just the back gardens of B&Bs or pubs; others are full-blown caravan sites with a few spaces put aside for tents. Showers are usually available, occasionally for a fee though more often than not included in the rate. Note that wild camping (ie not in a regular campsite) is not allowed.

Camping independently affords you a lot of freedom; if you find yourself ahead of schedule one day, you can simply push on to the next campsite. Likewise, if you're feeling particularly exhausted, you can stop earlier than planned if you pass a campsite halfway along that day's stage. However, carrying your accommodation around with you is not an easy option; the route is wearying enough without a huge, heavy rucksack on your back. So some hikers choose to employ one of the baggage-transfer companies mentioned on pp26-7. Of course this does mean it will cost more and that you will lose a certain amount of freedom as you have to inform the company, at least a day before, of your next destination – and stick to it – so that you and your bag can be reunited every evening. What's more, make sure that the baggage transfer companies deliver to campsites – not all of them do. Hadrian's Wall Ltd (see p28) offers a camping-based walking holiday.

Bunkhouses/camping barns and hostels

The terms '**bunkhouse**' and '**camping barn**' can mean many different things, though usually they are simple dormitory-style bunk-bed accommodation in a converted barn in a farmer's field or in the annex of a country house. Sleeping bags are usually necessary in these places, although some do provide bedding at extra cost. While not exactly the lap of luxury, a night in a bunkhouse is probably the nearest non-campers will get to sleeping outside, while at the same time providing campers with shelter from the elements should the weather look like taking a turn for the worse. Some of the better bunkhouses provide a shower and simple kitchen with running water and perhaps a kettle, and occasionally pots, pans, cutlery and crockery. You'll find bunkhouses/camping barns strung out most of the way along the Wall, including Bowness, Boustead Hill, Walton (where there's actually two of them), Gilsland and Once Brewed.

Hostels generally have a mix of dorms and private rooms; facilities are usually shared for dorms but some rooms are now en suite. They have self-catering facilities and rates may include a light toast-and-cereal breakfast. Independent hostels come with less restrictive rules regarding things like curfews and mixed dorms than YHA hostels do. However, since the first edition of this guide the number of YHA hostels (☎ 01629-592700, 🖳 yha.org.uk) on the trail has fluctuated wildly. For that first edition, there were enough youth hostels along the length of the trail to cover the whole trek. By the fifth edition, however, there was only one, at Once Brewed, and even that was closed for reconstruction. Thankfully, the situation has improved over the last few years: the YHA hostels at Once Brewed (now called YHA The Sill, see p148) and Newcastle are supplemented by independent hostels at Carlisle, Greenhead, and one more in Newcastle. Combine these with the odd night in a bunkhouse/camping barn and you can avoid staying in a tent or B&B for every night of your trek.

The cost of staying in a hostel usually works out at around £20-30 per person (pp) per night; the rate at a YHA hostel is about £3pp less for YHA members. For solo travellers, this is a lot cheaper than staying in a B&B. But if you are walking as a couple or in a group, and usually share the cost of a room, look at private rooms in a youth hostel – they're usually good value; and remember, too, that the price of a cheap B&B (or one of the nationwide hotel chains such as Travelodge or Premier Inn) may not be much more in total.

Bed and breakfast

Bed and Breakfasts (B&Bs) are a great British institution and many of those along the Hadrian's Wall Path are absolutely charming, with buildings often three or four hundred years old and some even made with Wall stones! There's nothing mysterious about a B&B; as the name suggests, they provide you with a bed in a private room and a (usually cooked) breakfast, though they range in style enormously.

Rooms usually contain either a double bed (known as a double room), or two single beds (known as a twin room) though sometimes twin beds can be pushed together to make a double bed. Some rooms sleep three (Tr) or four people (Qd); these are often called family rooms. Generally this means there is a double bed (which two people may need to share) with one or two single beds, or bunk beds. Rooms are often en suite but in some cases the facilities are shared or private, though even with the latter the bathroom is rarely more than a few feet away. Most rooms have a TV and tea/coffee-making facilities.

An evening meal (usually around £12-20) is often provided at the more remote or bigger places, at least if you book in advance. If not, there's nearly always a pub or restaurant nearby or, if it's far, the B&B owner may give you a lift to and from the nearest place with food.

B&B rates B&Bs in this guide start at around £30 per person (pp) based on two people sharing a room, but most charge around £35-45pp. Solo trekkers should take note: single rooms are not so easy to find so if you are on your own you will often end up occupying a double/twin room, for which you'll usually have to pay a single occupancy (sgl occ) rate, often amounting to the full room rate minus the cost of one breakfast (usually £10-15). Some places are more generous towards solo travellers, though, and will let you stay for closer to the per-person rate. Rates are sometimes discounted for stays of two or more nights. Do also check out nationwide chains such as Travelodge and Premier Inn.

❏ **SHOULD YOU BOOK YOUR ACCOMMODATION IN ADVANCE?**
Unless you're camping, it's essential that you have your night's accommodation booked by the time you set off in the morning. Nothing is more deflating than to arrive at your destination at the day's end only to find that you've then got to walk a further five miles or so, or even take a detour off the route, because everywhere in town is booked.

That said, there's a certain amount of hysteria regarding the booking of accommodation, with many websites, B&Bs and other organisations suggesting you book at least six months in advance. There really is no need for this, and it leaves you vulnerable to changing circumstances, which may lead to you being left with a trail of lost deposits. By not booking so far in advance, you give yourself the chance to shift your holiday plans to a later date should the unforeseen arise.

Unlike on some other national trails, the lack of accommodation is not as bad on the Hadrian's Wall Path, at least not outside the high season (ie the summer period coinciding with the long school holidays in the UK). Outside this period, and particularly in April/May or September, as long as you're flexible and willing to take what's offered, with maybe even a night or two in a hostel if that's all there is, you should get away with booking just a few nights in advance, or indeed just the night before. The exceptions to this rule are at weekends, when everywhere is busy, and where accommodation is very limited.

Campers, however, have much more flexibility and can usually just turn up and find a space, though phoning ahead in the morning gives you some reassurance. You should always phone ahead out of season, though, just to check your intended campsite is open.

Guesthouses, hotels, pubs and inns

The difference between a B&B and a guesthouse is minimal, though some of the better guesthouses are more like hotels, offering evening meals and a lounge for guests. Pubs and inns also offer bed and breakfast accommodation and prices are no more than in a regular B&B.

Hotels usually do cost more and some can be a little irritated with a bunch of smelly hikers turning up and treading mud into their carpet. Most on the Hadrian's Wall Path, however, are used to seeing walkers and welcome them warmly. Prices in hotels start at around £40pp, though occasionally you can get special deals with larger hotel chains (Travelodge, Premier Inn) in Newcastle and Carlisle that can be as low as £25 for a room (without breakfast). Hotel and pub rates usually include breakfast, but not always.

Airbnb

The rise and rise of Airbnb (💻 www.airbnb.co.uk) has seen private homes and apartments opened up to overnight travellers on an informal basis. While accommodation is primarily based in cities, the concept has spread to tourist hotspots in more rural areas, but do check thoroughly what you are getting and the precise location. While the first couple of options listed may be in the area you're after, others may be too far afield for walkers. At its best, this is a great way to meet local people in a relatively unstructured environment, but do be aware that these places are not registered B&Bs, so standards may vary, and prices may not necessarily be any lower than those of a regular B&B or guesthouse.

FOOD AND DRINK

Breakfast and lunch

Stay in a B&B and you'll be filled to the gills with a cooked **English breakfast**. This usually consists of a bowl of cereal followed by a plateful of eggs, bacon, sausages, mushrooms, tomatoes and possibly baked beans or black pudding, with toast and butter, and all washed down with coffee, tea and/or juice. Enormously satisfying the first time you have it, by the fourth or fifth morning your cholesterol-choked arteries may be crying out for a lighter continental breakfast. If you have had enough of these cooked breakfasts and/or plan an early start, ask if you can have a packed lunch instead of breakfast. Some B&Bs are happy to provide a **packed lunch** (indicated by the Ⓛ symbol in the text) at an additional cost (unless it's in lieu of breakfast), though of course there's nothing to stop you preparing your own (a penknife would be useful), or going to a pub or café.

Remember to plan ahead; certain stretches of the walk are virtually devoid of eating places (the stretch from Steel Rigg to Chollerford, for example, has nothing save for some snacks and a hot drinks machine that are available at Housesteads, and a coffee van that usually sets up in the car park by Brocolitia in summer) so read ahead about the next day's walk in Part 5 to make sure you never go hungry.

> ❏ **OPENING DAYS/HOURS**
> The opening days and hours for the pubs, restaurants and cafés mentioned in Part 5 are
> as accurate as possible. However, the pressures caused by shortage of staff and increas-
> ing energy costs – let alone if the weather is bad, or if there is no demand – mean that
> places may close early or not open at all, so it is essential to check in advance, partic-
> ularly if it involves a detour off the route and there are few other food options.

Cream teas

Whatever you do for lunch, don't forget to leave some room for a cream tea or
two, a morale, energy and cholesterol booster all rolled into one delicious package: a pot of tea accompanied by scones served with cream and jam, and sometimes a cake or two. The jury is out on whether you should put the jam on first
(the Creed of Cornwall) or the cream (the Devon Doctrine) but either way do
not miss the chance of at least one cream tea.

Evening meals

Pubs are as much a feature of the walk as pasture and sheep, and in some cases
the pub is as much a tourist attraction as any Roman fort or ruined priory. *Robin
Hood Inn* (see p174) at East Wallhouses, is one example, as are *The Keelman*
(see p185) at Newburn, the historic *Twice Brewed Inn* (see p148) at Once
Brewed, *Samson Inn* (see p132) at Gilsland, and *Drover's Rest* (see p101) in
Monkhill, near Beaumont.

Most pubs have become highly attuned to the desires of hikers and offer
lunch and evening meals (often with a couple of local dishes and usually some
vegetarian options), some locally brewed beers, a garden to relax in on hot days
and a roaring fire to huddle around on cold ones. The standard of the food varies
widely, though is usually served in big portions, which is often just about all
hikers care about at the end of a long day. In many of the villages the pub is the
only place to eat out. Note that pubs may close in the afternoon, especially in
the winter months, so check in advance if you are hoping to visit a particular
one, and also if you are planning lunch there as food serving hours can change.

There are also several great pubs in the towns and cities near the path, such
as *Golden Lion* and *The Wheatsheaf Hotel* (see p221) at Corbridge, the cosy
Black Bull Inn (see p144) at Haltwhistle, and the fabulously unassuming
Crown Posada (see p205) in Newcastle.

That other great British culinary institution, the **fish 'n' chip shop**, can be
found in Newcastle, Carlisle, and towns off the Wall such as Haltwhistle,
Brampton and Hexham; as can Chinese and Indian **takeaways**, which are usually the last places to stop serving food, staying open until at least 11pm.

Self-catering on the trail

Except for when the trail passes through the cities of Newcastle and Carlisle,
there aren't actually that many shops where you can buy provisions along the
path. There's a shop at Cottage & Glendale Holiday Park (see Map 1) near Port
Carlisle; while Heddon-on-the-Wall has a small supermarket that's combined

with its petrol station. The only other places where you can buy anything to eat are the gift shops at the forts of Chesters, Housesteads, Birdoswald and Carvoran, and at the informal **refreshment stalls** established at such places as Drumburgh, Grinsdale, Linstock, Crosby-on-Eden, Newtown, and Haytongate Farm. These refreshment stalls are, on occasion, absolute lifesavers: the biggest provide a small hut in which hikers can cower from the elements and take advantage of chilled cans, chocolate bars, crisps, even a hot drinks machine. Others are little more than small boxes in which the provisions are kept. All, however, are unsupervised, and thus rely on an honesty-box system (where you put the correct money into a tin or moneybox to pay for what you've consumed). As some of these 'stalls' are actually run by the children of local families, please don't abuse their trust by not paying. See Part 5 for more details.

❏ LOCAL BREWERIES (AND A DISTILLERY)

When it comes to drinking, there are any number of local breweries competing to slake the thirst of trekkers with real ales, stouts and bitters. Perhaps the most 'relevant' brewery for Wall walkers is the **Twice Brewed Brew House** (🖳 twice brewed-brewhouse.co.uk), next to the pub of the same name in the quintessential Hadrian's Wall stopover of Once Brewed. As the name of both pub and hamlet would suggest, they've been brewing beer for a long time around here – around 2000 years according to their website – and the names of several of their beers have a distinctly Roman flavour including a porter called Steel Rigg (4.9%), an amber called Ale Caesar (4.3%), a pale ale called Sycamore Gap (4.1%) and an IPA called Northern Frontier (5.3%). They also produce a selection of Hadrian's Wall gins.

    Hadrian Border Brewery (🖳 hadrian-border-brewery.co.uk) is based in Newcastle. A merger of two breweries, Hadrian and Border, their beers include Northumbrian Gold (4.5%) and the pleasantly light Tyneside Blonde (3.9%).

    Sticking near Newcastle, **Wylam Brewery** (🖳 wylambrewery.co.uk), once based in Heddon-on-the-Wall, has now relocated to Newcastle and is located just north of the city centre in the lovely Palace of Art in Exhibition Park (see map p200). Often very strong, brews are intriguingly named and include Hickey the Rake (4.2%) and Jakehead (6.3%). Brewery tours (£10) are held on Saturdays. Another that will be of interest to Wall Walkers is **Big Lamp Brewery** (🖳 biglampbrewers.co.uk), the North-East's oldest micro-brewery, based at The Keelman pub (see p185) just off the trail at Newburn. Brews include the delicious Summerhill Stout (4.4%) and the appropriately named Blackout (11%!). Another brewer from this neck of the Wall, **Mordue** (🖳 morduebrewery.com), produces the divine Workie (4.5%), formerly a Champion Best Bitter of Britain and a cracking pint.

    Moving further west but still in Northumberland, **Muckle Brewery** (🖳 muckle brewing.co.uk) is based outside Haltwhistle. According to their website all of their beers are inspired by the local landscape, including Whin Sill Blonde (3.5%) and their stout, Muckle Moss (4.3%), named after the boggy nature reserve near the western end of the path. Their beers are available at the Sill in Once Brewed, which is something of a marketing coup given that the Twice Brewed Brew House is just next door!

    Heading into Cumbria, another brewery of interest is Cockermouth's **Jennings Brewery** (🖳 jenningsbrewery.co.uk), the most ubiquitous brewer in Cumbria.

    For those who prefer spirits to beers, we should also mention Hadrian's Wall gin (🖳 hadrianswallgin.com), based a little away from the Wall in Alnwick.

Drinking water

There are plenty of ways of perishing on the Hadrian's Wall Path but given how damp the north of England is, thirst probably won't be one of them. Be careful, though, for on a hot day in some of the remoter parts after a steep climb or two you'll quickly dehydrate, which is at best highly unpleasant and at worst mightily dangerous. Always carry some water with you and in hot

> ❏ **INFORMATION FOR FOREIGN VISITORS**
>
> ● **Currency** The British pound (£) comes in notes of £50, £20, £10 and £5, and coins of £2 and £1. The pound is divided into 100 pence (usually referred to as 'p', pronounced 'pee') which come in 'silver' coins of 50p, 20p, 10p and 5p, and 'copper' coins of 2p and 1p. Cash is the most welcome form of payment though debit/credit cards are accepted in some places. Up-to-date currency **exchange rates** can be found on ▣ www.xe.com, at some post offices, and at most banks and travel agents.
>
> ● **Business hours** Most **village shops** are open Monday to Friday 9am-5pm and Saturday 9am-12.30pm, though some open as early as 7.30/8am; many also open on Sundays but not usually for the whole day. Occasionally you'll come across a local shop that closes at lunchtime on one day during the week, usually a Wednesday or Thursday; this is a throwback to the days when all towns and villages had an 'early closing day'. **Supermarkets** are open Monday to Saturday 8am-8pm (sometimes longer) and on Sunday from about 9am to 5 or 6pm, though main branches of supermarkets generally open 10am-4pm or 11am-5pm.
>
> Main **post offices** generally open Monday to Friday 9am-5pm and Saturday 9am-12.30pm; **banks** typically open at 9.30/10am Monday to Friday and close at 3.30/4pm, though in some places both post offices and banks may open only two or three days a week and/or in the morning, or limited hours, only. **ATMs** (**cash machines**) located outside a bank, shop, post office or petrol station are open all the time, but any that are inside will be accessible only when that place is open. However, ones that charge, such as Link machines, may not accept foreign-issued cards.
>
> **Pub hours** are less predictable as each pub may have different opening hours. However, most pubs on the Path open daily 11am-11pm (some close at 10.30pm on Sunday) but **some close in the afternoon**. The last entry time to most **museums and galleries** is usually half an hour, or an hour, before the official closing time.
>
> ● **Public (bank) holidays** Most businesses are shut on 1 January, Good Friday (March/April), Easter Monday (March/April), the first and last Monday in May, the last Monday in August, 25 December and 26 December.
>
> ● **School holidays** School holiday periods in England are generally: a one-week break late October, two weeks around Christmas/New Year, a week in mid February, two weeks around Easter, a week in late May/early June (to coincide with the bank holiday on the last Monday in May), and six weeks from late July to early September. Private-school holidays fall at the same time, but tend to be slightly longer.
>
> ● **EHICs and travel insurance** Although Britain's National Health Service (NHS) is free at the point of use, that is only the case for residents. All visitors to Britain should be properly insured, including comprehensive health coverage. Though Britain has left the EU, the European Health Insurance Card (EHIC) does still entitle EU nationals (on production of the EHIC, so ensure you bring it with you) to necessary medical treatment under the NHS while on a temporary visit here. To make sure this is still the case when you visit, however, contact your national social security institution. Also note that the EHIC is not a substitute for proper medical cover on

weather drink three or four litres a day. Don't be tempted by the water in the streams; if the cow or sheep faeces in the water doesn't make you ill, the chemicals from the pesticides and fertilisers used on the farms almost certainly will. Using iodine or another purifying treatment will help to combat the former, though there's little you can do about the latter. It's a lot safer to fill up from taps instead.

your travel insurance for unforeseen bills and for getting you home should that be necessary. Also consider cover for loss and theft of personal belongings, especially if you are camping or staying in hostels, as there may be times when you'll have to leave your luggage unattended.

• **Documents** If you are a member of a National Trust organisation in your country bring your membership card as you should be entitled to free entry to National Trust properties and sites in the UK. However, being a member of English Heritage (EH) is more useful for this walk as most of the forts/sites are managed by EH.

• **Weights and measures** Milk in Britain is still sometimes sold in pints (1 pint = 568ml), as is beer in pubs, though most other **liquids** including petrol (gasoline) and diesel are sold in litres. Road **distances** are given in miles (1 mile = 1.6km) rather than kilometres, and yards (1yd = 0.9m) rather than metres. The population remains divided between those who still use inches (1 inch = 2.5cm) and feet (1ft = 0.3m) and those who are happy with centimetres and millimetres; you'll often be told that 'it's only a hundred yards or so' to somewhere, rather than a hundred metres or so. Most **food** is sold in metric weights (g and kg) but the imperial weights of pounds (lb: 1lb = 453g) and ounces (oz: 1oz = 28g) are often displayed too. The **weather** – a frequent topic of conversation – is also an issue: while most forecasts predict temperatures in °C, some people continue to think in terms of °F (see temperature chart on p15 for conversions).

• **Time** During the winter the whole of Britain is on Greenwich Mean Time (GMT). The clocks move one hour forward on the last Sunday in March, remaining on British Summer Time (BST) until the last Sunday in October.

• **Smoking** Smoking in enclosed public places is banned. The ban relates not only to pubs and restaurants, but also to B&Bs, hostels and hotels. These latter have the right to designate one or more bedrooms where the occupants can smoke, but the ban is in force in all enclosed areas open to the public – even in a private home such as a B&B. Should you be foolhardy enough to light up in a no-smoking area, which includes pretty well any indoor public place, you could be fined £50, but it's the owners of the premises who suffer most if they fail to stop you, with a potential fine of £2500.

• **Telephones** The international access code for Britain is ☎ 44, followed by the area code minus the first 0, and then the number you require. Within the UK, to call a number with the same code as the landline phone you are calling from, the code can be omitted: dial the number only. It is cheaper to ring at weekends (from midnight on Friday till midnight on Sunday), and after 7pm and before 7am on weekdays. If you're using a **mobile (cell) phone** that is registered overseas, consider buying a local SIM card to keep costs down. Mobile phone reception is generally good on and around Hadrian's Wall Path; also remember to bring a universal adaptor so you can charge your phone.

• **Emergency services** For police, ambulance, fire and mountain rescue dial ☎ 999, or the EU standard number ☎ 112.

PLANNING YOUR WALK

MONEY

Although, since the pandemic, many more small businesses now accept card payments, you should still carry plenty of **cash** with you. Outside Newcastle and Carlisle, **banks** (and ATMs) are few and far between on the Hadrian's Wall Path – indeed, there are only two places, Heddon-on-the-Wall and Gilsland, which boast an ATM, though there are plenty in the towns (Hexham, Corbridge, Haltwhistle and Brampton) that lie a mile or two off the trail; see the table on pp32-3 for details. However, you can get cash (by debit card) for free at any **post office** counter if you bank with most UK banks or building societies; and there are post offices at Carlisle, Walton, Gilsland, Heddon-on-the-Wall and Newcastle. Note, however, that two of these (Walton and Gilsland) have very limited opening hours. For details see 🖥 www.postoffice.co.uk/branch-finder.

Another way of getting cash is to use the **cashback** system: find a shop that will accept a debit card and ask them to advance cash against the card. However, you will almost always need to buy something. Some pubs also do this.

Note that some B&Bs **don't accept credit cards** although you may be able to pay by **bank transfer**. It's always best to check this in advance.

OTHER SERVICES

Almost every B&B, hotel and hostel has **wi-fi** now, and even some of the larger campsites. (Indeed, pretty much the only places that didn't have wi-fi, we found, were the English Heritage-owned forts and accompanying tearooms along the route.) Although there are not many regular **grocery stores** at the western end of the Path, there are a number of **unmanned refreshment stalls** with honesty boxes. The **mobile phone reception** is generally good on and around the Path. There are **outdoor equipment shops** in Carlisle, Newcastle and Hexham; **pharmacies/chemists** in those towns as well as Corbridge and Brampton; while for **tourist information centres**, see box p45.

WALKING COMPANIES

It is, of course, possible to turn up with your boots and backpack at Bowness or Wallsend and just start walking, with little planned save for, perhaps, your accommodation (see box on p20). The following companies, however, are in the business of making your holiday as stress-free and enjoyable as possible.

Baggage transfer and accommodation booking

There are several baggage-transfer companies serving the Hadrian's Wall Path, from national organisations such as Sherpa Van Project to companies that consist of little more than one man and his van. With all these services you can book up to the last moment, usually up to around 8pm the previous evening, though it's cheaper if you book in advance. **Do shop around as the costs vary between the companies below**. It's usually around £8 to take your bag to your next destination but maximum bag weights vary (17-20kg). Most companies also stipulate a minimum number of bags that they will transfer from the same address (this is usually two). Nearly all these companies also offer accommodation booking, as do local tourist information centres (see box p45).

● **Brigantes Walking Holidays** (☎ 01756-770402, 💻 brigantesenglishwalks.com)
● **Hadrian's Haul** (☎ 07967-564823, 💻 hadrianshaul.com)
● **Sherpa Van Project** (baggage transfer ☎ 01748-826917, 💻 sherpavan.com)

Self-guided holidays

Self-guided basically means that the company will organise accommodation, baggage transfer, transport to and from the walk, and various maps and advice, but leave you on your own to actually walk the path. Most companies offer walks between March/April and the end of October. In addition to the 'standard' itineraries summarised on pp34-5, just about all the companies can tailor your holiday to suit your requirements and offer the walk in both directions.

● **Absolute Escapes** (☎ 0131-610 1210, 💻 absoluteescapes.com; Edinburgh) Trips of 5-8 days along the whole of the Wall in either direction.
● **Brigantes Walking Holidays** (see above) Complete Wall walks of 4-10 days.
● **British & Irish Walks** (☎ 01242-254353, 💻 britishandirishwalks.com; Glos) Offers an itinerary along the entire Wall in 7 days.
● **Celtic Trails** (☎ 01291-689774, 💻 celtictrailswalkingholidays.co.uk; Chepstow) A 4-day 'Best of the Wall' walk and complete Wall walks of 6-11 days. Also offers two standards of accommodation.
● **Contours Walking Holidays** (☎ 01629-821900, 💻 contours.co.uk; Derbyshire) Walks along the entire Wall (5-11 days) as well as Best of/ highlight tours (5-6 days/4-5 days) and a 'Short Break' (2-3 days) plus 'Dog-friendly' walks. Trail-running holidays also available.
● **Discovery Travel** (☎ 01983-301133, 💻 discoverytravel.co.uk; Isle of Wight) Offers standard self-guided walks of 6-9 nights as well as a 5-night 'Highlights of Hadrian's Wall' package.
● **Footpath Holidays** (☎ 01985-840049, 💻 footpath-holidays.com; Wilts) Runs single-centre guesthouse-based self-guided (selected parts) walks for 5-7 days with Hexham as the base and also the whole Path, inn-to-inn.
● **Freedom Walking Holidays** (☎ 07733-885390, 💻 freedomwalkingholidays .co.uk; Goring-on-Thames) Holidays of 5-10 days.
● **Great British Walks** (☎ 01600-713008, 💻 great-british-walks.com; Monmouth) Trips of 4-10 days along the whole of the Wall in either direction.
● **Hadrian's Wall Ltd** (☎ 07813-050344 💻 walkthewall.uk; Northumberland) As the name suggests, this company specialises in Hadrian's Wall. It offers all kinds of treks with a range of accommodation levels and even offers camping treks (May-mid Aug; 4-6 nights).
● **Hillwalk Tours** (☎ +353 91-763994, 💻 hillwalktours.com; Ireland) Walks (4-11 days) graded by level – gentle, moderate and challenging – and including the Hadrian's Wall Passport (see box p42).
● **Hooked on Walking** (☎ 01506-635 399, 💻 hookedoncycling.co.uk; West Lothian) Offers a 6-night itinerary along the whole Wall.
● **Let's Go Walking** (☎ 01837-880075, 💻 www.letsgowalking.com; Devon) Offers 7- to 10-day walks along the entire Wall, and a highlights tour.

PLANNING YOUR WALK

Self-guided holidays (cont'd)

● **Macs Adventure** (☎ 0141-530 8886, 🖳 macsadventure.com; Glasgow) A range of itineraries from a 'Best of the Wall' trip along the central section between Corbridge and Gilsland to the whole Wall in 6-11 days. Walkers also receive the Hadrian's Wall Passport (see box p42).

● **Mickledore Travel** (☎ 01768-772335, 🖳 mickledore.co.uk; Keswick) A number of self-guided tours ranging from a 3-day short break on the most dramatic central section of the wall, between Humshaugh and Gilsland, to a walk of 6-10 days (in either direction) over the entire length of the Path. Packed lunches are optional.

● **NorthWestWalks** (☎ 01257-424889, 🖳 northwestwalks.co.uk; Wigan) Itineraries from 6 nights/5 days' walking to 9 nights/8 days' walking.

● **Responsible Travel** (☎ 01273-823700, 🖳 responsibletravel.com; Brighton) Offers a 'Highlights of Hadrian's Wall' holiday; 5 days (3-4 days walking).

● **Roman Wall Walks** (☎ 07789 185049, 🖳 romanwallwalks.com; Heddon-on-the-Wall) A local company based on the Wall offering walks of any length according to clients' needs.

● **Shepherds Walks Holidays** (☎ 01669-621044, 🖳 shepherdswalksholidays .co.uk; Northumberland) Trips of 5-10 days along the whole of the Wall as well as 'highlights' tours. Also gives clients the Hadrian's Wall Passport (see box p42).

● **The Carter Company** (☎ 01296-631671, 🖳 the-carter-company.com; Buckinghamshire) Offers a luxury trip of 8 nights/7 days' walking.

● **Walkers' Britain** (☎ 020-8875 5070, 🖳 walkersbritain.co.uk; London) Offers 8- and 10-day 'Inn-to-Inn' walking tours along the whole Wall in either direction.

Group/guided walking tours

If you don't trust your map-reading skills or simply prefer the company of other walkers as well as an experienced guide, the following may be of interest. Packages nearly always include meals, accommodation, transport arrangements, minibus back-up and baggage transfer.

Have a good look at each of the companies' websites before booking as each has its own speciality. Note that there is likely to be a single supplement for solo travellers.

● **Hadrian's Wall Ltd** (see p27) Offers a range of guided and part-guided walks; the guide will accompany walkers for one day.

● **HF Holidays** (☎ 0345 470 8558, 🖳 hfholidays.co.uk; Herts) Offers a 'Best of the Wall' 6 nights, centre-based holiday located in Haltwhistle and a complete trail holiday over 7 nights.

● **Ramblers Walking Holidays** (☎ 01707-331133, 🖳 ramblersholidays .co.uk; Herts) A 6-day walk (May-Sept approx once a month; Heddon-on-the-Wall to Bowness) based at a hotel in Chollerford and one in Carlisle.

● **Shepherds Walks Holidays** (see above) Offers guided walks along the whole trail.

TAKING DOGS ALONG THE HADRIAN'S WALL PATH

Following the previous edition of this guidebook, a reader wrote in to tell us that we should emphasise the fact that the **Hadrian's Wall Path is actually not that dog-friendly**. He's not wrong. This is, after all, cow country, and much of the land through which the path passes is grazed by livestock so dogs must be kept on a lead.

The number of B&Bs, bunkhouses, guesthouses and even campsites that accept dogs is surprisingly low, too, and even the odd pub refuses to allow dogs inside, leaving you to sup your shandy in a storm while other walkers crowd around the open fire inside. And if you're still not convinced about the wisdom of leaving your dog at home, then remember that some of the forts don't allow dogs and, if they do, they tend not to be allowed in every part of the fort. And, assuming you're a responsible dog owner, you should know that there are few litter bins on the trail where you can throw away poo bags after you've cleaned up after your dog.

It's fair to say that dog owners must be a resilient breed to put up with the privations they suffer for the sake of their pet. Still, despite all the moans it *is* possible to walk from one end to the other with your dog and many are the rewards that await those prepared to make the extra effort required to bring their best friend with them.

But don't underestimate the extra work involved in bringing your pooch to the path. Just about every decision you make will be influenced by the fact you've got a dog: how you plan to travel to the start of the trail, where you're going to stay, how far you're going to walk each day, where you're going to rest and where you're going to eat in the evening etc etc. You may not believe it as you watch it haring around the fields but dogs do have a finite amount of energy, so consider whether yours really is up to walking for 10-20 miles a day.

For detailed information about taking a dog along the path see pp230-1.

DISABLED ACCESS

While many stretches of the path are inaccessible to the majority of wheelchair and scooter users, either because of the terrain or the not inconsiderable number of stiles and kissing gates to be negotiated, some sections are more forgiving. For more on access for the disabled, contact the Disabled Ramblers (🖥 disabled ramblers.co.uk). Though some of their website needs updating, it does mention a couple of accessible routes that coincide with parts of the Hadrian's Wall Path: a stretch from Walltown to Cawfields Quarry (7.8 miles/12.8km), and a loop beside Housesteads Fort (2.9 miles/4.6km).

Budgeting

England is not a cheap place to travel in and while the north may be one of the less expensive regions, the towns and villages on the Hadrian's Wall Path are more than used to seeing tourists and charge accordingly. You may think before you set out that you are going to try to keep your costs to a minimum by camping every night where possible and cooking your own food but it's a rare trekker who sticks to this rule. Besides, the B&Bs and pubs on the route are amongst the path's major attractions and it would be a pity not to sample the hospitality in at least some of them.

If the only expenses of this walk were accommodation and food, budgeting for the trip would be a piece of cake. Unfortunately, in addition, there are all the little **extras** that push up the cost of your trip: getting to and from the path, beer, coffees, cream teas, stamps and postcards, buses here and there, baggage transfer, laundry, souvenirs and entrance fees (to minimise these it is worth becoming a member of English Heritage and, to a lesser extent, National Trust; see box p77). It's surprising how much these add up.

CAMPING

You can survive on less than £20pp per day if you use the cheapest campsites, don't visit any pubs, avoid all the museums and tourist attractions in the towns, cook all your own food – and generally have a pretty miserable time of it. Even then, unforeseen expenses will probably nudge your daily budget above this figure. Include the occasional pint, and perhaps a pub meal every now and then, and the figure will be nearer £30 a day.

BUNKHOUSES/CAMPING BARNS AND HOSTELS

The charge for staying in a bunkhouse/camping barn or hostel varies according to its quality and range of facilities, but they tend to cost £15-35 per person. Breakfast is usually extra, at least in the cheaper bunkhouses. Overall, it is likely to cost around £35-60 per day, factoring in the odd beer and going out for the occasional meal.

B&Bs, PUBS, GUESTHOUSES AND HOTELS

B&B rates start at £35pp per night but can easily be at least twice this, particularly if you are walking by yourself and are thus liable to pay single supplements. Add on the cost of lunch and dinner and you should reckon on about £60pp minimum per day. Staying in a guesthouse or hotel would probably push the minimum up to £70pp unless those hotels are part of the Premier Inn, Travelodge or Easy Inn chains, which can be cheaper if booked well in advance.

Itineraries

Part 5 of this book (the Route Guide) has been written so that it can be used by hikers walking the Hadrian's Wall Path in either a westward or eastward direction, following a colour coding: **E →** and **W ←**. However, the general orientation of the chapter is **from west to east**. Of course there is nothing to stop you from tackling the Path in the opposite direction, and there are advantages in doing so – see below.

To help you plan your walk the colour maps at the back of the book have **profile charts**; there is also a **distance chart** and a **planning map**. The **table of village/town facilities** (pp32-3) gives a run-down on the essential information you will need regarding accommodation possibilities and services.

You could follow one of the suggested itineraries (see pp34-5) which are based on preferred type of accommodation and walking speeds or, if tackling the entire walk seems a bit ambitious, you can do it a day or two at a time, using public transport to get to the start and end of the stage. The public transport map and service details are on pp48-51. Once you have an idea of your approach turn to Part 5 for detailed information on accommodation, places to eat and other services in each village and town on the route. Also in Part 5 you will find summaries of the route to accompany the detailed trail maps.

WHICH DIRECTION?

These days it is more common for Wall walkers attempting the entire trail to start from Bowness and finish at Wallsend in Newcastle. This is only sensible – as any experienced walker in the UK will tell you, the prevailing winds tend to blow from west to east across the island, and it's often a lot easier to have these carrying you along the trail rather than trying to push against them. Practically, it probably makes more sense too. Getting away from Newcastle at the end of the trail is a far simpler task than getting away from Bowness – and struggling to find a bus or lift that will take you away from the Solway and back to 'civilisation' is not something you want to be doing after you've walked 84 miles.

Having walked the trail in both directions several times, I also think that, aesthetically, it's better heading east along the trail. I like starting at peaceful Bowness, and beginning my adventure with a meal at the pub there before heading off the next morning, particularly as it's often full of other trekkers who are similarly about to start their trek – or have just finished it and want to share their stories. I also think there's something suitably celebratory about finishing your trek by walking under the Tyne bridges in Newcastle before strolling onto Segedunum to get that final stamp in the passport. Newcastle is also, of course, a great place to celebrate the end of your adventure with bars and bistros aplenty. *(cont'd on p36)*

VILLAGE AND TOWN FACILITIES
Bowness to Newcastle – Walking East   E ▶ FROM BOWNESS

PLACE*	DISTANCE* MILES/KM	ATM	POST OFFICE	TOURIST INFO*	EATING PLACE*	FOOD SHOP	CAMP-SITE	BUNK/ HOSTEL*	B&B* HOTEL
Bowness-on-Solway					✓✓		✓	B	✓✓
Port Carlisle 1/1.6					✓(r)				
Drumburgh 3.5/5.6					✓(r)				
(Boustead Hill) (0.3/0.5)							✓	B	✓
Burgh-by-Sands 2.5/5					✓				
Beaumont (& Monkhill) 1.5/2.4					✓		✓		
Grinsdale 2/3.2					✓(r)				
Carlisle 3.5/5.6		✓	✓	TIC	✓✓	✓		H	✓✓
Crosby-on-Eden 5/8					✓	✓(r)	✓		
(Irthington) (0.6/1)					✓				✓
Newtown 5/8.1						✓(r)			✓
(Brampton) (2/3.2)		✓	✓	VC	✓✓	✓			✓
Walton 2/3.2			(✓)		✓		✓	BB	✓
(Lanercost Priory)(0.75/1.25)				VC	✓				
Banks 2.5/4							✓		
Birdoswald 2.5/4.1					✓				
Gilsland 2/3.2			(✓)		✓			B	✓
(Greenhead/Holmhead) (0.3/0.5)					✓		✓	H&B	✓
Carvoran 2.5/4.1					✓(m)				
(Haltwhistle) (2/3.2)		✓	✓	TIC	✓✓	✓			✓
(Once Brewed) (0.25/0.4)				NPC/TIC	✓		✓	YHA&B	✓
Steel Rigg 5.5/8.9									
Housesteads 4/6.4					✓				✓
(Old Repeater Stn) (0.5/0.8)							✓(u)		✓
Black Carts 7/11.3							✓	B	
Chollerford 2/3.2					✓		✓		✓
(Humshaugh) (1/1.6)					✓	✓			✓
Wall 1/1.6							✓		✓
Acomb–Hexham–Corbridge alternative route									
(Acomb)(1.5/2.4 + 2.25/3.5 to Path)					✓✓				✓
(Hexham) (4.5/7.2)		✓	✓	TIC	✓✓	✓			✓✓
(Corbridge)(3/4.8 from Halton)	✓	✓	✓	TIC	✓✓	✓			✓✓
Port Gate (A68) 4/6.4					✓				
East Wallhouses 4/6.4					✓✓		✓		✓
Heddon-on-the-Wall 6/9.7		✓£	✓		✓✓	✓			✓✓
(Wylam) (1/1.6)		✓	✓		✓✓	✓			✓✓
Newcastle/Wallsend 15/24.2	✓	✓			✓✓	✓		YHA&H	✓✓

TOTAL DISTANCE 84 miles/135.5km

*NOTES

> **PLACE** Places in brackets eg (Haltwhistle) are a short walk off the route.
> **DISTANCE** Distances given **in bold** are between places directly on the route.
> (from Steel Rigg to Housesteads, for example, is 4 miles/6.4km)
> Distances in (brackets) are the distances off the path but not necessarily
> from the previous place mentioned.
> **ATM)** £ = charges a fee for withdrawals
> **POST OFFICE** (✓) = pop-up post office and/or limited service

PLANNING YOUR WALK

VILLAGE AND TOWN FACILITIES

Newcastle to Bowness – Walking West ◀ W FROM NEWCASTLE

PLACE*	DISTANCE* MILES/KM	BANK (ATM)	POST OFFICE	TOURIST INFO*	EATING PLACE*	FOOD SHOP	CAMP-SITE	BUNK/ HOSTEL*	B&B/ HOTEL
Newcastle/Wallsend		✔	✔		✔✔	✔		YHA&H	✔✔
Heddon-on-Wall 15/24.2		✔£	✔		✔	✔		H	✔
(Wylam)	(1/1.6)	✔	✔		✔✔	✔			✔
East Wallhouses 6/9.5					✔		✔		✔
Port Gate (A68) 4/6.4					✔				
Corbridge–Hexham–Acomb alternative route									
(Acomb)(1.5/2.4 + 2.25/3.5 to Path)					✔✔				✔
(Hexham)	(4.5/7.2)	✔	✔	TIC	✔✔	✔			✔✔
(Corbridge)(3/4.8 from Halton)✔			✔	TIC	✔✔	✔			✔✔
Wall	4/6.4						✔		✔
Chollerford	1/1.6				✔	✔			✔
(Humshaugh)	(1/1.6)		✔			✔			✔
Black Carts	2/3.2						✔	B	
Housesteads	7/11.3				✔				✔
(Old Repeater Stn)	(0.5/0.8)						✔(u)		✔
Steel Rigg	4/6.4						✔	YHA&B	✔
(Once Brewed)	(0.25/0.4)			NPC/TIC	✔				
(Haltwhistle)	(2/3.2)	✔	✔	TIC	✔✔	✔			✔✔
Carvoran	5.5/8.9				✔(m)				
(Greenhead/Holmhead)	(0.3/0.5)				✔		✔	H&B	✔
Gilsland	2.5/4.1	✔	(✔)		✔✔			B	✔✔
Birdoswald	2/3.2				✔				
Banks	2.5/4.1						✔		✔
(Lanercost Priory)(0.75/1.25)				VC	✔				
Walton	2.5/4.1		(✔)		✔		✔	BB	✔✔
(Brampton)	(2/3.2)	✔	✔	VC	✔✔	✔			✔✔
Newtown	2/3.2				✔(r)				✔
(Irthington)	(0.6/1)				✔				✔
Crosby-on-Eden	5/8.1				✔(r)	✔			✔
Carlisle	5/8	✔	✔	TIC	✔✔	✔		H	✔✔
Grinsdale	3.5/5.6				✔(r)				
Beaumont (& Monkhill) 2/3.2					✔	✔			
Burgh-by-Sands	1.5/2.4				✔				
(Boustead Hill)	(0.3/0.5)						✔	B	✔
Drumburgh	2.5/5					✔(r)			
Port Carlisle	3.5/5.6				✔	✔(r)			
Bowness-on-Solway 1/1.6					✔✔		✔	B	✔✔

TOURIST INFO	TIC/VC = Tourist Information/Visitor Centre NPC = National Park Centre
EATING PLACE	✔ = one place ✔✔ = two ✔✔✔ = three or more ✔(m) = café for museum visitors only
FOOD SHOP	✔(r) = unmanned refreshments stall with honesty box or vending machine
CAMPING	(u) = no official campsite though can camp nearby; ask locals
BUNK/HOSTEL	YHA = YHA hostel H = independent hostel B = bunkhouse
B&B/HOTEL	✔ = one place ✔✔ = two ✔✔✔ = three or more

PLANNING YOUR WALK

PLANNING YOUR WALK

SUGGESTED ITINERARIES – Bowness to Newcastle – Walking East

The itineraries below are suggestions only and should be adapted to suit your own preferences. **Don't forget** to add the travelling time before and after the walk.

CAMPING

E ▶ FROM BOWNESS

	Relaxed		Medium		Fast	
Night	**Place**	**Approx Distance** miles/km	**Place**	**Approx Distance** miles/km	**Place**	**Approx Distance** miles/km
0	Bowness		Bowness		Bowness	
1	Beaumont	8.5/13.7	Beaumont	8.5/13.7	Crosby-on-Eden	19/30.6
2	Crosby-on-Eden	10.5/16.9	Walton	17.5/28.1	Once Brewed	22/35.4
3	Walton	7/11.3	Once Brewed	15/24.2	E Wallhouses	22/35.4
4	Greenhead	9/14.5	Wall	14/22.5	Newcastle *	21/33.8
5	Once Brewed	6/9.7	Heddon *	14/22.5		
6	Chollerford	13/20.9	Newcastle *	15/24.2		
7	Heddon *	15/24.2				
8	Newcastle *	15/24.2				

* No campsites in Newcastle or Heddon but bunkhouses or hostels available

STAYING IN BUNKHOUSES/CAMPING BARNS/HOSTELS

	Relaxed		Medium		Fast	
Night	**Place**	**Approx Distance** miles/km	**Place**	**Approx Distance** miles/km	**Place**	**Approx Distance** miles/km
0	Bowness		Bowness		Bowness	
1	Boustead Hill	6/9.7	Boustead Hill	6/9.7	Carlisle	14/22.5
2	Carlisle	8/12.9	Carlisle	8/12.9	Walton	12/19.3
3	Walton	12/19.3	Walton	12/19.3	Once Brewed	15/24.2
4	Greenhead	9/14.5	Greenhead	9/14.5	Chollerford	13/20.9
5	Once Brewed	6/9.7	Old Repeater Stn	15/24.2	Heddon	15/24.2
6	Black Carts	11/17.7	Heddon	19/30.6	Newcastle	15/24.2
7	Heddon	17/27.4	Newcastle	15/24.2		
8	Newcastle	15/24.2				

STAYING IN B&B-STYLE ACCOMMODATION

	Relaxed		Medium		Fast	
Night	**Place**	**Approx Distance** miles/km	**Place**	**Approx Distance** miles/km	**Place**	**Approx Distance** miles/km
0	Bowness		Bowness		Bowness	
1	Carlisle	14/22.5	Carlisle	14/22.5	Carlisle	14/22.5
2	Newtown	10/16	Walton	12/19.3	Gilsland	19/30.6
3	Gilsland	9/14.5	Once Brewed	15/24.2	Chollerford	21/33.8
4	Once Brewed	8/12.9	Chollerford	13/20.9	Heddon	15/24.2
5	Chollerford	13/20.9	Heddon	15/24.2	Newcastle	15/24.1
6	E Wallhouses	9/14.5	Newcastle	15/24.2		
7	Newburn	9/14.5				
8	Newcastle	12/19.3				

SUGGESTED ITINERARIES – Newcastle to Bowness – Walking West

The itineraries below are suggestions only and should be adapted to suit your own preferences. **Don't forget** to add the travelling time before and after the walk.

CAMPING

◄ W FROM NEWCASTLE

Night	Relaxed Place	Approx Distance miles/km	Medium Place	Approx Distance miles/km	Fast Place	Approx Distance miles/km
0	Newcastle *		Newcastle *		Newcastle *	
1	Heddon *	15/24.2	Heddon *	15/24.2	E Wallhouses	21/33.8
2	Chollerford	15/24.2	Wall	14/22.5	Once Brewed	22/35.4
3	Once Brewed	13/20.9	Once Brewed	14/22.5	Crosby-on-Eden	22/35.4
4	Greenhead	6/9.7	Walton	15/24.2	Bowness	19/30.6
5	Walton	9/14.5	Beaumont	17.5/28.1		
6	Crosby-on-Eden	7/11.3	Bowness	8.5/13.7		
7	Beaumont	10.5/16.9				
8	Bowness	8.5/13.7				

* No campsites in Newcastle or Heddon but bunkhouses or hostels available

STAYING IN BUNKHOUSES/CAMPING BARNS/HOSTELS

Night	Relaxed Place	Approx Distance miles/km	Medium Place	Approx Distance miles/km	Fast Place	Approx Distance miles/km
0	Newcastle		Newcastle		Newcastle	
1	Heddon	15/24.2	Heddon	15/24.2	Heddon	15/24.2
2	Black Carts	17/27.4	Old Repeater Stn	19/30.6	Chollerford	15/24.2
3	Once Brewed	11/17.7	Greenhead	15/24.2	Once Brewed	13/20.9
4	Greenhead	6/9.7	Walton	9/14.5	Walton	15/24.2
5	Walton	9/14.5	Carlisle	12/19.3	Carlisle	12/19.3
6	Carlisle	12/19.3	Boustead Hill	8/12.9	Bowness	14/22.5
7	Boustead Hill	8/12.9	Bowness	6/9.7		
8	Bowness	6/9.7				

STAYING IN B&B-STYLE ACCOMMODATION

Night	Relaxed Place	Approx Distance miles/km	Medium Place	Approx Distance miles/km	Fast Place	Approx Distance miles/km
0	Newcastle		Newcastle		Newcastle	
1	Newburn	11/18	Heddon	15/24.2	Heddon	15/24.2
2	Wallhouses	7.5/12	Chollerford	15/24.2	Chollerford	15/24.2
3	Chollerford	11.5/18.5	Once Brewed	12/19.3	Gilsland	21/33.8
4	Once Brewed	12/19.3	Walton	16/26	Carlisle	19/30.6
5	Gilsland	9/14.5	Carlisle	12/19.3	Bowness	14/22.5
6	Newtown	9/14.5	Bowness	14/22.5		
7	Carlisle	10/16				
8	Bowness	14/22.5				

PLANNING YOUR WALK

I also think – although others may disagree – that the trail looks slightly better from the west; in particular, you get a much better idea of just what an imposing natural barrier the crags are when looking at it from the west (and yes, of course, you can just look back and see the same view if travelling westwards – but it's a rare hiker who actually does). And finally, isn't there something poetic about finishing a walk along the Wall at a place called Wallsend?

So for all these reasons, the guide section of this book is ordered from west to east. But those who want to walk westwards from Newcastle shouldn't despair. This book is a two-direction guide, with walking routes written in both directions and maps tailored to suit those walking westwards as well as those walking eastwards. Those choosing to start their walk in Newcastle could argue that it feels more natural to walk out of a big city and into open country. The turrets and milecastles are also numbered from east to west (see box p124) as that is the direction that the Romans built the Wall – so you could argue that, in

PLANNING YOUR WALK

❏ VISITING THE FORTS – A WALKER'S VIEW

To many or even most people on the Hadrian's Wall Path, the various forts and museums are little more than milestones on the trail: places to tick off as they pass by rather than places to actually stop at and visit. However, some of our readers – many not even particularly interested in Roman history (or at least not before the trail) – write in to tell us how much they enjoyed the various museums on the way. The following from Jane Johnson is a good example:

'To get an idea of the Roman remains we decided it would be good to have visited the sites before commencing the walk, establishing their location as well as those of the Roman roads. We camped for a week, basing ourselves at Haltwhistle; this enabled us to visit Chesters, Vindolanda (5hrs), Corbridge etc as well as the smaller off-route places such as the bridge abutment across from Chesters. From Haltwhistle it was an easy train ride to Newcastle to visit the sites along the West Road and the Great North Museum: Hancock with its new displays.

We didn't do the actual walk until the following year but even with the gap in time we really appreciated having been to the main sites as we had some knowledge of things. Before setting off we spent two nights in Newcastle to see the rest of the sites around there. Arriving at the station in the early afternoon we hopped on the metro to South Shields to reach Arbeia, well worth visiting, before settling in to the city.

The next day we went to Segedunum and then did the short walk back to the city (not the most inspiring start to a walk!) leaving a 10-mile stretch to Heddon on the second day. This means you can visit Segedunum and walk the first five miles without baggage. What an easy start to the walk. Both Arbeia and Segedunum are great, especially having the reconstructions as they give an idea of the size of buildings. We wanted to stay in B&Bs for the actual walk and used a baggage transfer company to take our bags. Of course all this could be done in about two weeks' holiday if you have both the time and finance.'   **Jane Johnson**

While Jane's itinerary and her determination to see the forts may be a bit too detailed and comprehensive for some, we heartily agree with her sentiments; if nothing else, her email is at least further testimony that it is worth visiting some of the forts on the way.

one sense at least, you're following the timeline of the Wall by walking in this direction. And I have to say that, whenever I've started the trail in Newcastle, I don't think I've enjoyed it any less when compared to starting in Bowness.

Overall, I think your decision about which direction you're going to walk should depend on whichever is more convenient. If you find it easier or cheaper to book your transport to and from the Wall by starting at a certain end, or the accommodation you have chosen along the way is available if you head one way but not if you head the other, then these should be the deciding factors in choosing which way to go. Because whatever way you trek, it's going to be fun.

What to take

Deciding how much to take can be difficult. You've probably been told that you should take only the bare essentials but at the same time you must ensure you have all the equipment necessary to make the trip safe and comfortable.

KEEP YOUR LUGGAGE LIGHT

Experienced backpackers know that there is some sort of complicated formula governing the success of a trek, in which the enjoyment of the walk is inversely proportional to the amount carried. Carrying a heavy rucksack slows you down, tires you out and gives you aches and pains in parts of the body that you never knew existed. It is imperative, therefore, that you take your time while packing and that you are ruthless when you do; if it's not essential, don't take it.

HOW TO CARRY IT

If you are using one of the baggage-transfer services (see pp26-7), you must contact them beforehand to find out what their regulations are regarding the weight and size of the luggage you wish them to carry. Even if you are using one of these services, you will still need to carry a small **daypack**, filled with those items that you will need during the day: water bottle or pouch, this book, map, sun-screen, sun hat, wet-weather gear, some food, money and so on.

If you have decided to forego the services of the baggage carriers you will have to consider your **rucksack** even more carefully. Ultimately its size will depend on your plans for where you will stay and what you will eat. If you are camping and cooking for yourself you will probably need a 70- to 95-litre rucksack, which should be large enough to carry a small tent, sleeping bag, cooking equipment, crockery, cutlery and food. Those not carrying their home with them should find a 40- to 60-litre rucksack sufficient.

When choosing a rucksack, make sure it has a stiffened back and can be adjusted to fit your own back comfortably. Don't just try the rucksack out in the shop: take it home, fill it with things and then try it out around the house and take it out for a short walk. Only then can you be certain that it fits. Make sure the hip belt and chest strap (if there is one) are fastened tightly as this helps distribute the weight more comfortably, with most of it being carried on the hips. Include a small daypack inside the rucksack, as this will be useful to carry things in when leaving the main pack at the hostel or B&B.

Don't forget to bring a **waterproof rucksack cover**. Most rucksacks these days have them 'built in' to the sack, but you can also buy them separately for less than a tenner. Lining your bag with a strong **bin liner** is another sensible, cut-price idea. Finally, it's also a good idea to keep everything wrapped in plastic bags inside the rucksack; that way, even if it does pour with rain, everything should remain dry.

FOOTWEAR

Boots
Most hikers choose to wear a decent pair of strong, durable trekking boots, but it is perfectly possible to hike the trail in running shoes or cross-trainers, which are usually much more comfortable. The downside is that they are much less waterproof, if waterproof at all, so you will find you spend many an evening trying to dry them out in preparation for your next day's walk. Many hikers prefer boots with a good ankle support; the ground can occasionally be rough and stony and twisted ankles are commonplace. Whatever footwear you choose, it is essential that your shoes or boots are thoroughly 'broken in' so they're comfortable and not likely to cause blisters. Never, under any circumstances, attempt to start a hike like this one in new boots!

In addition, some people bring an extra pair of shoes or trainers (or even just sandals or flip-flops) to wear off the trail. This is not essential but if you've got room in your luggage, why not?

Socks
❏ *I have sent you ... pairs of socks from Sattua, two pairs of sandals and two pairs of underpants ...* Tablet 346 of the **Vindolanda Tablets** (see p149)

If you don't have a pair of the modern hi-tech walking socks the old system of wearing a thin liner sock under a thicker wool sock is just as good. Bring a few pairs of each; you certainly don't want to start any day of hiking in socks that are anything other than clean and bone dry.

CLOTHES

In a country notorious for its unpredictable climate it is imperative that you pack enough clothes to cover every extreme of weather, from burning hot to bloomin' freezing. Modern hi-tech outdoor clothes come with a range of fancy names and brands but they all still follow the basic two- or three-layer principle, with an inner base layer to transport sweat away from your skin, a mid-layer for warmth and an outer layer to protect you from the wind and rain.

A thin lightweight **thermal top** of a synthetic material is ideal as the base layer as it draws moisture (ie sweat) away from your body. Cool in hot weather

Of course, leg wear is very much an individual choice, but personally, I like those 'zip-off' trousers where you can remove the trouser beneath the knee. However, it must be said that my partner, for whom sartorial choice is less about a garment's practicality than its look, is not so keen. Indeed, I've noticed that whenever I wear them, she tends to walk a few yards behind me and on more than one occasion I've even heard her denying that we're together. But maybe I'm wrong to blame my trousers...

and warm when worn under other clothes in the cold, pack at least one thermal top. Over the top in cold weather a mid-weight **polyester fleece** should suffice. Fleeces are light, more water-resistant than the alternatives (such as a woolly jumper), remain warm even when wet and pack down small in rucksacks; they are thus ideal trekking gear. Over the top of all this a **waterproof jacket** is essential. 'Breathable' jackets cost a small fortune (though prices are falling all the time) but they do prevent the build-up of condensation.

Leg wear
Some hikers find trekking trousers an unnecessary investment and any light, quick-drying trouser should suffice. Jeans are not recommended as they are heavy and dry slowly. A pair of **waterproof trousers** *is* more than useful, however, while on really hot sunny days you'll be glad you brought your **shorts**.

Thermal **long johns** take up little room and could be vital if the weather starts to close in. **Gaiters** are not essential but, again, those who bring them are always glad they did, for they provide extra protection when walking through muddy ground and when the vegetation around the trail is dripping wet after bad weather.

Other clothes
Three or four changes of **underwear** is fine. Any more is excessive, any less unhygienic. Because backpacks can cause bra straps to dig painfully into the skin, women may find a **sports bra** more comfortable.

You may like to consider a woolly **hat** and **gloves** – you'd be surprised how cold it can get up on the moors, even in summer – and a **sun hat**.

TOILETRIES

Once again, take the minimum. **Soap**, **towel** (quick-dry micro-fibre camping towels are particularly useful as they pack up very small) a **toothbrush** and **toothpaste** are pretty much essential (although those staying in B&Bs will find that most provide soap and towels anyway). Some **toilet paper** could also prove vital on the trail, particularly if using public toilets (which occasionally run out).

Other items: **razor**; **deodorant**; **tampons/sanitary towels** and a high factor **sun-screen** should cover just about everything.

FIRST-AID KIT

A small first-aid kit could prove useful for those emergencies that occur along the trail. This kit should include **ibuprofen** or **paracetamol**; **plasters** for minor cuts; **moleskin**, **Compeed**, **Second Skin** or some other treatment for blisters; a **bandage** or elasticated joint support for supporting a sprained ankle or a weak knee; **antiseptic wipes**; **antiseptic cream**; **safety pins**; **tweezers** and **scissors**.

You may sometimes encounter biting midges in the early morning or late evening between June and August so it's worth taking **insect repellent**.

GENERAL ITEMS

Essential

Everybody should have some **emergency food**, a **water bottle** or pouch, a **torch** and **spare batteries**, a **penknife**, a **whistle** (the international distress signal is six blasts on the whistle or six flashes with a torch), and an **alarm** on a watch or phone.

If you know how to use it properly you may find a **compass** handy. Most people find a **mobile phone** invaluable too, particularly if it's a **smartphone** with GPS capabilities and a camera. Phone reception is usually good on the trail and it's extremely handy to be able to phone ahead in the mornings to confirm your accommodation for that night, or to be able to arrange a lift from the Wall to your B&B at the end of the day. Just don't forget your **phone charger**!

Useful items and luxuries

Those with weak knees may find a **walking pole** or **sticks** useful. Other things worth considering include a **map** (though of course this book has that covered), a **book** for days off, or on train and bus journeys, a **camera** (if you don't have a smartphone with a reasonable camera), a pair of **sunglasses**, **binoculars** and a **vacuum flask** for hot drinks.

CAMPING GEAR

For both campers and those intending to stay in the various bunkhouses/ camping barns en route, a **sleeping bag** is essential. A two- to three-season bag should suffice for summer. Campers will also need a decent **tent** or bivvy bag, a **sleeping mat** and **cooking equipment** (fuel and stove, cutlery, pans, a cup and a scrubber for washing up). If you're more concerned about the weight of your bag than the cost of your trip, you could get away without bringing cooking equipment, as most campsites are either close to pubs or cafés that do food, or can provide food themselves. This does prove expensive, though, if you 'dine out' every night, and many will say that cooking is half the fun of a camping trip.

MONEY AND DOCUMENTS

(Also see Money, p26) ATMs (cash machines) are infrequent along the Hadrian's Wall Path and, apart from pubs, few places along the trail accept **debit** or **credit cards** as payment either – though some B&Bs now do, as do many shops, restaurants and cafés in the larger towns just off the trail. As a result, you should always carry a fair amount of **cash** with you, just to be on the safe side. Crime on the trail is thankfully rare but you may want to carry your money in a **moneybelt**, just to be safe.

Don't forget your **Hadrian's Wall Path Passport** (see box p42). If you are a member of **English Heritage** or the **National Trust** (see box p77), bring your **membership cards**; membership of English Heritage in particular will save you money, allowing free entrance to the Roman forts and other attractions.

MAPS

The hand-drawn maps in this book cover the trail at a scale of 1:20,000. This large scale, combined with the notes and tips written on the maps, should be more than enough to stop you losing your way. Nevertheless, some people like to have a separate map of the region; such maps can prove invaluable should you need to abandon the path and find the quickest route off the trail in an emergency. They also help in identifying local features and landmarks and devising possible side trips.

Perhaps the best map for the whole walk is the 52-page *Hadrian's Wall Adventure Atlas*, published by A–Z (🖳 az.co.uk); this booklet includes the OS maps (1:25,000) with the path clearly marked; also included are distances and an index. Also worth considering is *Hadrian's Wall Path* (XT40) strip map (1:40,000) published by Harvey Map Services (🖳 harveymaps.co.uk); the bonus for this map is that it is waterproof.

Ordnance Survey (🖳 ordnancesurvey.co.uk) also produce a waterproof strip map (Explorer OL43) that covers the central section of the trail (centred on

---

❏ DIGITAL MAPPING

There are numerous software packages now available that provide Ordnance Survey (OS) maps for a PC, smartphone, tablet or GPS. Maps are downloaded into an app from where you can view, print and create routes on them.

Memory Map (🖳 memory-map.co.uk) currently sell OS Explorer 1:25,000 and Landranger 1:50,000 mapping covering the whole of Britain with prices from £19.99 for a one year subscription. **Anquet** (🖳 anquet.com) has the full range of OS 1:25,000 maps covering all of the UK from £28 per year annual subscription.

Or you can go to the original source itself: for a subscription of £4.99 for one month or £28.99 for a year (on their current offer) **Ordnance Survey** (🖳 ordnancesurvey.co.uk) allows you to download and use their UK maps (1:25,000 scale) on a mobile or tablet without a data connection for a specific period.

Harvey (🖳 harveymaps.co.uk) currently use the US Avenza maps app for their Hadrian's Wall Path map (1:40,000 scale, $14.99).

It is important to ensure any digital mapping software on your smartphone uses pre-downloaded maps, stored on your device, and doesn't need to download them on-the-fly, as this may be expensive and will be impossible without a signal. Remember that battery life will be significantly reduced, compared to normal usage, when you are using the built-in GPS and running the screen for long periods.

PLANNING YOUR WALK

❏ **HADRIAN'S WALL PATH PASSPORT**

A simple piece of folded card, the Hadrian's Wall Path Passport not only provides walkers with a bit of fun, and proof that they walked the entire trail, but is also an important measure in protecting the Wall. It is available from May to October only, so encourages walkers to view the trail as a summertime-only activity, and the money raised from it goes towards support for the maintenance of the Path.

You can buy a Passport (£5) in person from Segedunum, Walltown Quarry Country Park, Carlisle TIC, or in Bowness at the King's Arms. They are also available online at 🖥 shoptwmuseums.co.uk or 🖥 www.trailgiftshop.co.uk (but allow plenty of time for delivery which has been known to take up to 2 weeks).

Open up the passport and you'll find seven blank spaces; the idea is to collect seven stamps from various places along the trail. Get the full set and you qualify for the right to purchase a commemorative badge and/or certificate; these are available from most of the above places or by post. The **'stamping stations'** are located at:

• **Bowness-on-Solway** (p88); stamp also at **Banks Promenade shelter** (p92)
• **Carlisle** (p106)
• **Birdoswald Roman Fort** (p129)
• **Housesteads** (p154)
• **Chesters Roman Fort** (p166)
• **East Wallhouses** (p174)
• **Segedunum** (p190)

Haltwhistle and Hexham) at a scale of 1:25,000 as part of their Explorer Outdoor Leisure series. In addition, you'll need Explorer 314, 315 and 316 to cover the rest of the trail. They also offer online maps which you can download and tailor to your requirements by plotting routes, adding notes and photos and so on. A one-month subscription for this service costs £2.99 (£23.99 for one year).

Historic England (🖥 historicengland.org.uk) publish *An Archaeological Map of Hadrian's Wall*. Beautiful, fascinating and insightful, the map includes sites both along and near the Wall. It's probably only for those with a specialist interest in the Wall's history and archaeology, but is arguably the most absorbing map on the Wall and its surroundings.

RECOMMENDED READING

There is a wealth of books on the Wall, as you'd expect, so the following is a mere overview of the better, or at least newer, works. Some of these books can be found in the tourist information centres and at the reception desks of the Roman forts en route. As well as stocking many of the titles listed here, these places also have a number of books about the towns and villages en route, usually printed by local publishers. Furthermore, each of the visitor centres of the major English Heritage historical attractions, such as Housesteads, Chesters and Corbridge, publishes their own guidebook to the site.

The journalist and author Hunter Davies, who grew up at the western end of the trail, wrote the historical travelogue *A Walk Along the Wall* (Frances Lincoln; originally published in 1974), the result of spending a year trekking along and studying the wall.

Hadrian's Wall, by David Breeze and Brian Dobson, is part of the Penguin History Series and deals with the history of the Wall as well as the day-to-day activities of those who lived in its shadow, both soldiers and locals, during the Roman occupation.

On a similar subject, *Hadrian's Wall in the Days of the Romans*, by Ronald Embleton and Frank Graham (WJ Williams & Son Books Ltd; 2003), does exactly what it says on the cover; *Hadrian's Wall AD122-410* by Nic Fields (Osprey Publishing) covers much the same ground but it has some great illustrations and they've also written a second in the series, *Rome's Northern Frontier AD 70-235: Beyond Hadrian's Wall*, which looks in greater detail at how the northern border of the empire moved over time, and the various fortifications the Romans built (the Gask Ridge, Antonine Wall etc) to defend it.

Newer, *The Wall: Rome's Greatest Frontier* (Birlinn Ltd) by Alistair Moffatt, also deals with the building of the Wall and has a good section on the Vindolanda tablets. One of the leading Wall experts, Anthony R Birley, has produced a biography of the enigmatic man behind the Wall: *Hadrian, The Restless Emperor* (Routledge), though it must be said that the text is a little dry.

If you're British and of a certain age you'll remember the Haynes series of car manuals. Well, as cars get more intelligent, thus reducing the potential for you to be able to fix them yourself, Haynes seem to have taken the rather sensible decision to concentrate on subjects other than vehicles, and that includes a tome on Hadrian's Wall entitled *Hadrian's Wall Operations Manual: From Construction to World Heritage Site (AD122 Onwards)*. Gimmicky though it may sound, it's also comprehensive and very accessible.

While researching for a previous edition I had the great good fortune to bump into Wall expert Alan Whitworth in Brampton. Alan has written two books on the Wall, both fascinating. The first, *Hadrian's Wall Through Time* (Amberley Publishing), concentrates on the work of local Quaker teacher James Irwin Coates, who visited the Wall on several occasions between 1877 and 1896, and each time drew the Wall as he found it, with incredible accuracy. Together his sketches form a complete record of the Wall as it then stood, and in his book Alan has juxtaposed the works of Coates with modern photographs by the author to show how the Wall has changed over the past 150 years. The drawings are charming, and Alan's book is absorbing. His second tome, *Saving the Wall: The Conservation of Hadrian's Wall, 1746-1987* (Amberley Press),

PLANNING YOUR WALK

☐ **'BOARD' WITH BOOKS ON HADRIAN'S WALL?**

Then help is at hand, for there is now a **Hadrian's Wall board game**. Made by Renegade Game Studios (🖳 uk.renegadegamestudios.com/hadrians-wall), it costs an eye-watering £66. For this amount, you have the privilege of playing the part of a Roman General in charge of constructing a milecastle and bits of the Wall. The action takes place over six rounds, or years, and in this time you must complete all building work as well as man the Wall. In additon, you are expected to woo the locals by providing services and entertainment. The player that can successfully complete all these tasks will win the game and be crowned *Legatus Legionis*: the head of a legion.

co-written with Stephen Leach, looks at the heroes of the last two centuries whose efforts together ensured that at least some of the Wall remains to this day.

The Great Wall of Britain – A Walk Along Hadrian's Wall (Hayloft), by the illustrator Anton Hodge, is a travelogue-cum-geographical-historical-tour of the Roman Wall. You may find it locally, or you can visit the author's website: 💻 antonhodge.co.uk. In a similar 'travelogue' vein is Bob Bibby's *On the Wall with Hadrian* (Eye Books).

For a greater insight into what it might have been to have actually lived and worked on the Wall, check out both *Hadrian's Wall: Everyday Life on a Roman Frontier* by Patricia Southern (Amberley Publishing) and *Everyday Life of a Soldier on Hadrian's Wall* by Paul Elliott (Fonthill Media). Both have their merits, but more comprehensive than either is the wonderful *Living on the Edge of Empire: The Objects and People of Hadrian's Wall* (Pen & Sword Archaeology). Author Rob Collins has contributions from various curators who work along Hadrian's Wall, including curators and keepers of archaeology from the Tullie House Museum in Carlisle (see p110) and the Great North Museum: Hancock (p208), as well as Arbeia (p212) and Segedunum forts (p190).

🖵 WALL- AND PATH-RELATED WEBSITES

💻 **nationaltrail.co.uk/hadrians-wall-path** The official site of the Hadrian's Wall Path and the essential first stop for those looking to walk the Wall. Check out the slideshow (trail gallery), trail officer's blog, maps, sections on accommodation and publications. Best of all, register with them and they'll send you newsletters.

💻 **hadrianswallcountry.co.uk** The most complete website on the Wall itself, this is the website of Hadrian's Wall Country with lists of tour agencies, accommodation, travel information, events, history and the latest news. Unlike the website above, it is not specifically for walkers, though it does have a page on walking.

💻 **bbc.co.uk/history/ancient/romans** The BBC's website on the Romans, includes some useful timelines and interesting articles by various boffins. However, do note that it is no longer updated.

💻 **walltogether.org.uk** The website for Hadrian's Wall Association; this aims to promote and support the management and maintenance of the Hadrian's Wall Frontiers including the National Trail. However, do note that the website is currently only one page and is 'under review'. What this means for the site, the organisation as a whole and the *Essential Services* guide that they publish is, as yet, unknown.

💻 **heartofhadrianswall.com** Gives information about places to stay and eat as well as services in the most central – and thus loveliest – area of the Wall.

💻 **visitlakedistrict.com** Official website for the Lake District, Cumbria, though does contain pages on Carlisle and the Hadrian's Wall Path.

💻 **romaninscriptionsofbritain.org** Granted, this may not be for everyone, but Wall geeks will love this site which documents every inscription on the Wall and, apparently, in the whole of Britain too.

💻 **youtube.com** Search this video-sharing website for 'Hadrian's Wall' and you'll find plenty of videos ranging from 'follow my walk' to historical background, but of particular interest are: *Hadrian's Wall 122-2022* by Jon Imrye, commemorating the Wall's 1900th anniversary; and *Roman Vindolanda: An Introduction* by the Vindolanda Trust, presented by Dr Andrew Birley, CEO of the Trust.

❑ **SOURCES OF FURTHER INFORMATION**

Tourist information centres (TICs)
Tourist information centres are based in towns throughout Britain and provide all manner of locally specific information. The centres listed here are on or close to the Hadrian's Wall Path: **Carlisle** (see p106), **Brampton** (see p119), **Haltwhistle** (p143), **Hexham** (see p217) and **Corbridge** (see p221). The National Landscape Discovery Centre at **Once Brewed** is essentially one giant tourist information centre too.

Organisations for walkers
● **Backpackers' Club** (🖳 www.backpackersclub.co.uk) A club aimed at people who are involved or interested in lightweight camping through walking, cycling, skiing and canoeing. They produce a quarterly magazine, provide members with a comprehensive advisory and information service on all aspects of backpacking, organise weekend trips and also publish a farm-pitch directory. Membership is £20 a year or £30 for families.
● **The Long Distance Walkers' Association** (🖳 www.ldwa.org.uk) An association of people with the common interest of long-distance walking. Membership includes a journal, *Strider*, three times per year giving details of challenge events and local group walks as well as articles on the subject. Individual membership is £18 a year (£26 for non-UK residents) whilst family membership for two adults and all children under 18 is £25.50 a year; a £3 discount is offered for those who pay by direct debit.
● **Ramblers** (🖳 www.ramblers.org.uk) Looks after the interests of walkers throughout Britain. They publish a large amount of useful information including their quarterly *Walk* magazine, also available in PDF and audio format. Annual membership costs from £36.60, or £49 for two.

Finally, I must mention two books that I find really useful summaries of Roman history. *The Roman Republic: A Very Short Introduction* (David M Gwynn; OUP) and *The Roman Empire: A Very Short Introduction* (Christopher Kelly; OUP) are perhaps the best fodder you can bring with you for the walk itself: relevant, informative, well-written and, best of all, pocket-sized and lightweight.

Flora and fauna field guides
Now in its 3rd edition, *Collins Bird Guide*, with its beautiful illustrations of British and European birds, continues to be the favourite field guide of both ornithologists and laymen alike. Its *Trees of Britain & Europe* is also OK if you've room in your rucksack and don't know your ash from your alder. As part of their *Gem* series – a collection of cracking guides that are only slightly larger than a pack of playing cards and thus ideal for hiking with – Collins also produces guides to *Mushrooms*, *Butterflies*, *Insects* and *Wild Flowers*.

A rather unusual book – but charming in its way – is John Miles's *Hadrian's Wildlife* (Whittles Publishing) which looks at the animals, birds and landscape that would have existed in the region when the Wall was being built.

There are also some field guide **apps** for smartphones and tablets, including those that can aid in identifying birds by their song as well as by their appearance.

Getting to and from the Hadrian's Wall Path

Carlisle and Newcastle are the main transport hubs for the trail and, conveniently, they all but bookend the path, with Carlisle near the western end and the Newcastle suburb of Wallsend at the eastern end. Both are well connected by public transport to the rest of the country and indeed Europe. However, it should be noted that some of the other places on the trail are less well connected, especially those destinations east and west of Carlisle.

NATIONAL TRANSPORT

By train
Both Newcastle and Carlisle lie on the main England–Scotland rail links. All timetable and fare information can be obtained from **National Rail Enquiries** (☎ 03457-484950 – operates 24hrs; 🖥 nationalrail.co.uk), or the relevant train companies. Tickets can be bought through the train companies or from websites such as 🖥 thetrainline.com.

● **To Newcastle** Newcastle is a stop on the **London North Eastern Railway** (**LNER**; 🖥 lner.co.uk) line between London King's Cross and Edinburgh /Aberdeen/Inverness. There are 2-3 services an hour between London and Newcastle and the journey takes around three hours. There are 2-4 trains per hour from Edinburgh to Newcastle, with the journey taking around 90 minutes.

In addition, the **TransPennine Express** (🖥 tpexpress.co.uk) operates from Liverpool/Manchester Airport, inc Manchester (daily approx 1/hr from both) to Newcastle (journey time 2-3hrs from Liverpool/Manchester Airport) via Leeds and York (additional services from Leeds and York).

● **To Carlisle** Carlisle is a stop on **Avanti West Coast Railway** (🖥 avantiwest coast.co.uk; daily 1-2/hr) services from London Euston to Glasgow via Warrington and also their Edinburgh service via Birmingham & Crewe; the fastest Euston to Carlisle service takes about 3¼ hours. **TransPennine Express** (🖥 tpexpress.co.uk) operates from Manchester Airport (inc Manchester) to Glasgow/ Edinburgh via Carlisle (daily approx 1/hr; 2-2¼hrs from Manchester Airport to Carlisle).

● **Newcastle to/from Carlisle** Now operated by **Northern Trains** (🖥 northern railway.co.uk), the Hadrian's Wall Country Rail Line connects Newcastle and Carlisle (see p50), with trains running 1-2/hr. The service also calls at Corbridge, Hexham and Haltwhistle, with the slower service also stopping at Wylam and Brampton.

By coach
The principal coach (long-distance bus) operator in Britain is **National Express** (🖥 nationalexpress.com). Coach travel is generally cheaper (though with the excellent advance-booking train fares and special deals offered by the train com-

---

❏ GETTING TO BRITAIN

• **By air** Newcastle International Airport (🖥 newcastleairport.com) is the closest to the Hadrian's Wall Path, especially if walking east to west. For those starting their walk at Bowness, the most convenient airport is Carlisle Lake District Airport (🖥 carlisleairport.co.uk) though it's never been busy and has been closed since the pandemic. Your best bet, therefore, for this end of the path is Manchester Airport (🖥 manchesterairport.co.uk), which has many flights and takes just over two hours by train to Carlisle from there. Manchester Airport is also connected to Newcastle by train (see opposite). Other airports that are fairly close include Leeds Bradford (🖥 leeds bradfordairport.co.uk) and Teesside International (formerly Durham Tees Valley Airport; 🖥 teessideinternational.com).

• **From Europe by train** Eurostar (🖥 eurostar.com) operates the high-speed passenger service via the Channel Tunnel between Paris/Brussels/Amsterdam and London. Conveniently, the terminal in London is St Pancras International, which is only a 5-minute walk from Euston, the station for trains to Carlisle; while King's Cross, the station for departures to Newcastle, is even closer to St Pancras, but in the other direction on Euston Rd. For more information about rail services from Europe, contact your national rail provider or Railteam (🖥 railteam.eu).

• **From Europe by coach** Eurolines (🖥 eurolines.com) has a huge network of long-distance coach services connecting over 500 cities throughout Europe to London. But check carefully: often, once expenses such as food for the journey are taken into consideration, it doesn't work out much cheaper than flying, particularly when compared to the prices of some of the budget airlines.

• **From Europe by ferry (with or without a car)** There are numerous ferries plying routes between ports around the UK and those in Ireland and continental Europe. However, the most convenient for Hadrian's Wall Path is DFDS Seaways (🖥 dfds.com) with a daily service connecting Amsterdam and Newcastle.

   A useful website for further information is 🖥 directferries.com.

• **From Europe by car** Eurotunnel (🖥 eurotunnel.com) operates 'le shuttle' train service for vehicles via the Channel Tunnel between Calais and Folkestone taking just 35 minutes. But you've got a long drive from Folkestone to get to the Wall.

PLANNING YOUR WALK

panies, that is not always the case now) but the journey time is longer than if travelling by train (both London to Newcastle and London to Carlisle take at least six hours). There are services to both Newcastle and Carlisle (see box p50).

Low-cost coach company **Megabus** (🖥 uk.megabus.com) runs services between London and Newcastle (and beyond; 5-6/day) but none to Carlisle.

By car

There are reasonable road connections to Hadrian's Wall. Access from the western side is along the M6 from the south (junctions 42, 43 and 44) and A74 (M) from Glasgow to Carlisle. Access from the eastern side is along the A1(M) to Newcastle; take the city-centre exit and follow signs for Wallsend; or take the A19 and follow the signs for Wallsend from there. The A68 links Edinburgh and Darlington and bisects the trail around Corbridge. Finally, the A69 between Newcastle and Carlisle runs parallel to the Wall, usually around 2-5 miles (3-8km) south of it, and is the main access route.

☐ PUBLIC TRANSPORT – BUS SERVICES

• 685 services may be on an Arriva or a Stagecoach bus and tickets are valid on both.

• Drivers of Tynedale Links (TL) services will stop where it is safe to do so. • Not all AD122 services stop at all the places on the route.

No	Operator	Route and frequency details
AD122	GNE	Hexham to Haltwhistle via Chesters Fort, Housesteads, Once Brewed (The Sill), Vindolanda, Milecastle Inn, Walltown (Roman Army Museum) & Greenhead, mid Apr to late Sep daily 5/day, winter Sat & Sun only 4/day
BR1	BR	Laversdale to Carlisle via Irthington, Newtown, Brampton, Linstock & Rickerby, Tue & Fri 1/day
BR3	BR	Brampton to Walltown via Lanercost, Banks, Birdoswald, Gilsland & Greenhead, Wed (& Thur summer only) 2/day, plus 1/day continues from/to Laversdale via Newtown & Irthington
X85	GNE	Newcastle to Hexham via Denton Burn & Corbridge, daily 1/day (Tynedale Xpress)
10	GNE	Newcastle to Hexham via Blaydon & Corbridge, Mon-Sat 2/hr, Sun 1/hr (Tyne Valley Ten)
22	SC	Throckley to Silverlink Retail Park via Lemington, Newburn (Mon-Fri only); Newcastle centre & Wallsend, Mon-Sat 6/hr, Sun 2/hr
74	GNE	Newcastle to Hexham via Matfen, Halton & Errington Coffee House (formerly Errington Arms), Mon-Fri 4/day, Sat 5/day plus 1/day Newcastle to Matfen (TL)
93	SC	Carlisle to Anthorn via Monkhill (out), Beaumont (return), Burgh-by-Sands, Dykesfield, Drumburgh, Glasson, Port Carlisle & Bowness-on-Solway, Mon-Sat 3/day plus 2/day Carlisle to Burgh by Sands via Monkhill (out) or Beaumont (return)
93A	SC	Carlisle to Anthorn via Moorhouse, Mon-Sat 2/day
680	GNE	Hexham to Bellingham via Acomb, Wall, Humshaugh & Wark, Mon-Sat 7-8/day
681	GNE	Alston to Birdoswald via Slaggyford, Haltwhistle, Greenhead & Gilsland & Walltown, Mon-Fri 2/day, Sat 3/day
684	GNE	Newcastle to Hexham via Denton Burn, Lemington, Throckley, Heddon-on-the-Wall, Wylam & Corbridge, Mon-Sat 1/hr (TL)
685	ANE/SC	Newcastle to Carlisle via Lemington, Heddon-on-the-Wall, Corbridge, Hexham, Haydon Bridge, Bardon Mill, Haltwhistle, Greenhead & Brampton, Mon-Sat 1/hr, Sun Newcastle to Hexham 1/hr, Hexham to Carlisle 5/day plus Brampton to Carlisle, Mon-Sat 1-2/hr, Sun 1/hr
686	GNE	Prudhoe to Corbridge via Wylam, Ovingham & Ovington, Mon-Sat 1/day plus 5/day to Wylam & 1/day to Ovington (TL)

Operator contact details: ANE = Arriva North East (⌨ arrivabus.co.uk/north-east); GNE = Go North East (⌨ gonortheast.co.uk); SC = Stagecoach (⌨ stagecoachbus.com); BR = Border Rambler (⌨ borderramblerbus.co.uk; volunteer-run services)

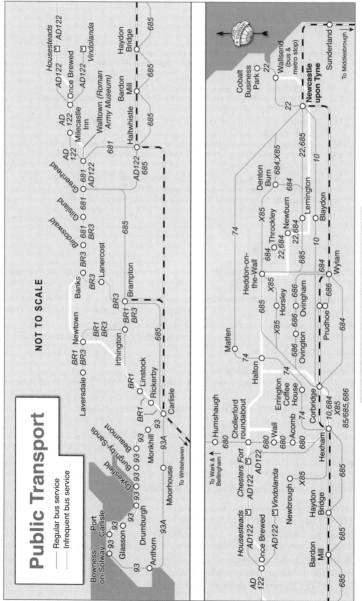

Public Transport

— Regular bus service
······ Infrequent bus service

NOT TO SCALE

❏ **NATIONAL EXPRESS COACH SERVICES**
The services listed below operate daily but not all stops are included. Places in bold are on the Hadrian's Wall Path. See 🖳 nationalexpress.com for more details.

172 Manchester to **Newcastle** via Leeds, Middlesbrough & Sunderland, 2/day
180 Birmingham to Glasgow via Leicester, Nottingham, Sheffield, Leeds, **Newcastle** & Edinburgh, 1/day travelling overnight
181 Birmingham to Glasgow via Manchester, Preston, Lancaster & **Carlisle**, 1/day travelling overnight
182 Birmingham to Edinburgh via Manchester, Preston, Penrith, **Carlisle** & Glasgow, 1/day
426 London to **Newcastle** via Leeds, Middlesborough & Sunderland, 3-4/day
435 London to **Newcastle** via Milton Keynes, Doncaster, Darlington & Durham, 1 day travelling overnight
590 London to Glasgow via Milton Keynes, Birmingham, Penrith & **Carlisle**, 1/day
591 London to Glasgow via Milton Keynes, Sheffield, Leeds, Darlington, **Newcastle**, Berwick-upon-Tweed & Edinburgh, 1/day

LOCAL TRANSPORT

With both a special Hadrian's Wall Country Bus service serving the middle section of the Wall, and good connecting bus services at either end as well as the Hadrian's Wall Country rail line (Newcastle to Carlisle – the oldest coast-to-coast service in the country), public transport along the trail is fairly good. That said, it has reduced in recent years and is constantly under threat of further cuts. At Hexham and Haltwhistle the services dovetail neatly, with the buses calling in at the railway stations.

Hadrian's Wall Country Bus AD122

This bus service, given the appropriate route number AD122, is operated (Easter to end Oct except bank holidays) by Go North East (🖳 gonortheast.co.uk/ad122). The AD122 operates a round-trip route between Hexham and Haltwhistle. In addition to the official stops the driver will stop en route if it is safe to do so. A one-day **AD122 Rover ticket** (£12.50/10/6/30 for adult/student/child/group of four adults) permits unlimited travel on the AD122. Three-day tickets (£25/20/12.50/50) are also available.

Present your AD122 ticket and you'll get 10% off at Vindolanda, Roman Army Museum, Housesteads, Chesters and Birdoswald.

Hadrian's Wall Country Rail Line

The rail line serving the Hadrian's Wall Path runs (very) approximately parallel to and and south of path. While the trail tends to pass through little villages where services are often in short supply – Crosby-on-Eden, Newtown, Walton, Wall, Chollerford, and Heddon – the railway line, in contrast, connects all the main towns where accommodation and eateries are much greater supply: Haltwhistle, Brampton, Hexham and Corbridge. All of these are connected by the Carlisle-Newcastle train line, and are all within walking distance of the trail.

Incidentally, in addition to Carlisle and Newcastle the railway also meets the trail at Greenhead and Gilsland. Unfortunately, the trains do not stop at either. That said, there is a campaign to reopen the station at Gilsland (🖳 rail future.org.uk/gilsland-station), which has been shut since 1967. At the start of 2021 the campaign actually received ministerial backing – so it's not a complete pipe dream. If it ever happens, it will open up a lot of opportunities for walkers.

Services on this line are operated by **Northern** (🖳 northernrailway.co.uk). A **Day Ranger ticket** allowing unlimited day travel on rail services between Sunderland and Whitehaven (which encompasses Newcastle to Carlisle) is available on trains, or from staffed stations, for £24.40/12.20/16.10 adult/child/railcard.

● Newcastle to Carlisle via Prudhoe, Hexham & Haltwhistle, Mon-Sat 1-2/hr, some services stop at Haydon Bridge, Bardon Mill & Brampton.

● Middlesbrough to Hexham via Newcastle, Blaydon, Wylam & Corbridge, Mon-Sat 1/hr.

● Middlesbrough to Carlisle via Newcastle, Hexham, Sun approx 1/hr but not all services stop at Blaydon, Bardon Mill or Brampton.

● Carlisle to Whitehaven, Mon-Sat 1/hr, Sun approx 1/hr.

PLANNING YOUR WALK

HADRIAN'S WALL

History

THE DECISION TO BUILD THE WALL

Though by far the most famous, Hadrian's Wall was in fact just one of four Roman frontiers built between the subjugated south of what is now called Britain and those tribes living in the northern part of the island, known collectively as the Caledones. Since their invasion in AD43, the Romans had at one time or another conquered just about all the tribes living on the island of Britannia. But the area we now call Scotland, once defeated, proved more difficult to keep under control. Even a potentially decisive victory in AD84, somewhere north of the Tay at a place they called Mons Graupius, failed to quell the ongoing insurrection by the Caledones.

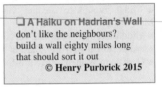

❏ A Haiku on Hadrian's Wall
don't like the neighbours?
build a wall eighty miles long
that should sort it out
© **Henry Purbrick 2015**

Emperors came and went before the pragmatic Domitian (who reigned AD81-96) decided that maintaining a grip over all of the island would ultimately require too many troops; troops that could be more usefully employed in other parts of the empire. It was thus decided to draw a line across the island and establish a border to separate the controllable south from those 'lawless' lands to the north. Initially that boundary was drawn to watch over the glens – the main gateways into and out of the Highlands – a border known as the **Gask Frontier**. However, as more and more troops were withdrawn from Britannia to fight in other parts of the Empire, by necessity the border receded south to the area now known, appropriately enough, as the Borders.

Soon after his accession, Emperor Trajan (AD97-117) decided to move the border still further south, choosing as his frontier the **Stanegate** (though this was not what the Romans called it), the east–west road that ran between the Roman settlements of Carlisle and Corbridge. Built during the governorship of Agricola in AD80, the Stanegate was an important trade route that needed protecting. Trajan's troops set about building a line of turf and timber forts to guard the Stanegate, including Vindolanda (see pp148-50) and Corbridge Roman Town (p223).

HADRIAN BUILDS HIS WALL

Having completely transformed the soldiers, in royal fashion, he made for Britain, where he set right many things and – the first to do so – drew a wall along a length of eighty miles to separate barbarians and Romans. **Aelius Spartianus**, *The Augustan History*

During Trajan's reign, his fortified border was used less as a defensive barrier than as a launchpad for incursions into Scotland; an *attacking* border, if you like. His successor and adopted son, Hadrian (AD117-138), however, saw it as more of a traditional border; as both a defensive barrier and a physical marker for the northern limit of his territories. Following a tour of his dominions in AD122, Hadrian ordered the refortification of Trajan's border with the building of a wall to the north of it along the line of the Whin Sill ridge, a geological fault running across the centre of Britain. This wall was to extend beyond the limits of the Stanegate, to stretch across the entire island. And thus the Wall that we know today began to take shape.

The building of the Wall was something of an organic process, evolving as the geology and political climate dictated. This is best illustrated by the curious size of the foundations, which for much of the eastern half of the walk (from Newcastle west to the River Irthing, which was the first section to be built) are far too broad for the wall that was eventually built upon them, suggesting, of course, that the Romans initially had plans to construct a much bigger barrier. The materials used in the Wall's construction changed too, depending on where it was built. In the east of the country, a core of rubble and puddled clay was used, whereas a limestone mortar core was prevalent in the middle of the country and at the western end an all-turf wall was built (though this, too, was later converted to stone sometime in the second half of the 2nd century AD as the infrastructure improved and the supply of building materials to the line of the Wall became more efficient). Surrounding this inner core the Romans used limestone in the east of the country, basalt around the Whin Sill and sandstone at the western end of the trail. Sandstone is easily eroded, so you won't see any examples of the sandstone Wall today, though you can see some sandstone Wall

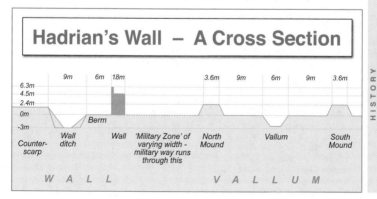

Hadrian's Wall – A Cross Section

HISTORY

stones in the fabric of other buildings built many centuries later, such as in the outer walls of Carlisle Castle, Lanercost Priory and several churches at the western end of the trail.

❏ HADRIAN'S WALL ... OR IS IT?

It should be stated here that there are some who believe that the refortification of Trajan's turf-and-timber wall by Hadrian actually took place *before* the latter visited Britain. The history of the Wall is full of minor controversies like this because, as you'll see when you read this book and other accounts, much of the history of Hadrian's Wall is still open to conjecture. Indeed, up until the 19th century or so, it was actually known as the **Wall of Severus** after the emperor who ruled at the beginning of the 3rd century AD. It was just prior to Severus's reign, in AD197, that the Wall was overrun for the first time, leading to an extensive overhaul and rebuilding of the Wall between AD205 and 208 – which explains why, until archaeological discoveries proved conclusively otherwise, the Wall was originally attributed to Severus.

Indeed, it was only in 1839 and the publication of *History of Northumberland* by **John Hodgson**, a local vicar, that people began to accept that the Wall might be Hadrian's baby after all. In the book, produced in six volumes over more than twenty years, the reverend wrote a lengthy footnote in the final volume presenting all the evidence he'd amassed that the Wall was Hadrian's – and nobody has convincingly argued against his theory ever since. (Unfortunately, Hodgson's health was failing him after working for so many years on a loss-making book, and he died while this final volume was being printed.)

While on the one hand people may find it astonishing that nobody knew who was responsible for such a massive feat of civil engineering, on the other hand it's perhaps not that surprising: there are no contemporary accounts of the construction of the Wall that have yet been discovered, with the earliest mentions having been written in the late 4th century, over 150 years later (such as that by Spartianus, as quoted on p53). What's more, these later authors weren't beyond rewriting history if it suited them. It is believed, for example, that Severus's son, Caracalla, could have been one of the sources for the rumour that his father was the originator of the Wall and not Hadrian. He and Severus had spent three years in northern Britain, and particularly Caledonia, trying to conquer the whole island without success. In AD211, the emperor himself was killed at York and Caracalla had to retreat back to Rome with his tail between his legs. However, in later texts this was portrayed as a victory, such as this example from the late 4th century:

'*... after driving out the enemy, he* [Severus] *fortified Britain, as far as it was useful, with a wall led across the island to each end of the Ocean.*'

Aurelius Victor, *Liber de Caesaribus*

One can only assume, therefore, that this and all the other histories written at this time that claim the Wall for Severus were using the same deceitful source, namely Caracalla or one of his followers, who wanted to present the campaign as a success.

All of which goes to prove just how difficult it is to compile an accurate chronology of the Roman Empire in Britain. So, with the following account of the Wall's construction and history, it's worth bearing in mind that not all of it should be taken as gospel but merely as a version of events currently accepted by the majority of Wall experts. Furthermore, don't be surprised if some of the 'facts' written here are contradicted by accounts in other books.

To carry out all this construction, three legions were employed: the Second Augusta from Caerleon in South Wales, the Twentieth Valeria Victrix from Chester and the Sixth Victrix from York. It was their task to clear the ground of trees and scrub where necessary and quarry, transport and organise the estimated 25 million facing stones that were used in the Wall, each approximately 10 inches long, 6 inches high and 20 inches deep (25cm by 15cm by 50cm respectively). These were then set into the core of the Wall. As a measure of the legions' efficiency, an experiment was conducted in the early 2000s in which a section of the Wall was rebuilt using some original facing stones. It concluded that a gang of 80 men needed 32 wagons and 64 oxen to keep them supplied with enough lime, water and stone to build the Wall. Yet despite all the effort required, the original construction took as little as six years to complete.

It's a level of efficiency that becomes even more impressive when one considers the sheer enormity of the Wall (or *Vallum Aelium* as the Romans may have called it, Aelium being Hadrian's family name). An estimated one ton of stone had to be dragged up for every single yard of it. Stretching from the Solway Firth to the North Sea, the Wall was 80 Roman miles long (73 modern miles) and stood at around 20ft (6m) high and just under 10ft (3m) thick. And just to ensure the security of the Wall, a 20ft (6m) **ditch** was dug on the northern 'Scottish' side along its length; Hadrian's ha-ha, if you will. (It should be noted here that the ditch was not quite an unbroken line; in particular, the ditch disappears around many of the crags, as the crags themselves were considered an adequate defence). A typical Roman defence, this ditch would probably have had a 'false floor' under which sharp spikes would have been concealed. Spikes were also placed in the **Berm**, the flat area between the ditch and the Wall.

Such manifold defences are impressive. Even so, Hadrian's Wall could act as an effective barrier only if it was sufficiently manned. So while the bulk of the men continued to be stationed in the old forts built by Trajan along the Stanegate road, **milecastles** (see box p56) with a capacity for 32 men were built along the entire length of the Wall at intervals of, as their name suggests, one Roman mile (the equivalent of a thousand paces); thus there were a total of 80 milecastles in all. And evenly spaced between each one were two **turrets** or observation posts, 161 all told along the Wall's entire length and always made of stone, regardless of the material of the Wall draped between them. Each could hold 10 men. Estimates suggest that it would have taken just 2½ minutes to run from one turret to the next, so messages could have been relayed along the Wall speedily.

Improving the Wall

Just a couple of years after the Wall was finished the defences were strengthened, possibly in response to pressure from either the Caledones north of the Wall or the Brigantes, whose territory the Wall crossed. Specifically, a series of **16 forts**, each housing 500 to 1000 men, was constructed at irregular intervals along the Wall. These, in many cases, replaced the forts along the Stanegate, which were either converted into supply bases or abandoned altogether. The Wall was extended at its eastern end too, beyond Pons Aelius to Segedunum (see pp190-3).

HISTORY

In addition, 50 to 100 yards (46 to 91 metres) south of the Wall two 10ft (3m) high walls of earth were constructed, with a 10ft (3m) deep, 120ft (36m) wide ditch between them. This earthwork is known as the **Vallum** which, confusingly, means 'wall' in Latin; the name was given by the Venerable Bede, an 8th-century monk and early English historian who was the first to write about the Wall's dimensions. (Incidentally, Bede wrote his *Ecclesiastical History of the English People* at his monastery in Jarrow, a building that was constructed, at least in part, from stones taken from the Wall.) Nobody is completely sure what the Vallum was for; as it is on the south side of the Wall it is unlikely to have been a defensive barrier; nor, with both the Stanegate and, later, the Military Way (see p61) nearby, would it have made much sense to construct a road here. Recent theories have suggested that the Vallum marked the border between the civilian territory and a sort of 'military no-go zone' surrounding the Wall. Another suggestion is that it was used to stop conscripted British soldiers, forced against their will to serve the Romans along the Wall, from running away.

The character of the Wall had now changed. From a lengthy but fairly flimsy construction whose primary purpose was a lookout from which to keep an eye on the locals, the Wall now became a defensive, heavily fortified barrier; while the number of soldiers stationed on the Wall went from a relatively measly 3000 to a much more intimidating 15,000 – a 500% increase in manpower. As a result, it is estimated that around 10% of the entire imperial Roman army was based in Britain, even though the island accounted for only 4% of their total territory.

It should be noted here that although Roman soldiers built the Wall, it was Rome's auxiliary legions who actually manned it. These soldiers were recruited from various parts of the empire – on the Wall alone you'll come across evidence of auxiliary legions from Belgium, Germany, Spain, Iraq, Syria and elsewhere. These auxiliary soldiers were not officially Roman citizens, at least not until they had served a certain length of time in the army (usually about 25 years, the minimum term of service for an auxiliary) and had retired.

HISTORY

❏ **A ROMAN MILE**
It may come to your notice as you're ambling along the Wall that the milecastles built by the Romans aren't actually a mile apart. This is not down to any inaccuracy by Hadrian's builders but merely because the definition of a mile has changed in the intervening 1900 years. The Roman mile was the equivalent of thousand paces of an adult male (hence the word 'mile', from the Latin *mille*, meaning 'one thousand'). In today's money it's about 1481m, or 1620 yards. That of course makes it slightly shorter than our own, modern mile, which is 1760 yards (1609.3m); in fact, one Roman mile is estimated to have been 0.92 modern miles. Thus though Hadrian's Wall was 80 miles long, and as a result had 80 milecastles originally, if it was still complete the Wall today would measure only 73 modern miles. Of course, the trail itself doesn't always follow the Wall exactly, which is why it's slightly longer, at 84 miles.

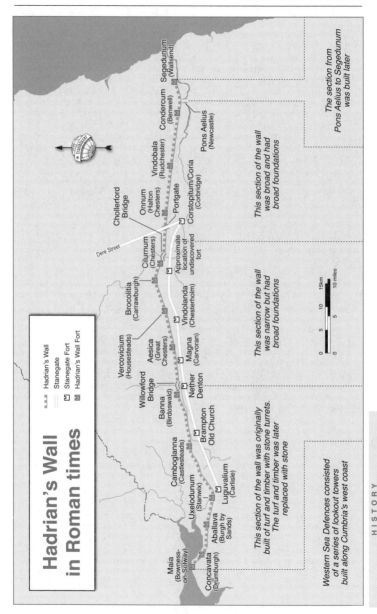

Hadrian's Wall in Roman times

Legend:
- ▬ Hadrian's Wall
- ⋯ Stanegate
- ⌂ Stanegate Fort
- ▣ Hadrian's Wall Fort

The section from Pons Aelius to Segedunum was built later

This section of the wall was broad and had broad foundations

This section of the wall was narrow but had broad foundations

This section of the wall was originally built of turf and timber with stone turrets. The turf and timber was later replaced with stone.

Western Sea Defences consisted of a series of lookout towers built along Cumbria's west coast

Places labelled:
Segedunum (Wallsend), Condercum (Benwell), Pons Aelius (Newcastle), Vindobala (Rudchester), Onnum (Halton Chesters), Chollerford Bridge, Portgate, Corstopitum/Coria (Corbridge), Dere Street, Cilurnum (Chesters), Approximate location of undiscovered fort, Brocolitia (Carrawburgh), Vindolanda (Chesterholm), Vercovicium (Housesteads), Aesica (Great Chesters), Magna (Carvoran), Willowford Bridge, Nether Denton, Banna (Birdoswald), Brampton Old Church, Camboglanna (Castlesteads), Uxelodunum (Stanwix), Luguvalium (Carlisle), Aballava (Burgh by Sands), Concavata (Drumburgh), Maia (Bowness-on-Solway)

Scale: 0 5 10 15km / 0 5 10 miles

❏ THE ROMANS IN BRITAIN

It took the Romans a while to reach Britain. Expanding in every direction from their base on the west coast of what we now call Italy, conquering the cold, windswept island in the top left-hand corner of the known world was never really a priority for them. And even when the Romans did eventually decide to invade, it wasn't the beauty of the land or the treasures it contained that lured them here. Instead, it could be said that the invasion was instigated by the whim of one man who was looking for a way to impress his friends and fellow citizens and strengthen his political position at home.

That man was Julius Caesar, and the year was 55BC. At that time Julius Caesar was one of a triumvirate, along with Pompey and Crassus, vying for supreme power in Rome; and the best way to improve your standing at home at that time was to win a battle abroad. So casting his eye around for a suitably easy yet seemingly impressive land to conquer, Julius hit upon Britannia.

Iron-Age Britain was a dynamic society of hillforts and nascent towns characterised by a grid of streets each flanked with houses, places of worship, forges and workshops, and populated by traders, craftsmen, warriors and druid priests. Metalwork was the Britons' signature craft, whether for vanity and decoration, such as the beautiful brooches that now sit in museums across the land, or for more belligerent purposes, such as horned helmets, swords and spears. The Romans described the country as 'uncivilised', but to them that simply meant that the inhabitants didn't live in cities.

To Caesar, Britain was the perfect victim for his invasion. He knew it wasn't the land of popular imagination, a land peopled by a barbaric yet united race that would fight tooth and nail to defend their homeland. Instead, he surmised that it was inhabited by a disparate set of tribes who were too busy with their own internecine squabbles to care too much about foreigners arriving on their shores, and whose squabbling would make them easy to divide, conquer and rule.

Unfortunately, things didn't quite pan out the way Caesar had imagined. Firstly, the weather – that most fickle of British facets – intervened. Storms across the channel smashed much of Caesar's army before it had even caught sight of land; those troops that did make it across found the locals would not stand and fight, as the Romans had hoped, but preferred instead to engage in guerrilla warfare, which hardly seemed fair at all. Thus their first invasion in 55BC was abandoned almost as soon as it had begun. A second campaign the following year was only slightly more successful: though they managed to get across the Channel in greater numbers this time, the might of the Roman Empire reached only as far as the Thames at Brentford – which, as anybody who's been to Brentford recently will agree, is a poor return for all that effort. Confronted with the might of the Catuvellauni tribe, the Romans were forced to retreat with their imperial tail between their legs, the only trophies they had to show for their invasion being a couple of tributes and taxes paid by a few piddling little tribes in southern England.

Claudius and the conquest

So it was left to one of Julius Caesar's successors, the divine Emperor Claudius, finally to invade and occupy in AD43, using a massive force of some 40,000 men. The disparate tribes of Britain in the 1st century AD were no match for the professionalism and discipline of the Roman legions. The Romans knew this; so, too, did many of the British tribes, or at least the smarter ones who, rather than engaging the Imperial legions in battle – a route that could lead only to certain defeat and possible annihilation – opted instead to live in peace and relative freedom, albeit under the rule of

Rome, and enjoy the advantages that acquiescence brings. Thus, for the first decade or two, things went pretty much to plan for the empire. True, the west and north of the island still lay beyond their control. But the tribes in that portion of Britain which they *had* conquered seemed to find living under the Romans to be no bad thing, and played the part of meek and obedient subjects rather well. And they probably would have done for much longer too, had Nero not ascended to the Imperial throne in AD54. Corrupt and oppressive, Nero's brutal administration caused the Britons to rise up against their rulers. The leader of this revolt was Boudicca (aka Boadicea), queen of the Iceni tribe, who rampaged through the province in AD60 destroying key Roman settlements one by one as she went, including Camulodunum (Colchester), Londinium (London; where thousands of Romans were massacred) and Verulamium (St Albans). Though the uprising was soon quashed the entire affair had exhausted both sides. Boudicca, witnessing the slaughter of her own troops at the final battle, took her own life and now lies buried, so some say, under Platform 10 of London's King's Cross Station. What's more, further upheaval back in Rome forced the empire to rethink its ambitions and a halt to its expansionist policy in Britain was called – even though the west and north still remained unconquered and alive with the enemies of Rome and its empire.

The accession of Vespasian in AD68 saw a return to stability and a consequent reinvigoration of Rome's ambitions to subjugate the British Isles; just a decade later Rome was again launching successful campaigns into the lands we now know as Wales, Cumbria and Scotland, under the rule of the new governor, Gnaeus Julius Agricola. Of the three regions, it was Caledonia (now called Scotland) that proved the most stubborn and even after a decisive victory against the Caledones at Mons Graupius (believed by some historians to be Bennachie in Aberdeenshire) the survivors were able to flee and regroup in the relative safety of the Highlands.

Recognising the difficulty of flushing out the Caledones from their remote base, Emperor Domitian opted instead for a policy of containment, building a line of fortifications known as the **Gask Frontier**, which ran south-west to north-east across Perthshire in Scotland. The idea of the frontier was to watch over the Scottish glens – the main exit and entry points into the Highlands – thereby effectively placing the Caledones under house arrest. Yet even this newer, more realistic strategy was soon deemed to be too ambitious and, as other parts of the empire came under attack from various tribes, the decision was made to withdraw one of the four legions stationed in Scotland and to pull back from the Gask Frontier.

Trajan and expansion

With the death of Domitian (possibly at the hands of his wife) in AD96, and the brief reign of Nerva, who ruled for less than two years, Marcus Ulpius Traianus, or Trajan, a career soldier, was anointed emperor in AD98. As his military background would suggest, Trajan's style was aggressive and focused largely on the continuing expansion of Rome's borders. Indeed, the empire was never larger than it was under his reign, as Armenia, Romania and Mesopotamia were brought under his rule.

Once again, however, in order to achieve these victories Trajan was forced to reduce his army's presence in Scotland, and in order to do this the empire's northern frontier was once again redrawn further south. This time a road known as the Stanegate (Saxon for 'Stone Road') was chosen as the frontier. Built in AD80 to link the towns of Corbridge and Carlisle, the road cut across the two main military routes heading north, one on either side of the Pennines. *(cont'd overleaf)*

HISTORY

THE WALL POST-HADRIAN

Whatever the original intentions of Hadrian, the defensive obligations of the Wall soon became rather secondary to more mundane yet lucrative duties. Following Hadrian's death in AD138 his successor, Antoninus Pius, decided to push the Empire's frontier further north once more, to a line stretching from the Clyde to the Firth of Forth.

Not to be outdone, Antoninus fortified his new border with a 'Wall' of his own (AD142-4), the **Antonine Wall**, made of turf. So, just 10 years after the completion of Hadrian's Wall, its primary purpose as a border-cum-defensive-barrier was all but finished. The character of Hadrian's original fortifications changed too. Some forts, such as Housesteads, no longer on the front line, were left to languish and developed more into trading posts than military positions. Others, such as Corbridge two miles south of the Wall, prospered as supply bases for the Roman troops stationed further north along Antoninus's border.

Markets were established near all the forts and the local tribe, the Brigantes, soon set up small villages, called *vici* (singular: *vicus*), in the shadow of the Wall to take advantage of the trading opportunities afforded them by the world's first professional army, staffed by regularly paid, full-time soldiers. The new, non-military character of these forts continued even after the Antonine Wall was

(cont'd from p59)   To suggest that Trajan ignored Britain, however, is wrong. Indeed, his unquenchable ambition simply would not allow him to be content with only half the island. So, while it is true that under his reign the northernmost boundary of his empire receded south into what we now know as England, Trajan did not view this Stanegate Frontier as a defensive border but more of an offensive one, as a base from which to launch further raids into Scotland. Indeed the Stanegate road became an essential military line of communication, enabling the Romans to move troops quickly across the Pennines from one major north–south road to the other. To guard the road, forts and watchtowers were placed at intervals along the Stanegate – the forerunner, of course, to Hadrian's Wall and its forts.

As for the land to the south of the Stanegate, Trajan was content to continue with what was known as the Flavian policy (the Flavians being the imperial dynasty that preceded Trajan and included Emperor Vespasian): allowing Roman culture and society to influence the development of the province, so that in time Britain would come to identify more closely with its masters and therefore, hopefully, be less inclined to rebel.

Hadrian and his Wall
With the death of Trajan in AD117, another Spanish military man and a relative of Trajan, Publius Aelius Hadrianus, was chosen as heir. Though no less competent, militarily speaking, than Trajan, where the latter was consumed by an ambition to push back the frontiers of his empire, Hadrian was content to adopt a more defensive approach and protect all the gains made in his predecessor's reign.

This change in policy heralded a period of almost 100 years of continuous peace; it also, of course, led to the building of one of the greatest military constructions of them all: a wall of stone along the empire's northernmost border, a frontier that up

H I S T O R Y

abandoned, about AD160, just 20 years after its inception, having been repeatedly overrun.

For the next 200 years after this, Hadrian's Wall remained the definitive limit of the Roman Empire. In addition, a second road, the **Roman Military Way**, was built around AD160 between the Stanegate and the Wall, often along the northern earthwork of the Vallum (which by now had been largely decommissioned). Such a road would be vital for the rapid transport of troops along the Wall and eventually replaced the Stanegate as the primary artery serving the neck of Britain.

It would be wrong, therefore, to think of the Wall purely as a means of defence, a place to shelter from the spears of the Barbarians to the north. Because, whatever Hadrian's original intention for his Wall, it had evolved to become more of a checkpoint, a place to watch the comings and goings of the locals as they crossed the border, and to collect tolls and customs duties from the traders.

Severus's restoration

That is not to say that the Wall had entirely forsaken its military duties; indeed, following a successful breach by invaders sometime around the end of the 2nd century AD, it was decided to restore, renovate and refortify Hadrian's Wall.

---

until now had been defended merely by hastily built turf and timber forts and watch-towers.

The end of Roman Britain

The Romans survived in Britain for almost another 300 years after Hadrian, until the start of the 5th century. Indeed, it's fair to say that they did more than just survive: they positively prospered. And so, too, did their subjects, who found that the Roman way of doing things, particularly when it came to matters of architecture, road-building, cooking, drinking, trading, educating and organising society in general, was often the best way (see box pp62-3). Far from an extended swansong, the last 200 years of Roman rule left behind some of the empire's most impressive pieces of work in Britain, such as the mosaics at Bignor Villa in West Sussex. In fact, some historians have even gone as far as to declare that, by the time the Romans departed, Britain was one of the most 'Romanised' of its territories, and its people the most prosperous and peaceful.

So what drove the Romans out from this most compliant of provinces? The truth is that nothing did, or at least nothing within Britain itself. Instead, as the Empire crumbled and its borders were attacked from all sides, the Romans found themselves unable to hold on to all their territories; just as Britain was one of the last places to succumb to Roman rule, so it became one of the first to be dispensed with when the going got tough.

As they withdrew, other invaders filled the vacuum. In particular, the Anglo-Saxons from across the North Sea, Picts from northern Scotland and invaders from Ireland all penetrated Roman Britain's borders. Attempts to restore some sort of Roman law and order went on for the next two centuries or so. But by then, the Golden Age of Roman Britain was well and truly over.

HISTORY

This took place at the beginning of the 3rd century under the reign of Emperor Severus. Amongst the improvements was a rebuilding of the Wall using a super-hard white mortar which allowed it to be much narrower than before. The Wall had never looked so good, nor so impregnable; it's been estimated that 3,700,000 tons (30,138,000kg) of stone was used in its construction. Indeed, so comprehensive was the renovation that the original construction of the Wall was for over 1500 years wrongly ascribed to – and even named after! – Severus; prior to conclusive proof that the Wall was built during the reign of Hadrian, it had always been assumed that Hadrian had ordered the construction of the Vallum only and that it was Severus who had built the actual Wall (see box on p54).

AFTER THE ROMANS

Unfortunately, after the Romans had gone their greatest monument on these shores suffered. Though it had been overrun only three or four times (nobody is sure exactly how many) since its original construction, when the Empire crumbled and the troops were withdrawn in AD409 the Wall was subjected to all man-

❏ LIFE IN ROMAN BRITAIN

Though the number of Roman troops who occupied Britannia was relatively small compared to the total population, their influence was all-pervasive. Roman cities sprouted on England's green and pleasant land, filled with quintessentially Roman buildings – basilicas, villas, baths and forums – that employed the latest Roman construction methods, exuded an architectural style that was intrinsically Roman, and were all crowded with local people who dressed in the Roman style, spent Roman money, measured distances in Roman miles (the word itself derived from the Latin for 1000 paces, the Roman mile being slightly shorter than the modern

Over the heather the wet wind blows,
I've lice in my tunic and a cold in my nose.

The rain comes pattering out of the sky,
I'm a Wall soldier, I don't know why.

The mist creeps over the hard grey stone,
My girl's in Tungria; I sleep alone.

Aulus goes hanging around her place,
I don't like his manners, I don't like his face.

Piso's a Christian, he worships a fish;
There'd be no kissing if he had his wish.

She gave me a ring but I diced it away;
I want my girl and I want my pay.

When I'm a veteran with only one eye
I shall do nothing but look at the sky.
                    WH Auden, *Roman Wall Blues*

one) and ate Roman food. Nor did Roman influence end there, for towards the end of their empire the descendants of many who had prospered under Roman rule even began to worship Roman gods and speak Latin as a first language!

And you can't blame them; without deriding the traditional British culture that had thrived before the invasion, life under the Romans certainly seemed a more comfortable affair. Rough, muddy tracks became sleek metalled roads. Buildings, previously made of timber, thatch and mud now became imposing, stone-made constructions with such novel features as windows and columns, with indoor plumbing and warmth provided by underfloor heating rather than the dangerous and unhealthy open hearth. The Romans brought with them a complete change in the organisation of ner of depredations and indignities. For one thing, local landowners started to remove the stone for their own purposes. Hexham Abbey was just one beneficiary of this pilfering, with the crypt constructed entirely of Wall stone. And where the locals left the Wall untouched, the elements took their toll as wind and rain gradually wore down the remaining structure. Today, only around 10 miles of the Wall are still visible.

And so it stood for centuries, forlorn and neglected if not exactly ignored. Soon it even lost its duty as a boundary between countries as the border gradually drifted north and the country beyond – now called 'Scotland' after the Scots tribe from Ireland who migrated centuries after the Romans had left – shrank.

Interest in the Wall was first revived, at least in print, in 1600 with the publication of *Britannia* by William Camden, then headmaster of Westminster School in London, who attempted to explain the form, function and construction of the Wall. His work was built on a century later by the Rev John Horsley and the publication of *Britannia Romana*, in which, of course, the Wall featured heavily.

British society, from the family-based 'clan' system so popular among the 'primitive' tribes to a highly stratified civil and military structure.

Other innovations that were introduced include canals, water mills, factories and even such basics as new cereals and vegetables. And when they went they took much of their technology with them, including glass-making (the secret of which wasn't rediscovered until the 13th century), lighthouses (reintroduced in the 19th century), lavatories and central heating (commonplace again only in the 20th century).

Indeed, so pervasive was their influence that their currency became the legal tender of Britain, as across the rest of the empire, and Latin became the *lingua franca* of traders in this remote northern outpost. Furthermore, as the merchants and traders of Britain learned Latin, so they learned the advantages of literacy and the written record. Nor was that the only benefit reaped by the traders of the occupied provinces. The fact that there were now thousands of foreign troops on their land was in itself a business opportunity and soon local villages were springing up near Roman strongholds to take advantage.

Of course, while Britain enjoyed great prosperity, it was still forced to play the part of the conquered; because while there was some integration and mixing of the two sides – an integration that grew the longer the Romans remained in Britain – there was still very much an 'us and them' mentality on both sides. For the Romans, inevitably, there was a sense of snobbery when it came to discussing the Brits, whom the former frequently came to sneer at as the Britunculli – a translation of which would be something like 'wretched little Brits'. The Brits, too, while happy to adopt much that was good about the Roman way of life, still identified themselves first and foremost with their tribes. The Brigantes occupied the region that today we think of as northern England (Lancashire, Yorkshire, Cumbria and parts of Derbyshire) while the Hadrian's Wall region was shared with the Carvetii. But the 'independence' of these tribes depended to a large extent on their obedience to Rome: the more supine the tribe, the greater the control they had over their affairs, with the more compliant even allowed to establish their own governing body, able to wield at least partial power over the affairs of their territory.

HISTORY

The General wades in

Horsley's work revived great interest in the Wall amongst the reading public but it was not enough to prevent further damage being visited upon it during the Jacobite Uprising. In 1745, Bonnie Prince Charlie smashed his way from Scotland down through Carlisle and on to Derby before turning back. The ease with which he was able to advance so far had much to do with the fact that his adversaries, General Wade and his men, were hunkered down in Newcastle waiting to ambush him there, having assumed that Charlie would choose the eastern road for his advance.

As a result of Charlie's success, Wade's troops constructed the Military Road (the modern B6318) across the Pennines to enable the swift movement of troops from one side of the country to the other. (This Military Road should not be confused with the Romans' Military *Way* – see p61 – though this lies nearby and performed much the same job almost 1700 years earlier.) To build this road, the Royal forces of George II removed sections of the Wall to pave their new highway. In fact, not only did they plunder the Wall for building material, they even built their road on top of it! (It should be noted that, though Wade is most associated with this road, it was actually built three years *after* his death.)

The Wall's modern pioneers

Once peace had returned to Britain, Camden's and Horsley's works encouraged others to look at the Wall anew. Among them was the shopkeeper William Hutton who in 1802 walked from his home in Birmingham to the Wall, walked along it and back, and then walked all the way home again – a total journey of about 600 miles (966km). Taking 35 days to complete, it was an impressive feat by any standards, particularly when one considers that he was 78 years old at the time and wore the same pair of socks for the entire walk.

The product of his adventure was a book, *The History of the Roman Wall which crosses the Island of Britain from the German Ocean to the Irish Sea, Describing its Antient* [sic] *State and its Appearance in the Year 1801* – a title almost as long as the Wall itself – in which his love of Severus's Wall (as it was still called) and his interest in its history shines through. John Hodgson and John Collingwood Bruce (whose *Wallet Book of the Roman Wall*, printed in 1863 and later renamed *Handbook to the Roman Wall*, was still being published over a hundred years later) also contributed to our knowledge, with texts on the history and archaeology of the Wall. Hodgson was also the man who first definitively proved that the Wall was built during Hadrian's reign and not Severus's.

Then there was John Clayton, a Newcastle town clerk in the late 19th century, who bought four of the Wall forts and to whom we owe a great debt of gratitude; without his excavation and restoration work much of the Wall still extant would have been lost. That's not to say Clayton's work is unanimously admired today. In particular, his attempts to rebuild much of the Wall, taking great liberties and using largely non-Roman methods and materials, make more than one modern archaeologist weep; Clayton preferred to rebuild without mortar, so in effect the sections of Wall he rebuilt resemble a 'modern' drystone

'Wall of Severus, near Housetead [sic], Northumberland' (19th century engraving)

wall, still common around northern England, rather than the original Roman Wall. Clayton's efforts may have ensured that there is more of the Wall visible today but it can also be argued that what we are looking at is not really the Roman Wall at all but a 19th-century reconstruction, with almost none of the Wall's original inner core remaining. Nevertheless, to the layman, Clayton's work is vital, the miles he 'reconstructed' helping us to imagine what the Wall must have looked like when first built. The work of Clayton was continued in the 20th century by individuals such as FG Simpson (of Stead & Simpson shoe shop fame), Eric Robin and Andrew Birley (see p151) and Sir Ian Richmond. Nor should we forget bodies such as the National Trust, English Heritage and the Tyne and Wear Museums Service, organisations which concentrated less on the Wall and more on its accompanying forts and other buildings.

A proper survey of the Wall, recording every surviving remain and ruin, was conducted in 1985 to ensure there was a complete record of what exactly the authorities had in their care. And then, in 1987, UNESCO announced that the Wall was to become a World Heritage Site, thereby placing it alongside such wonders as the magnificent ruined city of Petra in Jordan, the awe-inspiring Pyramids of Giza in Egypt, Cambodia's mesmerising temples at Angkor Wat, Peru's fabled lost city of Machu Picchu, the architectural dream that is India's

HISTORY

Taj Mahal and that other Great Wall, in northern China. The establishment in 2003 of a national trail running along the entire length of the Wall once more brought it into the spotlight, and its success should ensure that millions more will enjoy the Wall's grandeur for years to come.

❏ **HAPPY BIRTHDAY HADRIAN'S WALL**

The keen-eyed among you may have spotted that Hadrian's Wall recently celebrated a rather important anniversary. The year 2022 marked 1900 years since Hadrian ordered the building of his Northern Border across the island of Britain.

Running from January to December, the local authorities justifiably went all out to celebrate this milestone. Called the **1900 Festival** (🖳 1900.hadrianswallcountry .co.uk), they organised a series of events throughout the year including falconry displays, one-off historical exhibitions, art installations (the 'sound sculpture', Apertura, comprising of 1900 copper wind chimes at Walltown Crags, was particularly impressive) and the commissioning of a short story by Ann Cleeves, *Frozen*, written exclusively for the independent bookshop Forum. Even Radio 3 got in on the act, commissioning five podcasts by composer and sound artist Rob Mackay at five locations in Newcastle where remains of the Wall can be found.

Among the more unusual celebrations, there was the project to knit, crochet and sew 1900 flags of bunting, to be draped across Vindolanda's replica section of the Wall; and the nearby brewery, *Twice Brewed* (see p148), made a Roman-themed beer, using ingredients that would have been available to the Romans 1900 years ago. (Apparently, the result was a low strength ale made from barley, wheat and honey, all fermented with Belgian yeast – which, thanks to the Vindolanda postcards, we now know was a possibility since there was a Belgium-born brewer based at Vindolanda.)

Of course, there are few things more dreary than hearing about a party that you missed, and it's true that by the time you read this the bunting will be down, the wind chimes packed away, the falcons back in their cage and the beer all drunk. But hopefully a few of the exhibitions and installations will remain in situ for the time being. And if you don't find any evidence of the festivities, well at least you can comfort yourself with the fact that it's only 100 years to the next anniversary – and as that will be the 2000th, it should really be a party worth attending!

HISTORY

MINIMUM IMPACT & OUTDOOR SAFETY

3

Minimum impact walking

In April 2005 Britain was given a rude awakening by UNESCO, when it threatened to have Hadrian's Wall placed on their 'in danger' list of World Heritage sites. The warning was something of a national embarrassment, for at the time there were only 29 sites placed on this list, out of the then total 600 World Heritage sites; it was also only the second 'in danger' site in the so-called 'developed world' (alongside Cologne Cathedral in Germany).

Thankfully, the threat seems to have abated somewhat since 2005; the Wall (which is now officially entered on UNESCO's list as part of the 'Frontiers of the Roman Empire' which also covers the Antonine Wall) has stayed off the 'in danger' list, which now numbers 52 sites out of a total of 1154.

UNESCO's concern about the Wall arose largely because of the huge and sudden influx of walkers hiking alongside the Wall. The thousands of people who have walked along the National Trail since it opened (on 23 May 2003) have left their mark on the area, eroding the land and endangering the archaeological sites that have yet to be excavated (and the majority of the Wall and its fortifications remain unexcavated; indeed, according to one expert only about 5% of the Wall and it accompanying buildings have been examined). The soil in this part of the world is particularly thin and the climate rather damp. Combine this with thousands of pairs of boots and you have the recipe for some serious erosion. Vegetation is trampled, exposing not just the soil but also, over time, archaeological deposits.

Nor is the Wall itself exempt from the depredations of walkers: in 2004, a team of 800 bankers walked *on* the Wall between Steel Rigg and Housesteads as part of a team-building exercise, sparking fury amongst conservationists and historians alike. (To be fair to the bankers, they have returned since and abided by the Hadrian's Wall Code of Respect much more closely – see the box on pp68-9 – splitting their group up into more manageable sizes and keeping off the Wall itself.)

The controversy is only exacerbated by the fact that there was so much opposition to the creation of the path in the first place, particularly amongst historians worried about protecting the Wall. Their fears were allayed only when they received assurances that the Wall and its earthworks would be protected; unfortunately, the resources just haven't been available to protect it properly.

Though some may blame the authorities for the current crisis, accusing them of inadequate preparation and provision, this doesn't mean we as walkers can't do our bit as well. The Hadrian's Wall Code of Respect, known as **Every Footstep Counts** (see below), helps visitors minimise their impact on the trail. But the preservation of the Wall, while of overriding importance, should not be the only concern of walkers. The whole area is affected, economically, socially and culturally, by the arrival of walkers. By following a few simple guidelines while walking the trail, you can minimise your impact on it and have a positive effect on the local communities and the environment hereabouts.

ECONOMIC IMPACT

Rural businesses and communities in Britain have been hit hard in recent years by a seemingly endless series of crises. Most people are aware of the

---

❏ **CARING FOR THE WALL: THE HADRIAN'S WALL CODE OF RESPECT**
Overriding all other concerns about caring for the natural environment is the need to protect the Wall itself, and all the forts, milecastles, turrets, earthworks and ditches that go to make up the Roman defences – whether excavated or still buried beneath the soil.

With these considerations uppermost, the following code – known as **Every Footstep Counts** – has been formulated and endorsed by government agencies, English Heritage, the National Trust, local authorities, farmers, conservation and user groups concerned with the Wall.

● **Don't climb or walk on the Wall** Please don't walk on the Wall or climb it for a better view or to take a photograph of yourself, no matter how tempting.

● If walking only part of the trail, consider following a circular route or setting off from a place other than the usual starting points. This will limit the general wear and tear.

● **Don't walk the Wall in winter** The ground, and the unexcavated archaeological sites still buried within it, are more fragile and liable to damage then. Again, consider a nearby circular walk or visit one of the off-Wall Roman sites instead, such as Corbridge or Vindolanda. This is why the passport scheme runs only from May to October.

● **Visit the Roman forts along the way**, which will help to relieve the pressure suffered by the Wall itself.

● **Stay and eat locally** and use local services when visiting the Wall; that way the local economy will benefit from your visit.

● **Keep to waymarked and signposted paths** and trails only.

● **Keep dogs under close control** and on a lead when walking through fields with sheep; on National Trust land this is compulsory. Only let go of the lead if you're threatened by a farm animal.

Countryside Code (see p71), and not dropping litter and closing the gate behind you are still as pertinent as ever. But in light of the economic pressures that local countryside businesses are under, there is something else you can do: buy local.

Support local businesses

Look and ask for local produce to buy and eat; not only does this cut down on the amount of pollution and congestion that the transportation of food creates (the so-called 'food miles'), but also ensures that you are supporting local farmers and producers; the very people who have moulded the countryside you have come to see and who are in the best position to protect it. If you can find local food which is also organic then so much the better.

It's a fact of life that money spent at local level – perhaps in a market, or at the greengrocer, or in an independent pub – has a far greater impact for good on that community than the equivalent spent in a branch of a national chain store or restaurant. While no-one would advocate that walkers should boycott the larger supermarkets, which after all do provide local employment, it's worth remembering that businesses in rural communities rely heavily on visitors for their very existence. If we want to keep these shops and post offices, we need to use them.

- **Never light fires**, and **always take litter away** with you.
- **Use public rather than private transport** whenever you can.
- Leave all **farm gates** as you find them.
   In addition to the above rules, there are some other important guidelines that need to be followed to minimise the damage hikers do to the archaeological deposits.
- Camping is allowed only on official sites. **Don't 'wild camp'** near the Wall.
- If the path resembles a worn line in the grass, walk alongside it to avoid exacerbating the erosion. In other words, **keep on the grass**! This is one of the most important rules – and also one of the most unusual, for on most trails you are usually told to stick to the path to prevent a widening of the trail and the spreading of erosion. However, Hadrian's Wall is, of course, not your usual path and the authorities' main concern is not to preserve the state of the path but to protect the as-yet unexcavated archaeological treasures that lie beneath. This is why the path is a green sward, as it was felt that this was one of the best surfaces to protect the archaeology buried underground. But if that protective layer is eroded away, those treasures are put in danger. The erosion mats that have been placed on some of the muddier parts do a reasonable job but they can't be 100% successful. So avoid walking on a worn or eroded part of the trail and **walk side by side, not in single file**.
- Similarly, **don't walk on any nearby ridge or hillock**. Just as the trail cuts a delicate path through the Wall's numerous unexcavated mounds so you should avoid treading on any raised ground.
- If you find anything that might conceivably be of historical or archaeological interest on the trail, report your find(s) to a Wall guardian, trail officer or possibly a nearby museum. Do not, whatever you do, keep the find for yourself as a keepsake.
- Do not chip off a bit of stone or other matter from the Wall as a souvenir.

ENVIRONMENTAL IMPACT

A walking holiday in itself is an environmentally friendly approach to tourism. The following are some ideas on how you can go a few steps further in helping to minimise your impact on the environment while walking the Hadrian's Wall Path.

Use public transport whenever possible

Public transport along the Wall is not bad (though it can be infrequent), with most places served by at least one bus or train a day. If you need transport, try to use these in preference to private cars as it benefits everyone: visitors, locals and the environment.

Never leave litter

Leaving litter shows a total disrespect for the natural world and others coming after you. As well as being unsightly, litter kills wildlife, pollutes the environment and can be dangerous to farm animals. Please carry a degradable plastic bag so you can dispose of your rubbish in a bin in the next village. It would be very helpful if you could pick up litter left by other people too.

● **Is it OK if it's biodegradable?** Not really. Apple cores, banana skins, orange peels and the like are unsightly, encourage flies, ants and wasps and ruin a picnic spot for others.

● **The lasting impact of litter** A piece of orange peel left on the ground takes six months to decompose; silver foil 18 months; a plastic bag 10 years; clothes 15 years; and an aluminium can 85 years.

Respect all wildlife

Care for all wildlife you come across along the path; it has as much right to be there as you. As tempting as it may be to pick wild flowers, leave them in place so the next people who pass can enjoy them too. Don't break branches off or damage trees in any way.

If you come across wildlife, keep your distance and don't watch for too long. Your presence can cause considerable stress, particularly if the adults are with young, or in winter when the weather is harsh and food is scarce. Young animals are rarely abandoned. If you come across young birds, keep away so that their mother can return.

Outdoor toiletry

Public toilets are marked on the trail maps in this guide and you will also find facilities in pubs, cafés and campsites along the trail. As a result, there shouldn't be any need to 'go' outdoors. This is very important. Normally, when caught short outdoors and with no public facilities nearby, considerate hikers would dig a small hole in the ground in which to bury their excrement. However, as previously mentioned many of Hadrian's Wall's treasures are as yet unexcavated. For this reason, **it is forbidden to dig anywhere near the Wall**! And this point cannot be emphasised enough.

Toilet paper, **tampons and sanitary towels** take a long time to decompose, whether buried or not, and even if they are buried are easily dug up by animals and may then blow into water sources or onto the path. The best method for dealing with any of these is to **pack it out**. Put the used item inside a paper bag which you then place inside a plastic bag (or two if you're worried about ruptures). Then simply empty the contents of the paper bag at the next toilet you come across and throw the bag away.

Wild camping

Wild camping is not allowed along the Wall and, with the number of campsites serving the trail, there's no need to either.

ACCESS

Britain is a crowded cluster of islands with few places where you can wander as you please. Most of the land is a patchwork of fields and agriculture and the environment through which the Hadrian's Wall Path marches is no different. However, there are countless public rights of way, in addition to the main trail, that criss-cross the land. This is fine, but what happens if you feel a little more adventurous and want to explore the moorland, woodland and hills that can also be found near the walk?

Right to roam

The Countryside & Rights of Way Act 2000 (CRoW), or 'Right (or Freedom) to Roam' as dubbed by walkers, came into effect in full on 31 October 2005 after a long campaign to allow greater public access to areas of countryside in England and Wales deemed to be uncultivated open country. This essentially means moorland, heathland, downland and upland areas. Some land is covered by restrictions (ie high-impact activities such as driving a vehicle, cycling and horse-riding are not permitted) and some land is excluded, such as gardens, parks and cultivated land. For further details visit 🖥 gov.uk/right-of-way-open-access-land. With more freedom in the countryside comes a need for more responsibility from the walker. Remember that wild open country is still the workplace of farmers and home to all sorts of wildlife. Have respect for both and avoid disturbing domestic and wild animals.

❏ **THE COUNTRYSIDE CODE**

Respect other people
● consider the local community and others enjoying the countryside
● leave gates and property as you find them; follow signs and keep to paths unless wider access is available
● bear in mind the Hadrian's Wall Code of Respect (see box p68)

Protect the natural environment
● take your litter home – leave no trace of your visit
● do not light fires
● always keep dogs under control

Enjoy the outdoors
● check local conditions
● plan ahead and be prepared

Countryside code

The countryside is a fragile place which every visitor should respect. The Countryside Code, originally described in the 1950s as the Country Code, was revised and relaunched in 2004, in part because of the changes brought about by the CRoW Act; it has been updated several times since, the last time in 2022. The Code seems like common sense but sadly some people still appear to have no understanding of how to treat the countryside they walk in. The latest Code (🖳 gov.uk/government/publications/the-countryside-code), launched under the banner 'Respect. Protect. Enjoy.', is given in the box on p71.

Other points to consider on the Path

● **Keep to paths across farmland** Stick to the official path across arable or pasture land, though do bear in mind the Hadrian's Wall Code of Respect.

● **Use gates and stiles to cross fences, hedges and walls** The path is well supplied with stiles where it crosses field boundaries. On some of the side trips you may find the paths less accommodating. If you have to climb over a gate because you can't open it always do so at the hinged end.

● **Walk side by side and on healthy grass** In other words don't walk in single file and don't walk on worn areas.

● **Help keep all water clean** Leaving litter and going to the toilet near a water source can pollute people's water supplies.

● **Take special care on country roads** Drivers often go dangerously fast on narrow winding lanes. To be safe, walk facing the oncoming traffic and carry a torch or wear highly visible clothing when it's getting dark.

● **Protect wildlife, plants and trees** Care for and respect all wildlife you come across. Don't pick plants, break tree branches or scare wild animals. If you come across young birds that appear to have been abandoned leave them alone.

● **Make no unnecessary noise** Enjoy the peace and solitude of the outdoors by staying in small groups and acting unobtrusively.

Outdoor safety

AVOIDANCE OF HAZARDS

Though the Hadrian's Wall Path passes through some pretty wild countryside, the good waymarkings, proximity of the B6318 (the so-called Military Road) and the A69 highways to the south and the lack of any major highlands, fells or mountains mean that it is unlikely you're going to get lost or come to grief on the trail. Indeed, perhaps the biggest threat to your life is provided by the roads which cut across the path, particularly on the section between Heddon-on-the-Wall and Chollerford (there's already been one memorial erected by the Robin Hood pub to a walker who was hit and killed by a vehicle on this road).

That said, there are some hazards that beset trekkers on even the easiest trails. But with good planning and preparation these can be avoided. This information is just as important for those out on a day walk as for those walking the entire Hadrian's Wall Path. In addition to the points listed opposite, always make sure you have suitable **clothes** to keep you warm and dry whatever the conditions and a spare change of inner clothes. Carrying plenty of **food and water** is vital too. A **compass**, **whistle**, **torch**, **map** and **first-aid kit** should be carried; see p40.

Safety on the Hadrian's Wall Path

Sadly every year people are injured walking along the trail, though usually it's nothing more than a badly twisted ankle. The most dangerous section is from Sewingshields to Walltown, where the unpredictable weather can leave hikers in difficulty – though with a road never far away, there's nothing too serious to worry about. Abiding by the following rules, however, should minimise the risks:

● Avoid walking on your own if possible.

● Make sure that somebody knows your plans for every day you are on the trail. This could be a friend or relative whom you have promised to call every night or the B&B or hostel you plan to stay in at the end of each day's walk. That way, if you fail to turn up or call, they can raise the alarm.

● If the weather closes in suddenly and fog or mist descends while you are on the trail, particularly on the moors or fells, and you become uncertain of the correct trail, do not be tempted to continue. Just wait where you are and you'll find that mist often clears, at least for long enough to allow you to get your bearings. If you are still uncertain and the weather does not look like improving, return the way you came to the nearest point of civilisation and try again another time when conditions have improved.

● Always fill your water bottle or pouch at every available opportunity and ensure you have plenty of food such as high-energy snacks.

● Carry a torch, compass, map, whistle and first-aid kit. The **international distress signal** is six blasts on the whistle or six flashes with a torch.

● Always take wet-weather gear with you and a spare change of inner clothes.

● Use footwear with good grip, and consider wearing sturdy hiking boots with ankle support.

● Be extra vigilant with children.

● For information on walking safely with dogs, see pp230-1.

Dealing with an accident

● Use basic first aid to treat the injury to the best of your ability.

● Work out exactly where you are. If possible leave someone with the casualty while others go to fetch help. If there are only two of you, you have a dilemma. If you decide you must get help, leave all your spare clothing and food with the casualty.

● In an emergency dial ☎ 999 or ☎ 112.

WEATHER FORECASTS

The trail suffers from extremes of weather so it's vital that you always try to find out what the weather is going to be like before you set off for the day. Many B&Bs and tourist information centres will have pinned up somewhere a summary of the weather forecast. You can get an online forecast through 🖥 bbc.co.uk/weather or 🖥 metoffice.gov.uk. Pay close attention to it and alter your plans for the day accordingly. That said, even if the forecast is for a fine sunny day, always assume the worst and pack some wet-weather gear.

BLISTERS

It is important to break in new footwear before embarking on a long trek. Make sure your boots or shoes are comfortable and try to avoid getting them wet on the inside. Air your feet at lunchtime, keep them clean and change your socks regularly. If you feel any hot spots, stop immediately, apply a blister plaster and leave on until it is pain free or it starts to come off. If you have left it too late and a blister has developed you should make sure the wound is thoroughly clean (preferably apply some sort of antiseptic cream too) before applying a plaster.

HYPOTHERMIA, HYPERTHERMIA & SUNBURN

Also known as exposure, **hypothermia** occurs when the body can't generate enough heat to maintain its normal temperature, usually as a result of being wet, cold, unprotected from the wind, tired and hungry. It is usually more of a problem in upland areas such as the moors. Hypothermia is easily avoided by wearing suitable clothing, carrying and eating enough food and drink, being aware of the weather conditions and checking the morale of your companions.

Early signs to watch for are feeling cold and tired with involuntary shivering. Find some shelter as soon as possible and warm the victim up with a hot drink and some chocolate or other high-energy food. If possible give them another warm layer of clothing and allow them to rest until feeling better. If allowed to worsen, strange behaviour, slurring of speech and poor coordination will become apparent and the victim can quickly progress into unconsciousness, followed by coma and death. Quickly get the victim out of any wind and rain, improvising a shelter if necessary. Rapid restoration of bodily warmth is essential and best achieved by bare-skin contact: someone should get into the same sleeping bag as the patient, both having stripped to their underwear, putting any spare clothing under or over them to build up heat. Send urgently for help.

Hyperthermia occurs when the body generates too much heat, eg heat exhaustion and heatstroke. Not ailments that you would normally associate with the north of England, these are serious problems nonetheless. Symptoms of **heat exhaustion** include thirst, fatigue, giddiness, a rapid pulse, raised body temperature, low urine output and, if not treated, delirium and finally a coma. The best cure is to drink plenty of water. **Heatstroke** is more serious. A high body temperature and an absence of sweating are early indications, followed by symptoms similar to hypothermia such as a lack of coordination, convulsions and coma. Death will follow if treatment is not given instantly. Sponge the victim down, wrap them in wet towels, fan them and get help immediately.

Sunburn can happen, even up here and even on overcast days. The best way to avoid sunburn – and the extra risk of developing skin cancers that sunburn brings – is to keep your skin covered in light, loose-fitting clothing, and to cover any exposed areas of skin in sunscreen (with a minimum factor of 30). Sunscreen should be applied frequently throughout the day. Don't forget your lips, nose, ears and the back of your neck, and even under your chin to protect against rays reflected from the ground. Most important of all, always wear a hat!

4

THE ENVIRONMENT & NATURE

Conservation

GOVERNMENT AGENCIES AND SCHEMES

Natural England

Natural England (gov.uk/government/organisations/natural-england) is the single body responsible for identifying, establishing and managing: National Parks, Areas of Outstanding Natural Beauty, National Nature Reserves and Sites of Special Scientific Interest.

The highest level of landscape protection is the designation of land as a **national park** (www.nationalparksengland.org.uk), which recognises the national importance of an area in terms of landscape, biodiversity and as a recreational resource. At the time of writing there were 10 national parks in England. The Hadrian's Wall Path passes through one: the 1049 sq km Northumberland National Park (northumberlandnationalpark.org.uk), England's most remote national park, and an area that contains some of the best-preserved parts of the Wall. But as well as being deemed worthy of protection because of its 'landscape, biodiversity and as a recreational resource', there is an extra dimension to Northumberland National Park – the sky. In 2013, the park was awarded the title of **Northumberland Dark Sky Park** (see box p136).

The second level of protection is **Area of Outstanding Natural Beauty** (AONB; landscapesforlife.org.uk), of which there are 33 wholly in England (plus the Wye Valley which straddles the English-Welsh border) covering some 18% of the UK. The only AONB on the trail is the exquisite Solway Coast (solwaycoastaonb.org.uk), west of Carlisle, though the trail also brushes the northern edge of England's second largest AONB, North Pennines (northpennines.org.uk), which begins just to the south of the road running between Brampton and Hexham. Their primary objective is conservation of the natural beauty of a landscape.

Other levels of protection include: **National Nature Reserves** (NNRs), of which there are 225 in England, including Greenlee Lough NNR, the largest freshwater lake in Northumberland, situated north of Housesteads in Northumberland National Park; Muckle

Moss NNR, a 'mire' or peat bog close by between Stanegate and Vindolanda; Drumburgh Moss NNR, south of the trail and the hamlet of the same name; Finglandrigg Woods and South Solway Mosses NNR, just south of Bowness at the western end of the walk, which is a composite of three large lowland raised bogs – peat bogs.

Overlapping many of the NNRs are **Sites of Special Scientific Interest** (SSSIs). These range in size from little pockets protecting wild flower meadows, important nesting sites or special geological features, to vast swathes of upland, moorland and wetland. On the trail there are several that are either on – or at least associated with – the path (the following descriptions all assume you are heading east along the Path; those in bold are actually on the trail): the **Upper Solway Flats and Marshes**, Drumburgh Moss, **Glasson Moss** and **Bowness Common** at the western end of walk; **White Moss, Crosbymoor** (on the way out of Crosby-on-Eden); the **River Eden and its tributaries** (first encountered on the way into Carlisle); the **Tipalt Burn** that crosses the path at the lovely Thirlwall Castle; **Irthing Gorge**; **Walltown to Allolee** (beginning from the crags at Walltown and stretching for about 1¼ miles along the Wall until about half a mile west of Chesters fort); **Muckle Moss**,

---

☐ **CAMPAIGNING AND CONSERVATION BODIES**
● **English Heritage** (🖳 english-heritage.org.uk) English Heritage looks after, champions and advises the government on historic buildings and places. However, in April 2015 it was divided into a new charitable trust that retains the name English Heritage and a non-departmental public body, Historic England.

English Heritage is responsible for nearly all the Roman forts along the Wall that are open to the public, though in one notable instance (Housesteads Fort) shares this duty with the National Trust.
● **Historic England** (🖳 historicengland.org.uk) Created in April 2015 as a result of dividing the work done by English Heritage, Historic England is the government department responsible for looking after and promoting England's historic environment and is in charge of the listing system, giving grants and dealing with planning matters.
● **National Trust** (NT; 🖳 nationaltrust.org.uk) A charity which, through ownership, aims to protect threatened coastline, countryside, historic houses, castles and gardens, and archaeological remains for everybody to enjoy. In particular the NT cares for about 780 miles of British coastline, over 250,000 hectares of countryside and 500 historic buildings, monuments, parks, gardens and reserves, including: George Stephenson's birthplace in Wylam, Housesteads and six miles of the Wall itself!
● **Royal Society for the Protection of Birds** (RSPB; 🖳 rspb.org.uk) The largest voluntary conservation body in Europe focusing on providing a healthy environment for birds and wildlife and with over 150 reserves in the UK and more than a million members.
● **The Wildlife Trusts** (🖳 wildlifetrusts.org) The umbrella organisation for the 46 wildlife trusts in the UK. The two that are relevant to the Hadrian's Wall Path are **Cumbria Wildlife Trust** (🖳 cumbriawildlifetrust.org.uk) and **Northumberland Wildlife Trust** (🖳 nwt.org.uk).

THE ENVIRONMENT AND NATURE

Roman Wall Escarpments and Roman Wall Loughs which together form one large SSSI stretching from Cawfields Quarry to just east of Sewingshields; Brunton Bank Quarry, just to the north of the path just before Planetrees; and **Close House, Riverside,** the riverbank area by the Tyne after you've dropped down through the golf course.

Fauna and flora

Northumberland and Cumbria are England's two 'wildest' counties so, as you would probably expect, much of the nation's native flora and fauna is more abundant here than elsewhere. Furthermore, given the variety of habitats that you pass through on the trail, from woodland and grassland to heathland, moor and bog, the variety of flora and fauna present is also commensurately greater.

The following is not in any way a comprehensive guide, but merely a brief run-down of the more commonly seen flora and fauna on the trail, together with some of the rarer and more spectacular species.

Hazel (with flowers)

THE ENVIRONMENT AND NATURE

TREES

In the main, the Wall passes through bleak moorland bereft of any plantlife that can rise higher than the carpet of heather or pasture, though there are patches of woods and forest along the way, particularly in Northumberland National Park and towards the western end of the trail in Cumbria. Indeed, woodland in Cumbria is estimated to cover a surprisingly large 65,000 hectares, or 9.5% of the land in the county. Even more surprising, Cumbria's woodland cover has actually *increased* over the past two decades. Conifer woodland makes up the major-

❑ **ASH DIEBACK**
Described by The Tree Council as 'the most damaging tree disease since Dutch elm', Chalara ash dieback is caused by a fungus called *Hymenoscyphus fraxineus* which is native to eastern Asia. It was first identified in England in 2012 and initially causes blackening and wilting of leaves and shoots in mid- to late-summer, progressing from the leaves into the twigs, branches and eventually the trunk of the tree. It is now present in most parts of the UK, potentially leading to the decline and possible death of the majority of ash trees in the country.

See ⌨ treecouncil.org.uk for more information about the action plan, known as the Ash Dieback Toolkit, to deal with the problem.

ity, though there's also a fair bit of broadleaf woodland. Popular species include willow, oak, beech and maple.

Oak woodland is a diverse habitat and not exclusively made up of oak. Other trees that flourish here include **downy birch** (*Betula pubescens*), its relative the **silver birch** (*Betula pendula)*, **holly** (*Ilex aquifolium*) and **hazel** (*Corylus avellana*) which has traditionally been used for coppicing (the periodic cutting of small trees for harvesting).

Birch (with flowers)

Further east there are some examples of limestone woodland. **Ash** (*Fraxinus excelsior*) and oak dominate, along with **wych elm** (*Ulmus glabra*), **sycamore** (*Acer pseudoplatanus*) and some **yew** (*Taxus baccata*). The **hawthorn** (*Crataegus monogyna*) also

Alder (with flowers)

grows along the path, usually in isolated pockets on pasture. These species are known as pioneer species and they play a vital role in the ecosystem by improving the soil. It is these pioneers – the hawthorn and its companion the **rowan** (*Sorbus aucuparia*) – that you will see growing alone on inaccessible crags and ravines. Without interference from man, these pioneers would eventually be succeeded by longer-lived species such as the oak. In wet, marshy areas and along rivers and streams you are more likely to find **alder** (*Alnus glutinosa*). Finally, in Northumberland National Park there are a few examples of the **juniper** tree (*Juniperus communis*), one of only three native British species of conifer, the blue berries of which are used to flavour gin.

Juniper (with berries)

THE ENVIRONMENT AND NATURE

FLOWERS

Spring is the time to come and see the spectacular displays of colour on the Hadrian's Wall Path, when most of the flowers are in bloom.

Woodland, hedgerows and riverbanks

From March to May **bluebells** (*Hyacinthoides non-scripta*) proliferate in some of the woods along the trail, providing a wonderful spectacle. The white **wood anemone** (*Anemone nemorosa*) – wide open flowers when sunny, closed and drooping when the weather's dull – and the yellow **primrose** (*Primula vulgaris*) also flower early in spring. **Red campion** (*Silene dioica*), which flowers from late April, can be found in hedgebanks along with **rosebay willowherb** (*Epilobium angustifolium*) which also has the name fireweed due to its habit of colonising burnt areas.

In scrubland and on woodland edges you will find **bramble** (*Rubus fruticosus*), a common vigorous shrub responsible for many a ripped jacket thanks to the sharp thorns and prickles. **Blackberry** fruits ripen from late summer to autumn. Fairly common in scrubland and on woodland edges is the **dog rose** (*Rosa canina*) which has a large pink flower, the fruits of which are used to make rose-hip syrup.

In streams and rivers look out for the white-flowered **water crow-foot** (*Ranunculus penicillatus pseudofluitans*) which, because it needs unpolluted, flowing water, is a good indicator of the cleanliness of the stream.

Other flowering plants to look for in wooded areas and in hedgerows include the tall **foxglove** (*Digitalis purpurea*) with its trumpet-like flowers, **forget-me-not** (*Myosotis arvensis*) with tiny, delicate blue flowers, and **cow parsley** (*Anthriscus sylvestris*), a tall member of the carrot family with a large globe of white flowers which often covers roadside verges and hedgebanks.

Perhaps the most ubiquitous plant on the trail, however, is none of the above – nor is it even a British native. **Himalayan balsam** (*Impatiens glandulifera*) is a tall plant that can reach to well over head height and produces pink flowers with pods that 'explode' when squeezed, scattering their seeds. Introduced in 1839, it particularly enjoys riverbanks where it thrives, often suffocating out any other plant.

Grassland

There is much overlap between the hedge/woodland-edge habitat and that of pastures and meadows. You will come across **common birdsfoot-trefoil** (*Lotus corniculatus*), **Germander speedwell** (*Veronica chamaedrys*), **tufted** and **bush vetch** (*Vicia cracca* and *V. sepium*) and **meadow vetchling** (*Lathyrus pratensis*) in both. Often the only species you will see in heavily grazed pastures are the most resilient. Of the thistles, in late summer you should come across the **melancholy thistle** (*Cirsium helenoides*) drooping sadly on roadside verges and hay meadows. Unusually, it has no prickles on its stem.

The **yellow rattle** is aptly named, for the dry seedpods rattle in the wind, a good indication for farmers that it is time to harvest the hay.

Other widespread grassland species include **harebell** (*Campanula rotundifolia*), delicate yellow **tormentil** (*Potentilla erecta*), which often spreads onto the lower slopes of mountains along with **devil's-bit scabious** (*Succisa pratensis*). Also keep an eye out for orchids such as the **fragrant orchid** (*Gymnadenia conopsea*) and **early purple orchid** (*Orchis mascula*).

Herb-Robert
Geranium robertianum

Meadow Cranesbill
Geranium pratense

Heartsease (Wild Pansy)
Viola tricolor

Lousewort
Pedicularis sylvatica

Red Campion
Silene dioica

Common Dog Violet
Viola riviniana

Germander Speedwell
Veronica chamaedrys

Heather (Ling)
Calluna vulgaris

Harebell
Campanula rotundifolia

Common Knapweed
Centaurea nigra

Bell Heather
Erica cinerea

Bluebell
Hyacinthoides non-scripta

Gorse
Ulex europaeus

Meadow Buttercup
Ranunculus acris

Marsh Marigold (Kingcup)
Caltha palustris

Bird's-foot trefoil
Lotus corniculatus

Water Avens
Geum rivale

Tormentil
Potentilla erecta

Primrose
Primula vulgaris

Ox-eye Daisy
Leucanthemum vulgare

Cotton Grass
Eriophorum angustifolium

Common Ragwort
Senecio jacobaea

Hemp-nettle
Galeopsis speciosa

Cowslip
Primula veris

Yellow Rattle
Rhinanthus minor

Dog Rose
Rosa canina

Forget-me-not
Myosotis arvensis

Scarlet Pimpernel
Anagallis arvensis

Self-heal
Prunella vulgaris

Thrift (Sea Pink)
Armeria maritima

Ramsons (Wild Garlic)
Allium ursinum

Common Hawthorn
Crataegus monogyna

Sea Campion
Silene maritima

Rosebay Willowherb
Epilobium angustifolium

Yarrow
Achillea millefolium

Hogweed
Heracleum sphondylium

Common Vetch
Vicia sativa

Honeysuckle
Lonicera periclymemum

Rowan (tree)
Sorbus aucuparia

Foxglove
Digitalis purpurea

Early Purple Orchid
Orchis mascula

Himalayan Balsam
Impatiens glandulifera

A bank of bluebells east of the hamlet of Oldwall (see p117).

REPTILES AND FISH

The **adder** (*Vipera berus*) is the only common snake in the north of England, and the only venomous one of the three species in Britain. They pose very little risk to walkers – indeed, you should consider yourself extremely fortunate to see one, providing you're a safe distance away. They bite only when provoked, preferring to hide instead. The venom is designed to kill small mammals such as mice, voles and shrews, so deaths in humans are very rare but a bite can be extremely unpleasant and occasionally dangerous to children or the elderly. You are most likely to encounter them in spring when they come out of hibernation and during the summer when pregnant females warm themselves in the sun. They are easily identified by the striking zigzag pattern on their back. Should you be lucky enough to encounter one, enjoy it but leave it undisturbed.

Salmon (*Salmo salar*) thrive in the clean waters of Northumberland National Park.

MAMMALS

One of the great attractions of walking any long-distance trail in Britain is the opportunity it affords of seeing a native animal in its natural environment, and the Hadrian's Wall Path is no different. That said, actually spotting the wildlife is another matter. Many of Britain's native species are nocturnal and those which aren't are often very shy and seldom encountered. Then of course there are those – the otter, for example, or the water vole – that are few in number anyway and sightings are always very rare.

Nevertheless, with a bit of luck and patience, on the quieter parts of the trail you may be rewarded with a sighting or two of something fluffy, feathery, slippery or scaly. One creature that you will definitely see along the walk is the **rabbit** (*Oryctolagus cuniculus*). Timid by nature, most of the time you'll have to make do with nothing more than a brief and distant glimpse of their white tails as they race for the nearest warren at the sound of your footfall, though at some stage during your walk you may get close enough to observe them without being spotted. Trying to get a decent photo is a different matter.

Although the apparent decline in the local rabbit population (see box p82) is dismal news for the rabbits themselves, it seems to be good news for **hares** (*Lepus europaeus*), often mistaken for rabbits but much larger, with longer bodies, ears and back legs. I saw four in a week on this last trip where previously, in the 15 years I've been writing this book, I had only ever seen one before.

Northumberland and Cumbria play host to a number of creatures that are found in few other places in England. In particular, there's the **red squirrel** (*Sciurus vulgaris*), which I've seen on the Wall near Birdoswald Fort. Elsewhere in the country this small, tufty-eared native has been usurped by its larger cousin from North America, the **grey squirrel** (*Sciurus carolinensis*), but in the north of England, Scotland and a few other isolated locations the red squirrel maintains a precarious foothold. Fears for their survival on these shores have prompted the establishment of Red Alert, a charity aimed at protecting the species. For more information see 💻 rsst.org.uk.

THE ENVIRONMENT AND NATURE

Also subject to long-term protection programmes are the otter and the water vole. Previously persecuted because it was (wrongly) believed to have an enormously detrimental effect on fish stocks – indeed, it was hunted with dogs up until 1977 – the **otter** (*Lutra lutra*) is enjoying something of a renaissance thanks to some concerted conservation efforts. At home both in salt- and freshwater, they are a good indicator of a healthy unpolluted environment and are said to be well established on the banks of the North Tyne in Northumberland National Park. As for the **water vole** (scientifically known as *Arvicola terrestris*, but better known as 'Ratty' from Kenneth Grahame's classic children's story *Wind in the Willows*), this is another creature, like the red squirrel, that's fallen foul of an alien invader, in this case the **mink** from North America (*Mustela vison*) which has successfully adapted to the British countryside after escaping from local fur farms. Unfortunately, the mink not only hunts water voles but is small enough to slip inside their burrows. Thus, with the voles afforded no protection, the mink is able to wipe out an entire riverbank's population in a matter of months. This is another reason why protecting the otter is important: they kill mink.

You might see the ubiquitous **fox** (*Vulpes vulpes*), now just as at home in the city as it is in the country. While generally considered nocturnal, it's not unusual to encounter a fox during the day too, often lounging in the sun near its den. While another creature of the night that you may *occasionally* see in the late afternoon is the **badger** (*Meles meles*). Relatively common throughout the British Isles, these sociable mammals with their distinctive black-and-white striped muzzles live in large underground burrows called setts, appearing around sunset to root for worms and slugs.

One creature that is strictly nocturnal, however, is the **bat**, of which there are 17 species in Britain, all protected by law. Your best chance of spotting one is at dusk while there's still enough light in the sky to make out their flitting forms as they fly along hedgerows, over rivers and streams and around street lamps in their quest for moths and insects. The commonest species in Britain is the **pipistrelle** (*Pipistrellus pipistrellus*).

In addition to the above, keep a look out for other fairly common but little-seen species such as the carnivorous **stoat** (*Mustela erminea*), its diminutive

❏ **2000 YEARS OF RABBITS**

Rabbits and Romans have a shared history as the Romans brought rabbits with them to use as the main ingredient in gourmet dishes. And now, 2000 years later, the descendants of those first rabbits are said to be one of the main threats to the Wall, their burrows destroying its foundations from below ground just as the boots of hikers damage them from above. The situation is said to be so serious, some scientists are calling for a reintroduction of myxomatosis, the disease that wiped out 99% of the rabbit population in the 1950s. Interestingly, on my latest research trip in 2022 I was staggered to find that the rabbit population had shrunk dramatically. I have no idea why this is – and I could find no reports online about rabbits being culled in this part of the world. But something has definitely happened.

cousin the **weasel** (*Mustela nivalis*), the **hedgehog** (*Erinaceus europaeus*) – these days, alas, most commonly seen as roadkill – and any number of species of **voles**, **mice** and **shrews**.

Finally, a surprisingly large number of hikers encounter deer on their walk. Mostly this will be the **roe deer** (*Capreolus capreolus*), a small native woodland species, though it can also be seen grazing in fields. As with most creatures, your best chance of seeing one is very early in the morning, particularly in Northumberland National Park: there are said to be 6000 in nearby Kielder Forest alone! Britain's largest native land mammal, the **red deer** (*Cervus elaphus*), is rarely seen on the walk though it does exist in small pockets in Cumbria.

BLACK GROUSE
L: 580MM/23"

BIRDS

The woods, moorland and hedgerows along the Hadrian's Wall Path provide homes for a wealth of different species.

At the western end of the trail, the AONB (Area of Outstanding Natural Beauty) along the Solway Firth is renowned as a haven for birdlife. The most famous, or at least the most voluble, inhabitant is the **barnacle goose** (*Branta leucopsis*). The goose is actually only a winter visitor, as it flees its nesting sites on the cliffs of Svalbard, Norway, to enjoy Cumbria's milder climate. Up to 30,000 of the birds arrive in November, heading back to Norway in mid-April.

Other species you might encounter on this shoreline include **ducks**, **swans**, **ringed plovers** (*Charadrius hiaticula*), **oystercatchers** (*Haematopus ostralegus*) and **lapwings** (*Vanellus vanellus*). The latter is black and white with iridescent green upper parts and is approximately the size of a pigeon or tern. Its most distinctive characteristic, however, is the male's tumbling, diving, swooping flight pattern when disturbed, believed to be either a display to attract a female or an attempt to distract predators from its nest, which is built on the ground. Common in Solway, you can also find them on the moors in Northumberland.

Speaking of Northumberland, while the county is rich in birdlife, in order to appreciate this fecundity it's often necessary to leave the trail, either by heading to one of the offshore islands or visiting the forest

LAPWING/PEEWIT
L: 320MM/12.5"

at Kielder. Kielder has a wealth of bird species though it's fair to say that often you can't see the birds for the trees. Nevertheless, the area is particularly rich in raptors, including **sparrowhawks** (*Accipiter nisus*), **goshawks** (*Accipiter gentilis*), **merlins** (*Falco columbarius*), **peregrines** (*Falco peregrinus*) and **kestrels** (*Falco tinnunculus*).

Skylark
L: 185mm/7.25"

At the northern end of Kielder Water, Bakethin Reservoir has been declared a nature reserve and attracts **ospreys** as well as more common residents including wildfowl and gulls. The conifer forests at Kielder play host to the **crossbill** (*Loxia curvirostra*), while the deciduous, lower areas of the North Tyne Valley are popular with the **pied flycatcher** (*Ficedula hypoleuca*) and **redstart** (*Phoenicurus phoenicurus*).

Occasionally, some of these species may be glimpsed on the trail but in the main it's the usual 'garden' species that dominate: the **great tit** (*Parus major*), **coal tit** (*Parus ater*), **blue tit** (*Parus caeruleus*), **blackbird** (*Turdus merula*), **mistle thrush** (*Turdus philomelos*) and **robin** (*Erithacus rubecula*). You may also see, but are more likely to hear, the continuous and rapid song of the **skylark** (*Alauda arvensis*). They tend to move from moorland to lower agricultural land in the winter. Just bigger than a house sparrow, they have brown upper parts and chin with dark flakes and a white belly.

One of the most common birds seen on the path is the **pheasant** (*Phasianus colchicus*). The male is distinctive thanks to his beautiful long, barred tail feathers, brown body and glossy green-black head with red flashes, while the female is a dull brown. Another way to distinguish them is by the distinctive strangulated hacking sound they make together with the loud beating of wings as they fly off. Another moorland favourite is the rare **black grouse** (*Tetrao tetrix*). Feeding on cotton grass and tree shoots, in spring they gather together in 'leks' – display grounds – where the males conduct a spectacular courtship display. Its much commoner relative, the **red grouse** (*Lagopus lagopus scoticus*), is one of the few birds that stays on the moors year-round.

Less common but still seen by many hikers is the **curlew** (*Numenius arquata*). The largest of the British wading birds, it's the emblem of Northumberland National Park and lives on the moors there throughout spring and summer, returning to the coast in autumn. With feathers uniformly streaked grey and brown, the easiest way to identify this bird is by its thin elongated, downward curving beak. Other birds that make their nest on open moorland and in fields include the **redshank** (*Tringa totanus*), **golden plover** (*Pluvialis apricaria*), **snipe** (*Gallinago gallinago*), **dunlin** (*Calidris alpina*) and **ring ouzel** (*Turdus torquatus*).

Finally, though the Hadrian's Wall Path doesn't *quite* reach the coast, that doesn't mean that the coast doesn't occasionally come and meet the trail. There's a sign by the BALTIC Centre in Newcastle that says that the quay is home to 700 breeding pairs of **kittiwakes** – the furthest inland colony of these coastal birds in the world!

THE ENVIRONMENT AND NATURE

ROUTE GUIDE & MAPS 5

Using this guide

In this guide the trail has been described from west to east and divided into six stages. Though each of these roughly corresponds to a day's walk, do not assume that this is the only way to plan your trek. There are so many places to stay en route that you can pretty much divide up your hike however you want.

To enable you to plan your own itinerary, **practical information** is presented clearly on the trail maps. This includes walking times for both directions, waypoints (see pp226-9 for full list), all places to stay, camp and eat, as well as shops where you can buy supplies. Further **service details** are given in the text under the entry for each place. For **map profiles** and cumulative **distance chart** see the colour pages at the end of the book. For an overview of this information see 'Itineraries' pp34-5 and the village facilities table on pp32-3.

TRAIL MAPS [see key map inside cover; symbols key p237]

Direction

(See p31 for a discussion of the pros and cons of walking west to east or east to west.) In the text and maps that follow, look for the

E ⟶ FROM BOWNESS **E →** symbol which indicates information for those walking **east from Bowness to Wallsend** and the

W ⟵ FROM NEWCASTLE **W ←** symbol with shaded text (also on the maps) for those walking **west from Wallsend to Bowness**.

Scale and walking times

The trail maps are to a scale of 1:20,000 (1cm = 200m; 3⅛ inches = one mile). Walking times are given along the edge of each map and the arrow shows the direction to which the time refers. The black triangles indicate the points between which the times have been taken. **See important note below on walking times.** The time-bars are a tool and are not there to judge your walking ability. There are so many

---

❏ **IMPORTANT NOTE – WALKING TIMES**
Unless otherwise specified, **all times in this book refer only to the time spent walking**. You should add 20-30% to allow for rests, photos, checking the map, drinking water etc, not to mention time simply to stand and stare. When planning the day's hike count on 5-7 hours' actual walking.

variables that affect walking speed, from the weather conditions to the weight of the pack you're carrying, the state of your feet and how many beers you drank the previous evening. After the first hour or two of walking you will be able to see how your speed relates to the timings on the maps.

Up or down?
The trail is shown as a red dotted line. An arrow across the trail indicates the slope; two arrows show that it is steep. Note that the arrow points towards the higher part of the trail. If, for example, you are walking from A (at 80m) to B (at 200m) and the trail between the two is short and steep, it would be shown thus: A – – –>> – – – – B. Reversed arrow heads indicate a downward gradient.

Accommodation
Accommodation marked on the map is either on or within easy reach of the path. If arranged in advance, many B&B proprietors based a mile or two off the trail will collect walkers from the nearest point on the trail and take them back the next morning.

For **B&B-style accommodation** the number and type of rooms is given after each entry: **S** = single room (one single bed), **T** = twin room (two single beds), **D** = double room (one double bed), **Tr** = triple room and **Qd** = quad. Note that many of the triple/quad rooms have a double bed and either one/two single beds, or bunk beds, thus in a group of three or four, two people would have to share the double bed, but it also means the room can be used as a double or twin.

Unless stated otherwise, **rates** quoted for B&B-style accommodation are **per person (pp) based on two people sharing a room for a one-night stay**; rates are sometimes discounted for longer stays. Where a single room **(sgl)** is available the rate for that is quoted if different from the rate per person. The rate for single occupancy **(sgl occ)** of a double/twin may be higher and the per person rate for three/four sharing a triple/quad may be lower. At some places, generally chain hotels, the only option is a **room rate**; this will be the same whether one or two people (or more if permissible) use the room. Unless specified, rates are for bed and breakfast. See p20 for more information on rates. Some, but not all, B&Bs and campsites accept **credit/debit cards** but most guesthouses and nearly all hotels and hostels do.

Rooms either have **en suite** (bath or shower) facilities, or a **private** or **shared** bathroom, or shower room, just outside the bedroom. Most of these have only a shower. In the text � signifies that at least one room has a bathroom with a **bath**, or access to a bath, for those who prefer a relaxed soak at the end of the day.

Nowadays almost all places to stay or eat, including many campsites, have **wi-fi** which is free unless otherwise stated. If a business has a Facebook page **(fb)** it can be useful to check this for updates to opening times, especially for small and seasonal businesses.The text indicates if **dogs** (🐾 – see also pp230-1) are welcome in at least one room (subject to prior arrangement, additional charge may apply). And finally it shows if **packed lunches** (Ⓛ) can be prepared, again subject to prior arrangement.

Other features

Features are marked on the map when pertinent to navigation. In order to avoid cluttering the maps and making them unusable not all features have been marked each time they occur.

The route guide

E ▶ FROM BOWNESS If you're doing this walk in an **easterly direction** (from west to east starting in Bowness and ending at Wallsend), follow the maps in an ascending order (from 1 to 33) and the text as below, looking for the **E →** symbol on overview text and on map borders.

◀ W FROM NEWCASTLE If you're walking in a **westerly direction** (Wallsend to Bowness) follow the maps in a descending order (from 33 to 1) and the text with a **red background**, looking for the **← W** symbol on overview text and on map borders. **Turn to p195 to start your walk in this direction**.

BOWNESS-ON-SOLWAY
[Map 1, p92]

Bowness is a low-key, peaceful place. In fact, it's almost eerily quiet. Many hikers, itching to get on the trail or head for home, see little of the place but there are a couple of places to stay and the pub is a magnet for Wall walkers.

The name Bowness comes from the bow-shaped corner of the *ness*, or peninsula here. As the last place where the Solway is fordable, it is understandable why the Romans decided to finish their Wall here, and a large 7-acre (2.8-hectare) fort was built where the village now stands. This was **Maia**, the second largest fort on the Wall (indeed, 'Maia' can be translated as 'Larger'). Originally, the Wall was supposed to continue a little way beyond the fort at Bowness, for the Romans were wary that the Caledones and Irish could sneak by the Wall and land on Cumbria's west coast. But they soon decided to build a series of towers on that coastline instead, including one at Maryport, that are now known as the Western Sea Defences.

Today, there's very little evidence of the Romans. There are some purloined stones from the Wall in the fabric of St Michael's, the village's striking Norman church, which stands on the site of the fort. The destruction of the Wall around here seems to be quite a recent event: in 1801 there were said to be 500 yards (about 450 metres) of Wall just outside the village; while the old Roman altar that used to stand above a blocked-up byre door has now disappeared thanks to the building works going on at the farm.

In the absence of any Wall or fort remains it's fair to say that Bowness is a little lacking in tourist attractions, though the church has a couple of bells inside at the back behind the font which were stolen from villages across the Solway in the 17th century. It is apparently a tradition for every new vicar across the water to formally ask the parish for the bells back. There's also a **visitor centre** at Bowness House Farm Holiday Complex.

But if you just want to relax for an hour or two before starting or finishing your adventure, there are a couple of tearooms, a decent selection of accommodation – and the pub is a good one!

Services

Visiting Bowness requires a bit of forward planning. There's no ATM for one thing,

---

although the pub and at least one of the B&Bs takes cards. And there is no post office or public telephone. Also, the transport links are few and seldom (see Transport). That said, the locals do the best they can. The pub has a small **convenience store** (daily noon till the pub closes) inside. You can also buy **Hadrian's Wall passports** if you're starting your walk here, or **completion certificates**, if this is the end of your walk. They also sell a few Hadrian's Wall souvenirs and T-shirts. Note, you can also get your Hadrian's Wall passports stamped at Banks Promenade (pp91-2).

There are public **toilets** inside Lindow Hall (Nov-Mar 8am-5pm, Apr-Oct 8am-8pm).

Transport
Note: bus times are liable to change so it is essential to check them in advance.

To Bowness Getting to or from Bowness-on-Solway is straightforward unless it's a Sunday. Stagecoach's No 93 **bus** service from Carlisle bus station (*not* the railway station) to Anthorn travels via the trailhead and takes about 47 minutes to reach Bowness. **Don't panic when you first look at the bus timetables**, which would seem to suggest that the first bus that actually travels via Bowness doesn't leave Carlisle until 12.50pm – leaving you insufficient time to walk the 14 miles back to the city before nightfall. It's true that the two morning buses, leaving Carlisle at 6.35am and 9.30am, don't travel via Bowness on the way out; but after they've reached Anthorn they turn round and *do* visit Bowness on their return journey to Carlisle, arriving at the King's Arms at 7.34am and 10.32am respectively.

(Incidentally, some of these buses to Bowness used to be numbered **Bus 93A**, and while they *seem* to have stopped calling them that now, you will still find reference to bus 93A on the internet and on old timetables – and there is a possibility Stagecoach will return to calling some of the services on this route 93A again.)

If it's a Sunday or a Bank Holiday, there'll be no public transport, so you'll be forced to take a **private taxi** – expect to pay about £35 for a trip to/from Carlisle. You'll find adverts for the local taxi companies up inside the entranceway of Lindow Hall opposite the public toilets. Try Airstream Taxis (☎ 07808 778599). Bowness House Farm Holiday Complex (see opposite) also offer the trip for £35.

To Carlisle Those travelling to Carlisle from Bowness should find the procedure similarly straightforward. From Monday to Saturday the No 93 calls in by the King's Arms. There are six buses each day – three to Carlisle and three to Anthorn; as before, for Carlisle just jump on any one as even the ones heading to Anthorn will then loop back to Carlisle.

Where to stay
There's **bunkhouse** accommodation at *Lindow Hall* (☎ 07908466850 or ☎ 01228-576157, 🖳 lindowhall.org.uk; 16 beds, £14pp; advance booking essential), just up from the church. Lottery funding was used to convert the old reading room upstairs into a simple but spacious bunkhouse. There can be separate male and female shower facilities (£1); rates include use of the kitchen (with free tea and coffee) and dining area. A continental breakfast 'bag' costs an extra £5. Bedding isn't provided, but can be rented for an extra £4.

Of the B&Bs, *Wallsend Guest House* (☎ 016973-51055, 🖳 thewallsend.co.uk, **fb**; 1S/3D or T/1D, all en suite; ✦; (L)) is the smartest and most established (from £60-62.50pp, sgl £90) in town, and is housed in a lovely building, the Old Rectory, at the western end of the village just below the church. The new owners have done some extensive redecorating, including the introduction of an honesty bar. There is also a fabulous **campsite** (🐾; from £12.50pp) in a back field with communal toilet and shower block, and they offer breakfast boxes (£10) for campers. There are five en-suite glamping **pods** (5D; 🐾; from £60pp; min 2 nights), which have double beds plus sofa beds for children, as well as kitchenettes with cooking facilities, and bedding, towels and crockery are all provided. They can accept payment by card and the owners can also pick up guests from the trail if it's all getting too much.

Also providing good-quality B&B is *Shore Gate House* (☎ 016977-44622, shoregatehouse.co.uk, **fb**; 2D/3T, all en suite; ⓛ), on the north side of the village and with sumptuous views of the estuary; rates here are from £47.50pp in a twin (sgl occ £75), £60pp in a double.

The pub offers accommodation too. Rooms at the *King's Arms* (☎ 016973-51426, 🖥 kingsarmsbowness.co.uk, **fb**; 2T or D/1Tr/1F, share facilities; 🖤; ⓛ) are simple but clean and fair value (from £50pp, sgl occ £65). There are views over the houses opposite to the estuary from some rooms.

All of the above are being rather overshadowed by the development going on at the farm below the pub. Now run by Hunter Leisure Group Ltd, *Bowness House Farm Holiday Complex* (☎ 016973-52418; 🖥 bownesshousefarmholidaycomplex.co.uk)

has **camping** (£20 per tent) and four cute **shepherd's huts** (from £90 per hut; 4Tr en suite; 1 small 🐾; ⓛ), which sleep three people in bunkbeds (a double lower bunk under a single upper bunk) and which are equipped with log burners, showers and even a small oven and hob – all watched over by some very free-range chickens. There are also four very spacious self-catering **apartments** (from £150; 1 small 🐾; ⓛ), with a double bed and sofa bed, equipped with a full kitchen (with washing machine, fridge freezer, and microwave) housed in a former old barn. In addition, in the farmhouse itself there are 10 en suite **B&B** rooms (2D/3T/5F; 🐾; ⓛ) charging from £50pp in the double, £140 for the family rooms that sleep up to 5 (sgl occ £85).

Where to eat and drink

Pear Tree Farm Tearoom (**fb**; Thur-Mon 10.30am-3.30pm) is a sweet little place just up the road from the pub serving, as they put it, 'tea, coffee, cold drinks, light lunches and cake cake cake!'.

There's also a bar/bistro (daily 8am-11pm) that's part of the *Bowness House Farm Holiday Complex* (see Where to stay). However, for a filling lunch or a proper evening meal (including vegetarian, gluten-free and dairy-free options) then your best choice is currently the *King's Arms* (see Where to stay; food Mon-Fri noon-2pm, 5-9pm, Sat & Sun noon-9pm). The menu is large and specialises in pub classics, starting at £7.95 for the ham, eggs and chips. Incidentally, on the outside wall they have a map showing where the original Roman fort would have stood, with the pub lying almost at its heart.

🔲 HAAF NETTING

If you're lucky, when visiting Bowness you may come across the strange sight of several men standing chest-deep in the waters of the Solway holding large nets secured to wooden frames. This practice, known as haaf netting, is the traditional means of fishing in the estuary. The practice is believed to have come from the Vikings in around the 10th century AD, and indeed the very word 'haaf' comes from the Norse word for channel. The haaf net itself is a wooden frame, or 'beam', 5.5m long, which is said to be the length of an old Viking oar without the blade. The net is then suspended from this beam, and the fishermen, usually in groups of about six, form a line across the channel to catch any fish, usually sea trout and Atlantic salmon, that pass their way.

E → BOWNESS-ON-SOLWAY TO CARLISLE   [Maps 1-6]

If you were to describe the ideal first stage to any national trail, one that allows you to eat up the miles without being too strenuous, then this initial section from Bowness-on-Solway to Carlisle pretty much fits the bill. Bowness is a lovely place to start, and from there the walk is flat, peaceful and picturesque as you stroll along path and pavement, tarmac and track, with the first hill of any note not occurring until Beaumont, almost eight miles into the walk.

But while this stage may be ideal as a warm-up for the later, more arduous stretches, in other ways we have to admit that it's also a little disappointing. Where, for example, is the Wall that you've travelled so far to see? There's simply no sign of it throughout this **14-mile (22.5km; 5¼hr** hike, nor any trace of

❏ WHERE TO EAT ON THIS STAGE

This stage has always suffered from a lack of places to eat. It's a situation that has been exacerbated by the permanent closure of the Highland Laddie at Glasson, and the Hope & Anchor at Port Carlisle which seems to change owners more times than most pubs change their menus.

Thankfully, the Greyhound Inn at Burgh-by-Sands has managed to survive for a couple of years now and it's hoped that it'll become a permanent fixture on the trail. But even so, walkers are still left with few choices for lunching and dining along this stretch – particularly on a Monday and Tuesday when, at the time of writing, the Greyhound doesn't serve food.

The situation is somewhat alleviated by the increasing number of honesty boxes en route, including at the **Methodist church on the outskirts of Port Carlisle** and the long-standing snack-shed, called *Laal Bite*, at Drumburgh, around 4½ miles from Bowness, where you can make yourself a hot drink and buy chocolate, tray bakes, ice cream etc. There's also an honesty box at **Grinsdale** where you can find more snacks. Plus, of course, there's the food shop at the holiday park in Glasson (Map 1, p93), 2½ miles from Bowness. So it is possible that those walking this stage in one go can find enough sustenance to complete it.

Where it becomes more tricky is if you plan to break this stage into two halves by spending a night at a B&B along the way (eg at Boustead Hill); while the accommodation at Boustead Hill is most pleasant they usually don't offer dinners. Which is where Colin Smithson comes in. The enterprising Colin is the landlord of *The Bush* (☎ 016973-98001, 🖳 innatthebush.co.uk, **fb**) at Kirkbride, 4 miles (6.4km) south of Bowness-on-Solway, and for the past couple of years he has been providing lifts to walkers from the trail or their B&B to his pub for dinner, and back afterwards too. He doesn't charge for the transport. Food-wise (food daily 5-9pm) it's standard pub fare but very good value, with most mains from just £10. The pub also provides some smart rooms upstairs (1D/2D or T/1F; en suite; 🛏; 🐾; 🄻) with rates from £47.50pp (sgl occ £95), again, with transport from/to the trail included. The Bush is also offering 2-day/3-night packages between Carlisle and Bowness, where you are picked up from the trail every evening to eat and sleep at the pub, before being dropped off again the next morning to continue the walk. You may well find you can complete this section of the trail without Colin's services. But there's no doubt he runs a fine pub with good food and smart rooms, and whether you're just eating there or staying overnight too, it's a great option to bear in mind.

❏ **HIGH TIDE IN THE SOLWAY ESTUARY**

For the section between Bowness-on-Solway and Carlisle it's worth checking before-hand to see when the high tides occur in the Solway Estuary. Parts of the trail between Drumburgh and Burgh-by-Sands (Map 3) are sometimes flooded during very high tides. To be sure of a dry passage, it's worth avoiding walking on this stretch an hour either side of the high-tide point. Note that this flooding doesn't happen very often, and most of the time you can get away with just turning up and hoping luck is on your side. But a flooded path can seriously ruin your itinerary (and it's annoying too), hence the recommendation to check in advance.

You can find out when high-tide times are in a number of ways: many B&Bs and hostels have a **booklet** of tide times; there are **noticeboards** at Bowness-on-Solway and Dykesfield (where the trail floods; see Map 2) with the times printed on; or you can **check online**. Visit ▣ easytide.admiralty.co.uk and search for Silloth. Alternatively check ▣ www.tidetimes.org.uk/silloth-tide-times. If walking during British Summer Time (late Mar to late Oct) you will need to add two hours (one hour in winter) to the high-tide times given as Silloth, while the nearest port to the trail, is not located on the path.

---

the two forts that bookend this stage, at Bowness and Carlisle. Secondly, from a practical point of view it's not perfect either, for there aren't many places where you can get food on the way: currently the Methodist church at the western end of Port Carlisle, the long-running snack shed at Drumburgh, an honesty box at Grinsdale and the shop at the holiday park in Glasson (Map 1, p93) are the only places to buy food, and The Greyhound Inn pub in Burgh-by-Sands is the only place open daily where you can get a meal – see box opposite.

Nevertheless, though you don't see any of the Wall, the path adheres as best it can to *where it would have once been*. And there is some evidence on the ground of this. Not much, admittedly: a bit of Vallum, a few Roman altars, and a dedication stone all crop up en route, and all in places where you wouldn't expect them (by a muddy track near a caravan site, outside and above a couple of front doors, and in a church wall respectively). The church at Burgh-by-Sands is also clearly made from Wall stones (which goes some way to explaining why there is no Wall left on this stage – see p100). The region's subsequent history, when bandits terrorised the local communities and residents were forced to build fortified houses to keep themselves safe, is also fascinating and several of these mini-castles remain today. This may not be the most scintillating of stages but there's beauty and interest enough to make the day an enjoyable one – and, I promise you, the trail does gets better!

Banks Promenade The official westernmost extremity of the trail is a small shelter on **Banks Promenade**. How you approach it, of course, depends to a great degree on whether you're starting the trail, or finishing it. If you're just setting off, the Latin text above the western entrance translates as 'Good Luck', and, having checked your luggage, tied your shoelaces and practised in the mirror beforehand the look of steely determination that you're going to wear throughout your trek, it's time to set off, pausing only within the shelter itself to

stamp your Hadrian's Wall passport and admire some Roman-style mosaic flooring depicting the local birdlife.

If you're coming from the east, however, then the Latin text facing you above the shelter's eastern entrance translates as 'Welcome to the end of the Hadrian's Wall Path', and for you this humble hut will be a place replete with celebratory cheers, high-fives and group hugs. Because you've done it: you've just walked the Hadrian's Wall Path.

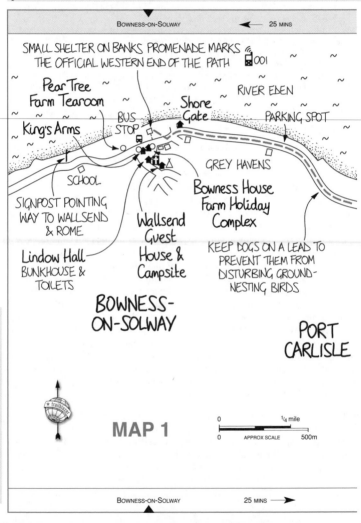

BOWNESS-ON-SOLWAY   ← 25 MINS

SMALL SHELTER ON BANKS PROMENADE MARKS THE OFFICIAL WESTERN END OF THE PATH 001

Pear Tree Farm Tearoom

King's Arms

BUS STOP

Shore Gate

RIVER EDEN

PARKING SPOT

SCHOOL

GREY HAVENS

SIGNPOST POINTING WAY TO WALLSEND & ROME

Wallsend Guest House & Campsite

Bowness House Farm Holiday Complex

Lindow Hall BUNKHOUSE & TOILETS

KEEP DOGS ON A LEAD TO PREVENT THEM FROM DISTURBING GROUND-NESTING BIRDS

BOWNESS-ON-SOLWAY

PORT CARLISLE

MAP 1

0   ¼ mile
0   APPROX SCALE   500m

BOWNESS-ON-SOLWAY   25 MINS →

PORT CARLISLE [Map 1]

The path chooses to ignore Port Carlisle, preferring instead to go round the back of the village by the water's edge. That's a bit of a shame, as it's one of the more interesting on this stage. Once upon a time there were big plans for Port Carlisle, with both a canal and, after that shut down, a railway

line terminating here – each of them following the line of the Wall. Stephenson's *Rocket* actually travelled along the line in 1829. Indeed it was hoped that the village would become a major port for goods to and from Scotland and Ireland. However, factors conspired against Port Carlisle and

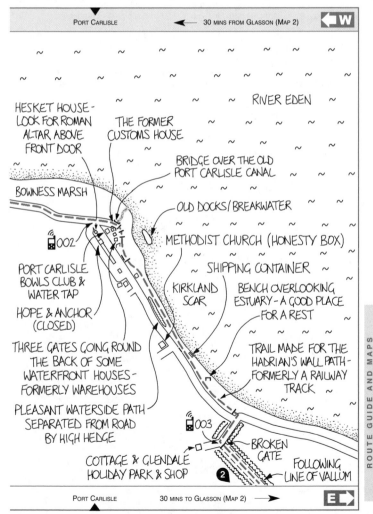

PORT CARLISLE   ◄— 30 MINS FROM GLASSON (MAP 2)   ◄W

~ ~ ~ ~ ~ ~ ~ ~ ~
~ ~ ~ ~ ~ ~ ~ ~
~ ~ ~ ~ ~ RIVER EDEN ~
HESKET HOUSE – THE FORMER ~ ~ ~ ~ ~
LOOK FOR ROMAN CUSTOMS HOUSE ~ ~ ~
ALTAR ABOVE ~ ~ ~
FRONT DOOR ~ BRIDGE OVER THE OLD ~ ~
~ ~ ~ PORT CARLISLE CANAL ~ ~
BOWNESS MARSH ~ ~ ~ ~
~ OLD DOCKS / BREAKWATER ~ ~
📱002 METHODIST CHURCH (HONESTY BOX) ~
~ ~ ~ ~ ~
PORT CARLISLE ~ SHIPPING CONTAINER ~
BOWLS CLUB & KIRKLAND BENCH OVERLOOKING ~
WATER TAP SCAR ESTUARY – A GOOD PLACE
HOPE & ANCHOR FOR A REST ~
(CLOSED)
THREE GATES GOING ROUND TRAIL MADE FOR THE
THE BACK OF SOME HADRIAN'S WALL PATH –
WATERFRONT HOUSES – FORMERLY A RAILWAY
FORMERLY WAREHOUSES TRACK ~
PLEASANT WATERSIDE PATH ~
SEPARATED FROM ROAD 📱003
BY HIGH HEDGE BROKEN
GATE
COTTAGE & GLENDALE ② FOLLOWING
HOLIDAY PARK & SHOP LINE OF VALLUM

the canal was abandoned after just 30 years, while the railway line held out for a century before it, too, closed down.

Thereafter, Port Carlisle slipped back into being one of the sleepier backwaters of the British Isles. Today, you can see the remains of the lock and port, and you cross the last vestiges of the canal on the walk. Look out across the water too, and just a few metres away are the remains of the harbour walls.

At the northern end of the village is Hesket House, formerly the Steam Packet Inn, and notable for the small grey stone **altar**, distinctly Roman, set into the brickwork above the door. It fits in rather well.

For facilities, the Methodist Church at the far eastern end of the village has drinks and biscuits inside, which are for sale using the **honesty box** system. The village is home to the Port Carlisle Bowls Club, which has a **water tap** on the wall of its clubhouse that you can use. The pub opposite, the Hope & Anchor, has closed again.

Stagecoach **bus** No 93 calls in Port Carlisle; see pp48-9 for details.

GLASSON [Map 2]
Since the demise of the Highland Laddie Inn there's been little of interest for walkers to Glasson, though to the north-west of the village itself and right by the trail is Cottage

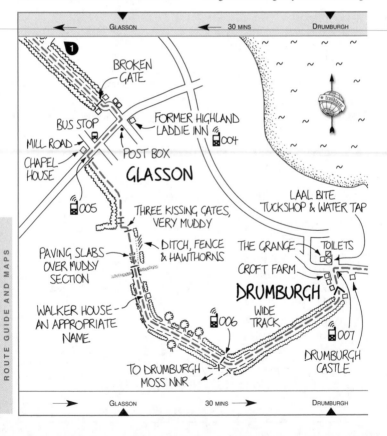

and Glendale Holiday Park (Map 1, p93). Camping is not allowed here but it does have a handy, well-stocked **shop** (Sun-Thur 9am-3.30pm, Fri & Sat 9am-5.30pm).

Incidentally, on the walk between the caravan park and village you're actually following the line of the **Vallum**.

Stagecoach **bus** No 93 stops here; see pp48-9 for further information.

DRUMBURGH [Map 2]
Drumburgh ('Drumbruff'), an unassuming little farming community, is situated where once a small Roman fort stood. This fort was known as **Congabata** or Concavata, built to watch over the salt flats nearby.

Before that, Milecastle 76 would also have stood where Drumburgh now stands.

Today the hamlet's highlight is **Drumburgh Castle**, at the eastern end of the hamlet, a bastle house (see p225) built in 1307 to provide protection against reivers (see box p96) – yet another manifestation of the antipathy and distrust that simmered for centuries between neighbours in this part of the world. The livestock would be housed on the ground floor, with the family living upstairs. Note the heraldic crest above the door, the griffins perched on the roof and not one but *two* Roman altars out front.

Drumburgh has little else to interest walkers except a **serve-yourself tuckshop**

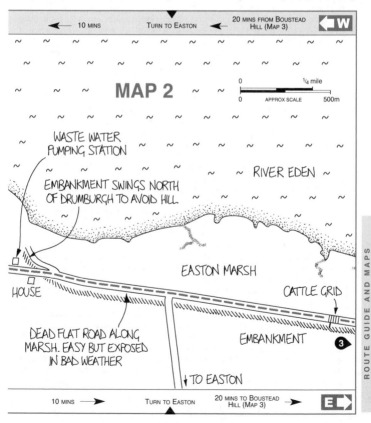

❏ THE REIVERS

The Middle Ages, particularly the 300 years or so between the War of Scottish Independence (c1315) and the Union of the Crown in 1603, was a tempestuous and bloody time for the Wall region. The almost constant warring between Scotland and England meant that those poor souls who chose to live in the borderlands between the two were subject to frequent harassment by one side or another. Their crops were regularly destroyed or appropriated by the troops and their livestock slaughtered to feed the army. As a result, many locals chose to engage in sheep and cattle rustling, a practice known as **reiving**, in order to eke out a living and ensure their survival.

Such was the ubiquity of this practice that reiving eventually became a way of life and one that local borderers regarded as a profession rather than a crime. Nor was it merely English families raiding Scottish ones and vice versa, for they were happy to steal from their compatriots too. Nor, for that matter, was reiving confined merely to the destitute and desperate – local nobles condoned and occasionally even indulged in the practice themselves, as did the Wardens of the Marches, the very people who were supposed to be upholding the rule of law in the region!

As the reiving continued through the generations, various laws were put in place to try to regulate the situation. For example, a victim of a reive had two courses of action open to him. The first was to file a complaint with the warden who would then be compelled to investigate. Or, and this was by far the more common choice, the victim could raise a raiding party of his own and pursue the reivers himself. It became enshrined in Border Law that anyone encountering this counter-raid was compelled to ride along with them and offer such help as they could, or else stand accused of being complicit in the original raid. If this counter-attack caught the reivers within 24 hours they could fight to retrieve their livestock. If, however, the 24 hours passed without any encounter with the thieves, the reivers could keep their booty.

Eventually, to try to combat the worst excesses of reiving, the two countries decided to set up armies, known as Borderers, as a first line of defence against 'foreign' raiding parties. Heavily armed, the Borderers were recruited from local families and travelled on horseback, using their intimate knowledge of the local area to launch guerrilla attacks on local reiving parties.

The whole phenomenon of reiving effectively ended with the accession of James VI of Scotland to the English throne. His attempts to unify the two countries included appropriating the land of reiver families, the introduction of a ban on weapons and a drive to arrest and execute notorious reivers. There was even talk of rebuilding Hadrian's Wall to limit and control cross-border movement. Whereas before the reivers could raid in one country then cross into another for safety, with the two countries unified no such safe haven existed and the reivers could be pursued relentlessly. The construction of the Military Road in the mid-18th century also helped the authorities police the region more efficiently.

But though the phenomenon of reiving no longer exists, echoes of this troubled period in the region's history can still be heard. The terms 'kidnapping' (a favourite pastime of the reivers), 'blackmail' (originally protection money paid to the reivers, as opposed to legitimate rent paid to a landowner which was called 'greenmail') and 'bereaved' (which originally meant to lose a loved one by the hand of the reivers) are all words that come from this period. And the remnants of some imposing fortifications built by well-to-do families to protect themselves from reivers can still be seen today. Buildings such as bastle houses (see p225), pele towers, and even larger fortifications such as the wonderful Thirlwall Castle were all designed with the reivers in mind.

called *Laal Bite* (Easter to Oct daily 8am-6pm) at The Grange, opposite where the trail turns off the road. They sell ice-creams, tray bakes and chocolate bars and have facilities for making yourself a cup of tea or coffee, a tap for refilling water bottles and a toilet. Laal Bite, incidentally, trans-lates as *Little Stand*, a 'stand' being a posi-tion allocated to a fisherman from where he can fish and which are traditionally given names by the locals.

Stagecoach's No 93 **bus** service calls here; see pp48-51 for further details on local transport.

Easton Marsh This area of the trail is liable to flooding at certain times of the year (see box p91). It can also be one of the most interminable stretches, a wearying trek over flat terrain with a floodbank blocking your views to the south and the wind whipping off the shore to chill your marrow from the north. If it all becomes too much for you, stand in a safe place and any passing Stagecoach's 93 **bus** service (see pp48-9) will stop. But if the weather's fair and the traffic's minimal it can be quite pleasant, with herons swooping above sun-basking cows. You can vary the walk slightly by walking atop the embankment to the south of the road – one of the last vestiges of the old railway that ran through here to Port Carlisle – where at least you can get a better view of Skiddaw and the Lake District peaks to the south (though watch your step as the embankment is precarious in places).

It's worth mentioning here, as you continue your yomp along the marsh, that there has never been any evidence of the Wall, nor milecastles nor turrets, uncovered on this stretch. Of course, just because nothing has been found yet that doesn't mean there isn't anything to find…an absence of evidence is not evidence of absence, as clever archaeologists are wont to say.

BOUSTEAD HILL **[Map 3, p98]**
Most people whizz through this stage between Bowness and Carlisle, making the most of the largely flat terrain. But those who take their time are rewarded with some very pleasant accommodation, good food and lovely people; and Boustead Hill, at approximately halfway between Bowness and Carlisle, is a logical place to stop. True, it's little more than a line of rather grand houses, amongst which you'll find a camp-site, two B&Bs and a bunk barn. But the accommodation, the people and the views across the marshes to the estuary are reason enough to stop for a night.

Hillside Farm (☎ 01228-576398, 🖳 hadrianswalkbnb.co.uk; 1T/1D shared facil-ities; ➷; 🐾; Apr-Oct) is a welcoming place. As well as two **B&B** rooms (from £50pp, sgl occ full room rate), they also have a **bunk barn** (open all year; sleeps about 12) with its own spacious kitchen-cum-living room (including microwave, crockery, cutlery and electric cooker), shower and toilet; they charge £15pp. The owner is typical of the sort of person you meet at this end of the trail – chatty, friend-ly, and helpful in a very unfussy way. Breakfasts (£5) are available to barn guests if requested in advance. The wi-fi is excel-lent too, and the showers in the bunkhouse are wonderfully hot and powerful.

The other **B&B**, just down the hill, is *Highfield Farm* (☎ 01228-576060, ☎ 07976-170538, 🖳 highfield-holidays.co.uk; 1D or T en suite/1D or Tr with a spa bath; ➷; ☪; Mar-end Oct), a smarter affair that's good value when considering the quality of the accommodation (from £50pp, sgl occ £90). The double room has a sofa bed so can sleep a third person. They even have their own family of barn owls living on their 300 acres of land and a **campsite** (🐾 if on lead; Mar-end Oct) out back charging from £10 for a pitch and one person (extra people £5 each), including use of showers, hot and cold water and kitchen facilities. If arranged in advance breakfast (£7) is available for campers.

Stagecoach's No 93 **bus** service passes here (request stop); see pp48-51 for further details.

Dykesfield The path continues along the road and along the line of the Vallum through this village (Map 3), though the only suggestion that this is the case is the name of one of the houses – 'Vallum House' – along the way. For walkers, the only other possible points of interest in the village are the bus stops (bus No 93 stops here) and, if you're heading across the marshes, the tide times (see p91) that are printed on the board at the village's westernmost point.

BURGH-BY-SANDS
[Map 3 & Map 4, p102]
Burgh-by-Sands (pronounced 'Bruff-by-Sands') is the largest settlement on this stage, though it's still little more than a collection of houses strung out along the main road. The 12th-century **St Michael's Church** is the main focus for Romano-philes, with its walls largely made from

Wall stones and its location at the centre of what was once a five-acre (two-hectare) Roman fort. This was **Aballava**, garrisoned for much of its history by auxiliary troops of Moors from North Africa. Comparatively little is known of Aballava, though we do know that the bathhouse (which, as is typical, would have been outside the fort) was

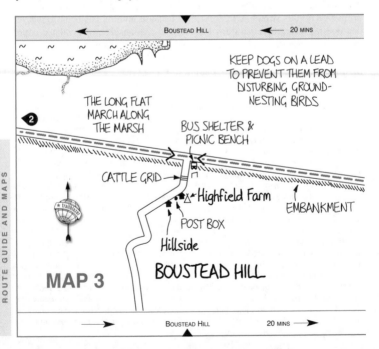

❏ WHY DOES THE WESTERN WALL DODGE AROUND SO MUCH?

In all, this westernmost section of Hadrian's Wall changes direction 34 times over the course of the 14 miles between Carlisle and Bowness. By comparison, the Wall to the east of Carlisle changes direction just 19 times in 17 miles.

One theory, and it seems to be the only one we have at the moment, is that 2000 years ago the River Eden, which the Wall roughly follows on this westernmost stage of the walk, was itself full of kinks and changes in direction. (It is interesting to note, too, that the Vallum strays from the line of the Wall after leaving Carlisle – again nobody is entirely sure why.) Despite all this zig-zagging, the path continues in its mission to stick to the original line of the Wall. The bridge stones in Carlisle, the various churches along the way that have been built from Roman masonry – not to mention the occasional Roman altar that now finds secondary employment in local homes as a lintel decoration or garden ornament – are all proof that the trail has not forsaken its duty and continues to adhere, as closely as it can, to the line of the Wall.

located where the vicarage is today, and excavations have revealed a number of Roman artefacts, including glassware and metalwork. In 1928 a section of Wall foundations was uncovered in the graveyard too.

Today, some stone slabs line the churchyard path and recount the history of the village for visitors. There's more evidence of Roman occupation within the church itself, where the face of a pagan god

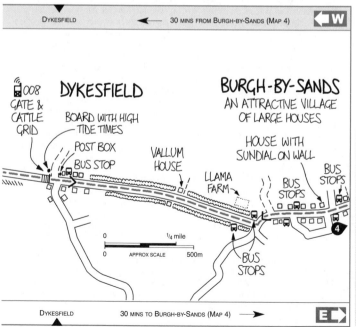

DYKESFIELD   ◀—— 30 MINS FROM BURGH-BY-SANDS (MAP 4)   ◀ W

⌨ 008
GATE &
CATTLE
GRID

DYKESFIELD

BOARD WITH HIGH
TIDE TIMES

POST BOX

BUS STOP

VALLUM
HOUSE

BURGH-BY-SANDS
AN ATTRACTIVE VILLAGE
OF LARGE HOUSES

HOUSE WITH
SUNDIAL ON WALL

LLAMA
FARM

BUS
STOPS

BUS
STOPS

4

0   ¼ mile
0   APPROX SCALE   500m

BUS
STOPS

DYKESFIELD   30 MINS TO BURGH-BY-SANDS (MAP 4) ——▶   E ▶

ROUTE GUIDE AND MAPS

❏ SO WHERE'S THE WALL?

One of the most noticeable aspects of the walk on this stage between Bowness and Carlisle is the lack of any concrete evidence (or more accurately, facing-stone-on-rubble-and-puddled-clay-or-limestone-mortar evidence) of the actual Wall on this stretch of the trail. It comes as a bit of a disappointment to many of those walkers who start in Bowness that the first bit of Roman architecture they will come across (outside Carlisle) is the bridge abutment after Walton. (And even here you'll find that the abutment has now been turfed over for its own protection; so even here the Wall, while extant, remains hidden.) Thus, for a distance of some 26 miles (42km), which equates to almost a third of the whole route, walkers have to make do without any visible evidence of the Wall. Which is, of course, the main reason why the trail exists in the first place!

This fact is all the more remarkable when one considers that the path on this stage sticks more closely to its historical line than almost anywhere else on the entire walk. One look at an archaeological map of the Wall proves that the route here continues to follow, as faithfully as the modern landscape and the current laws on rights-of-way allow, the line of Rome's northernmost frontier. And it is even more curious considering that this stage was bookended by the two largest Roman forts on the entire Wall (with Carlisle's Stanwix being the largest, and Bowness's Maia Fort the second). There was also a third fort located at Burgh-by-Sands and a fourth at Drumburgh. Indeed, Carlisle was the headquarters of the entire frontier, with not one but two forts located within the boundaries of the modern city (see p105).

Logic would therefore suggest that this would have been the most populated and heavily fortified part of the Wall – so you'd be forgiven for thinking that this area would yield the greatest amount of evidence that the Romans were here. So why then, is there so little left of Hadrian's greatest architectural achievement around these parts?

Well, part of the answer can be found in the churches passed on this stage. St Mary's at Beaumont, St Michael's at Burgh-by-Sands and St Martin's at Bowness are all clearly built with Roman masonry, the very fabric of the churches made up from bits of the Wall (indeed, at Beaumont the church's exterior wall is said to include a 'building stone' inscribed by the 5th cohort of the 20th legion; the stone is in the left-hand wall as you head up the hill). One can also point to the marshes east of Bowness, where no evidence of a Wall has ever been found between Milecastles 73 (at Dykesfield) and 76 (at Drumburgh). That's not to say that the Wall *definitely* wasn't built on the marshes. But is there, perhaps, a case to be made that the Wall builders decided that the mud and sand of the Solway would be defence enough and thus never bothered to construct a Wall here?

Nevertheless, though there's no Wall, there are some charming little Roman 'curios' that provide some sort of proof that they were here; the two Roman altars, for example, at the front of Drumburgh Castle (see p95) and above a door at Port Carlisle. And some of the best artefacts currently in the new Roman Gallery at Carlisle's Tullie House Museum are also from the west of the city, including a tiny figure of Mars found on the site of Aballava Fort in Burgh-by-Sands; a rough sandstone head of the goddess Minerva with her classical Corinthian helmet, found at Sourmilk Footbridge (see p102) and now in Carlisle's Tullie House Museum; and a small stone altar dedicated to the Goddess Latis, deity of the pool and found in Kirkbampton. There is also said to be a fragment of an altar dedicated to Hercules at Cross Farm in Burgh, which sits above the stable door. All of which actually amounts to very little – but with archaeologists claiming that only about 5% of the Wall has been properly studied, there's hope that plenty more will emerge from this western end of the trail.

can clearly be discerned on the east wall of the chancel behind the altar, emerging from the blank plaster that covers the rest of the wall. Presumably the builders of the church weren't fussy about which Roman stones they used, hence the pagan face. Isn't it curious how it hasn't been removed, especially as, when the faithful face the altar and bow, they are also bowing to this pagan god? At the opposite end of the aisle, note how the church tower has no exterior door and only tiny slit windows, presumably because it was once a pele tower used to protect the locals against raiders.

There's a **drinking water tap** outside the east wall of the church. You can also fill up water bottles at The Greyhound Inn.

Virtually opposite the church, a road leads up to the **Edward I monument**, marking the spot where the so-called Hammer of the Scots died from dysentery while waiting to cross the Solway Firth on 7 July 1307. The king's body lay in state in the church before being buried in Westminster Abbey. There's also an impressive **statue of Edward** outside the Greyhound Inn that was erected on the 700th anniversary of the same event.

Welcoming **pub *The Greyhound Inn*** (☎ 01228-575168; ✹) is open every day from 11am (from noon on Sundays), though sometimes has reduced opening hours in winter. There's a selection of real ales and good **food** (Wed-Sun noon-8pm).

Stagecoach's Nos 93 **bus** stop here en route to Bowness or Carlisle; see pp48-51 for further information.

BEAUMONT & MONKHILL
[Map 4, p102]

Beaumont and its church are situated at the top of the 'beautiful mountain' that gives the village its name. Unsurprisingly, the church is largely built with Wall stones and is in fact the only church on the whole route that lies directly on the line of the Wall.

There's nothing in the village for walkers but a six-minute walk south of Beaumont in **Monkhill** is *Roman Wall Lodges* (☎ 07784-736423, 🖳 hadrianswall-accommodation.co.uk, **fb**; ✹; Ⓛ), a small, friendly, well-equipped **campsite** (from £15pp) with five smart wooden 'cabins' (sleep 4; from £65 for walkers), two of which are en suite (from £95 for walkers) in a small field by the quiet roadside. The owners are very amiable and can conjure up a cooked breakfast if requested. The communal facilities are great here. A large wood cabin houses two bathrooms, a dining room (plates and cutlery provided), a reading room (with a fine selection of books to browse), a drying room and a wood-decked terrace; all of which makes things so much more manageable for campers caught out in the rain.

The campsite also has the advantage of being a stone's throw from one of the best pubs on the whole trail: *Drover's Rest* (☎ 01228-576141, 🖳 droversrestinn.com, **fb**; food Wed-Fri noon-2pm & 5-8.45pm, Sat noon-8pm, Sun noon-7pm; ✹) at Monkhill (Map 4) is an award-winning real-ale pub with a good selection of fairly fancy, hearty mains (from £12.45). It's the beers that are the main focus, though; they hold monthly beer-tasting evenings (£15) and always have some great ales from across the world.

Stagecoach's No 93 **bus** service (see pp48-51) calls at Beaumont and also stops outside Drover's Rest.

The diversion between Beaumont and Kirkandrews-on-Eden
There is currently a diversion in place on the path east of the village of Beaumont (see Map 4). I say 'currently' but, in truth, this is one temporary footpath that is probably anything but! There is even a smart new wooden signpost in the centre of Beaumont that points to the new route and makes no reference to it being a 'diversion' from the proper path – which surely wouldn't have been installed if this 'diversion' was not now the official permanent path. Looking at the

planning notice on the signpost, it says this diversion was first put in place in 2012! That said, you will still see other signs in the village that still call it 'temporary' – so that's what we'll call it here. The diversion was put in place after the path, which originally was located on a steep slope overlooking the River Eden, was washed away after heavy rain. Apparently there is some sort of dispute between the trail authorities and the landowner and, as a result, the path is now diverted south away from the river for about three-quarters of a mile.

Sourmilk footbridge The trail still follows the line of the Wall where it can, invisible though the Wall is. Proof of this is in the appearance of the Vallum, the dip in the field to the south as you cross the little Sourmilk footbridge (Map 4).

BURGH-BY-SANDS ← ← 30 MINS

BURGH-BY-SANDS

↑ TO EDWARD I MONUMENT, ½ MILE

FORTALOO TOILET (HIGH SEASON ONLY)

EDWARD I STATUE

PATH PARALLEL TO ROAD BUT IN FIELD

KEEP TREES TO NORTH OF YOU HERE

BUS STOP

NOT THIS WAY

010

CLOSELY FOLLOWING THE LINE OF THE WALL, THOUGH YOU'LL SEE LITTLE EVIDENCE OF THIS

WALKING ON A MUDDY BRIDLEWAY BETWEEN HEDGES

❸

VILLAGE GREEN

DRINKING TAP

Greyhound Inn 009

BLACK & WHITE HOUSE

KISSING GATE; THE END, OR BEGINNING, OF THE LONGEST SECTION OF ON-ROAD WALKING ON THE TRAIL

NO FOOTPATH ALONG THIS MAIN ROAD

ST MICHAEL'S. BETTER TO GO THROUGH CHURCHYARD TO AVOID PAVEMENT-LESS STRETCH OF ROAD

0   ¼ mile
0   APPROX SCALE   500m

BURGH-BY-SANDS   30 MINS →

ROUTE GUIDE AND MAPS

It's funny how such a seemingly unremarkable footbridge should have been dignified with its own name, though the bridge does have some importance for archaeologists: it was here that a sandstone head of Minerva, Roman goddess of wisdom and warfare, was found in the 19th century. It can now be found in Carlisle's Tullie House Museum (p110).

Grinsdale The village of Grinsdale (Map 5) has little for trekkers save for a **wooden honesty box** with drinks and snacks (and CCTV to make sure you remain honest!). Milecastle 69 is supposed to have been built around here but you won't see any evidence of it today. Even the local church, St Kentigern's, fails to have any Wall stones within its fabric, disappointing for a church along the trail.

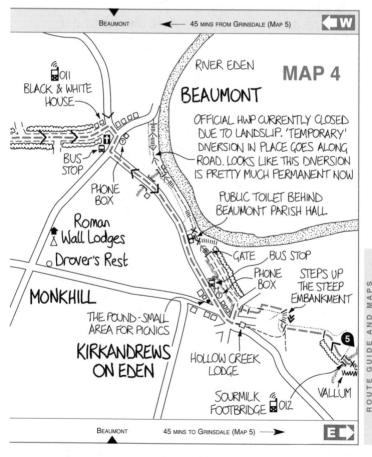

BEAUMONT ← 45 MINS FROM GRINSDALE (MAP 5) W

RIVER EDEN   **MAP 4**

011
BLACK & WHITE HOUSE

BEAUMONT

OFFICIAL HWP CURRENTLY CLOSED DUE TO LANDSLIP. 'TEMPORARY' DIVERSION IN PLACE GOES ALONG ROAD. LOOKS LIKE THIS DIVERSION IS PRETTY MUCH PERMANENT NOW

BUS STOP

PHONE BOX

PUBLIC TOILET BEHIND BEAUMONT PARISH HALL

Roman Wall Lodges
Drover's Rest

GATE   BUS STOP

PHONE BOX

STEPS UP THE STEEP EMBANKMENT

MONKHILL

THE POUND - SMALL AREA FOR PICNICS

KIRKANDREWS ON EDEN

HOLLOW CREEK LODGE

5

SOURMILK FOOTBRIDGE 012

VALLUM

BEAUMONT   45 MINS TO GRINSDALE (MAP 5) →

ROUTE GUIDE AND MAPS

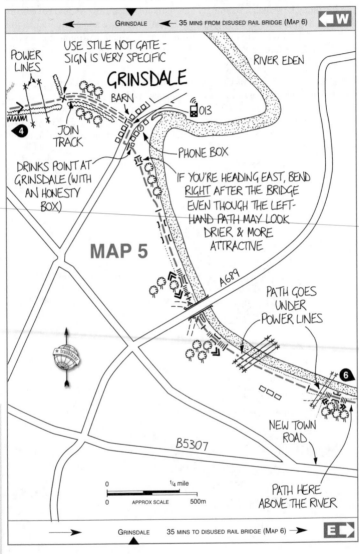

POWER LINES

USE STILE NOT GATE –
SIGN IS VERY SPECIFIC

GRINSDALE

RIVER EDEN

BARN

013

JOIN TRACK

PHONE BOX

DRINKS POINT AT
GRINSDALE (WITH
AN HONESTY
BOX)

IF YOU'RE HEADING EAST, BEND
RIGHT AFTER THE BRIDGE
EVEN THOUGH THE LEFT-
HAND PATH MAY LOOK
DRIER & MORE
ATTRACTIVE

MAP 5

A689

PATH GOES
UNDER
POWER LINES

NEW TOWN
ROAD

B5307

0   ¼ mile
APPROX SCALE
0   500m

PATH HERE
ABOVE THE RIVER

W ← CARLISLE TO BOWNESS-ON-SOLWAY   [Maps 6-1]

This is an unusual end to the walk. There are no ruins, either of Wall or forts, and only occasional glimpses of Vallum and ditch. There are no moors either, nor crags, nor even really any gradients worth moaning about. Nevertheless, there are some delights in store on this **14-mile (22.5km; 5¼hr)** stage, including a couple of cute villages, some great views over the River Eden to Scotland, and a stroll through an Area of Outstanding Natural Beauty; and if the weather holds, the walk is both a peaceful, gentle pleasure and the perfect way to finish and reflect upon the epic journey you've just completed.

CARLISLE   [map p109]

Though it cannot compare in scale with Newcastle, the trail's other Wall city, Carlisle, is a pleasant place to visit, with a fair amount to see and do and a compactness and modesty that means it never feels intimidating or overwhelming. It has in the last few years also become very keen to celebrate its Roman connections and as you walk along the path through Bitts Park you'll see several pillars emblazoned with the word 'Luguvalium' – the name of the original Roman fort at Carlisle.

There is a distinct lack of any significant Roman ruins within the city boundaries today, save a small huddle of 90 or so stones lying to the north of the trail in Bitts Park that were dredged up from the Eden and which were, apparently, the remains of an old Roman Bridge. There are also, inevitably, Roman stones in the fabric of both Carlisle's Castle and cathedral, and an archaeological dig at the castle in 2010 discovered over 80,000 Roman artefacts! But there are very few Roman ruins left in situ; the most extensive example you'll find is the sunken shrine in the grounds of Tullie House Museum (see p110) – an essential port of call in Carlisle for anyone interested in the Romans and their Wall.

The lack of Roman remains is remarkable when one considers two salient facts: first, that when St Cuthbert visited the city in AD685 (see p107) he was taken to see a 'remarkable' Roman fountain; and, second, that 2000 years ago this city was the headquarters for the whole Wall and the home of two forts, one of which was the largest of them all. Uxelodunum, commonly known as Stanwix after the suburb that exists today

in this location on the north side of the Eden, measured 9.3 acres (3.72 hectares) in total and was garrisoned by the 1000-strong Ala Petriana cavalry – said to be the largest body of calvary stationed anywhere in the entire empire!

Stanwix was not the first fort in town, however. That was Luguvalium, stretching from Botchergate, near the railway station, to the castle – covering pretty much the whole of the city centre. This first fort here was built around AD72 by governor Cerialis to defend the Stanegate. (There is some evidence that Agricola had a turf fort here around AD80.) Despite the presence of Stanwix, built around 50 years later when the Wall was constructed, Luguvalium (the name is derived from the sun god, Lug) continued to be used until the 4th century or so, although it filled a role that was less military and more civic as time went on.

The local tribe, the Carvetii, saw the presence of such a large garrison not as a threat but an opportunity, and began trading with the Romans and inhabiting the land near Luguvalium Fort. This continued until the Carvetii's settlement became their unofficial capital – and Carlisle was born (though the name, Caerluel, is a post-Roman invention meaning 'Castle of Luel'), rising to provincial capital status by the end of the 4th century.

Despite such rich Roman history, there are few sights in Carlisle that demand your time (apart from the essential and absorbing Tullie House Museum, and perhaps a visit to the castle, see p111) – which leaves you free to enjoy the city's shops, restaurants, cafés and bars, of which there are plenty.

Services

The focus of the city centre is Market Cross, the cobbled pedestrian-only junction where you'll find the Old Town Hall, now home to the **tourist information centre** (TIC; ☎ 01228-598596, 🖳 www.discover carlisle.co.uk; Mar-May & Sep-Oct Mon-Sat 9.30am-5pm, Jun-Aug to 5.30pm & Sun 10.30am-3pm, winter hours shorter). They sell a few Wall-related souvenirs and Hadrian's Wall passports here.

There are **banks** and **ATMs** dotted around the city centre, especially on English St, where you'll also find the **post office** (Mon-Sat 9am-5.30pm, Sun 10.30am-2.30pm) inside a branch of WH Smith.

There's a Boots **pharmacy** (Mon-Sat 9am-5.30pm, Sun 10.30am-4.30pm) on English St. For **hiking gear** you have a couple of choices: Millets (Mon-Sat 9am-5.30pm, Sun 10am-4pm), 110 English St, and Trespass at 64 Scotch St (Mon-Sat 9am-5.30pm, Sun 10.30am-4.30pm).

For a **supermarket**, Tesco Metro is near the train station (Mon-Fri 7am-10pm, Sat 7am-8pm, Sun 10am-4pm).

Johnson's **laundrette** (Mon-Sat 8.30am-5.30pm) is right in the city centre on Market St, though when I asked how much they would charge for a single load of washing they quoted me £20! Better to wait until you get home if you can…

You can *usually* get your **Hadrian's Wall Passport stamped** at reception in Sands Centre, by Eden Bridge. However, at the time of writing the whole site was closed for major redevelopment, so in the meantime you'll find the Carlisle stamp at Bowness and Birdoswald.

Transport

[See pp48-51] Those arriving by public transport will alight in town, or at the **bus station** on Lonsdale St, home to both local and National Express buses. Stagecoach's No 685 is a very useful **bus** service, but perhaps of most interest is Stagecoach's No 93 service to Bowness-on-Solway (see p48 for further details). The limited BR1 service also stops in Carlisle.

Train services run twice an hour to Newcastle via Brampton, Haltwhistle, Hexham and Corbridge. For a **taxi** try AAA Taxis (☎ 01228-808777, 🖳 aaa-taxis.com), or Carlisle Taxis (☎ 01228-247365, 🖳 carlisle-taxis.com).

Where to stay

Finding somewhere to stay in Carlisle is not as easy as it should be. B&Bs are relatively plentiful but often book up quickly, there's only one hostel, and the nearest campsite is in Beaumont (see p101).

The one hostel is *Carlisle City Hostel* (☎ 07914-720821, 🖳 carlislecityhostel.com, **fb**; 2 x 6-bed dorms shared facilities, 2Qd, 1 en suite), at 36 Abbey St, an independently run hostel with a great location, overlooking the back of Tullie House Museum and just a stone's throw from the cathedral and the castle. Both quad rooms have a double bed and a bunk bed. They charge from £23 per dorm bed (private room sgl occ £53-56, two adults sharing £53-63) and a light breakfast is included. There are also self-catering facilities and a laundry service (£8-10).

For a **B&B**, the first area to look is Victoria Place, just a 5-minute walk from Eden Bridge and the trail, where a couple of listed buildings stand next to each other: *Cartref* (☎ 01228-522077, 🖳 cartrefguest house.co.uk; 2S shared facilities, 1S/2D/3Tr, all en suite; 🐾;ⓛ), at No 44, is perhaps the smartest of these, a large and attractively furnished home. The owners work really hard to make this place as comfy as possible

---

❑ **WHERE TO STAY: THE DETAILS**
In the descriptions of accommodation in this book: 🛏 means at least one room has a bath; ⓛ means a packed lunch can be prepared if arranged in advance; 🐾 signifies that dogs are welcome in at least one room but also subject to prior arrangement, an additional charge may also be payable; **fb** indicates a Facebook page. See also p86.

> ❏ **THE WALL'S FIRST TOURIST?**
> According to the Venerable Bede, in AD685 St Cuthbert came to Carlisle to visit an
> English queen staying in a nunnery in town. Whilst there, Cuthbert was taken by the
> citizens of Carlisle to look at the town walls and the 'remarkable fountain, formerly
> built by the Romans'. Thus, with this brief mention by Bede, Cuthbert becomes the
> first recorded tourist to visit the Wall. The 'remarkable fountain', incidentally, has
> never been found, though in the 1930s a building was excavated with a fountain in
> its central courtyard, which dated back to AD78 and the reign of Vespasian. Could
> this be the fountain Cuthbert was shown?

(each room comes equipped with a foot spa)
and they succeed. The rates (from £37.50pp,
sgl £32-37, or £40-45 en suite) don't include
their award-winning breakfast, but it only
costs £7.50pp.

By the side of Cartref, at No 42, is
Brooklyn House (☎ 01228-590002, 🖥
brooklynhousecarlisle.co.uk; 3S/3D or T/
2Qd, all en suite or with private bathroom,
🖤; ⓛ). They have introduced a two-night
minimum policy, but this needn't be a problem as you can spend one night in Carlisle,
then travel to Bowness early the next morning and walk back to Carlisle the next day.
This also allows you to leave your luggage
behind in your room, of course. B&B costs
from £45pp per night (sgl £45).

Down Howard Place at No 6, is the
friendly **Langleigh Guest House** (☎ 01228-
530440, 🖥 langleighhouse.co.uk; 3S/4Tr/
1Qd en suite, 1Tr private bathroom; 🖤;
ⓛ). It has huge, immaculate, furniture-
filled rooms and is run by a trained chef, so
the breakfasts should be decent. They will
provide an evening meal if requested at
least 24-48hrs in advance. They charge
from £42.50pp (sgl £55).

At the southern end of Howard Place,
at 90 Warwick Rd, **Howard Lodge Guest
House** (☎ 01228-529842, 🖥 howard-lodge
.co.uk; 2S/1D/1T/2Tr, most en suite; ⓛ)
prides itself on its large breakfasts. B&B
costs from £37.50pp (sgl from £45).

Further down Warwick Rd, at No 107,
amiable **Cornerways Guest House** (☎
01228-521733, 🖥 cornerwaysbandb.co.uk;
6S/1D/3Tr, most en suite, some shared
facilities; ⓛ) charges from £40pp (sgl £40-
55, sgl occ £65).

Down in Botchergate, the road running

south from near the station, are several larger hotels. They include **Ibis Carlisle City
Centre** (☎ 01228-587690, 🖥 all.accor
.com; 65D/15T/17Tr, all en suite; 🖤), a
depressingly ugly place on the outside but
comfortable inside. Rates are fair, starting
at about £45 for the room, with the cheapest rates through their website. There's also
Travelodge Carlisle Central (☎ 08719
846374, 🖥 travelodge.co .uk; mix of D, T
& Tr, all en suite; WI-FI 30 mins free then
£3/24hrs; 🖤), just off Botchergate on Cecil
St, with rooms for as little as £26. Note that
at both these places, breakfast is extra.

Where to eat and drink
Cafés & tearooms As you walk into
Carlisle from the path through Bitts Park
you may well stroll past a new venue/art
gallery/workspace/bar/restaurant space
called **Tribe** (🖥 tribecarlisle.co.uk). It's
early days yet but the vision of the design-
ers is clear. Whether it catches on remains
to be seen – there are only a few eateries
here currently, serving Mexican, Lebanese
and Greek food. But it might just be one of
the go-to places for a drink or bite to eat in
the coming years.

Cafés abound in Carlisle, but the best
of them are often hidden away down little
side streets and alleyways away from the
main shopping precinct. Perhaps the best of
the lot in terms of the quality of its teas and
coffees is **John Watt & Son** (☎ 01228-
521545, 🖥 johnwatt.co.uk; Mon-Fri 9am-
4.30pm, Sat 8am-4.30pm, Sun 10am-
3.30pm), coffee-roaster and tea-blender
extraordinaire that was first established in
Carlisle in 1865. The aroma of freshly
ground coffee beans envelopes you as soon

as you walk in the door and they have single-origin coffees and loose-leaf teas from all over the world. The food is excellent too, and unlike the tea and coffee, sourced locally (within a 30-mile/50km radius) wherever possible. Breakfasts (from £6) are served until 11.30am, at which point they start serving from their lunch menu which includes homemade soups (£3.95), sandwiches (£7.25) and jacket potatoes (£8.25). You can also buy tea, coffee and other related items from their small **shop** (Mon-Fri 9am-5pm, Sat 8am-5pm, Sun 10am-4pm) by the entrance.

The same owners have now taken over *Cakes & Ale* (**fb**; Mon-Sat 9.30am-4.30pm, Sun 11.30am-4pm), a charming little place with friendly staff and decent coffee, lunches and cakes. Add in the pleasant garden, reasonably priced food (sandwiches for £6.50, toasted ciabattas £6.75) and the fact that it's attached to an independent **bookshop** and you have an eatery that pretty much ticks every box for most walkers. This place has always been my favourite in Carlisle – so if it had to be taken over by somebody else, I'm glad that it's the people behind John Watt. The easiest way to find it is to look for the attached **bookshop**, Bookcase (⌨ bookcasecarlisle .co.uk), on Castle Street; the front door of the café is down the alley, Long Lane, that runs alongside it.

A third great café is *The Old Engine House* (☎ 01228-510741, **fb**; 9.30am-3pm), a cute little family-run place slightly away from the town centre on West Walls, serving teas, coffees, sandwiches,

scones and the like from what was an old fire engine house. Nor must we forget the *Cathedral Café* (**fb**; daily 9am-3.30pm) in the grounds of the cathedral itself, a simple place with pretty good food – though the setting, and the tranquility, are what really stay with you.

Alexandros Greek Deli (☎ 01228-592227, ⌨ thegreek.co.uk; Tue-Sat 9.30am -3pm) is attached to the Greek restaurant (see Pubs & restaurants) of the same name, and the perfect place to pick up an espresso and some Mediterranean-flavoured lunch-box fillers.

Those looking for an early start are pretty much confined to the national chains that you'll see on every High Street up and down the country, including *Greggs* (on English St; Mon-Sat 6.30am-6pm, Sun 9am-4pm), *McDonald's*, just up the hill (daily 6am-10pm), and both *Costa* (Mon-Fri 6.30am-7pm, Sat 7.30am-6pm, Sun 9am-5pm) and *Caffe Nero* (Mon-Fri 8am-5.15pm,Sat to 5.30pm, Sun to 4.15pm). But there is also one local eatery that opens early: *Henri's Baguettes* (Mon-Sat 7.30am-3pm), at the entrance to Market Hall, with filled baguettes for £3-4.

Don't forget the Victorian Market Hall (8am-4.30pm), at the northern end of the town centre just five minutes from the trail. There are plenty of food stalls here (and booths in which to eat your purchases) including fish and chips, Chinese and Thai; and not forgetting *Romano Pizzeria*, the best pizzeria, according to one aficionado, outside of Italy.

CARLISLE – KEY

Where to eat & drink

1 The Turf
2 Adriano's
3 Market Hall, inc. Romano Pizzeria
4 Greggs
5 Mama's Fish Restaurant
6 Henri's Baguettes
7 McDonald's
8 Costa
9 Franco's
10 Cakes & Ale
12 Cathedral Café
13 The Old Engine House
14 Caffe Nero
15 John Watt & Son
16 Apple Tree
22 Alexandros & Alexandros Greek Deli
23 Davids
25 Yummy's
26 Royal Outpost
27 La Mezzaluna
28 Home & Away
29 William Rufus

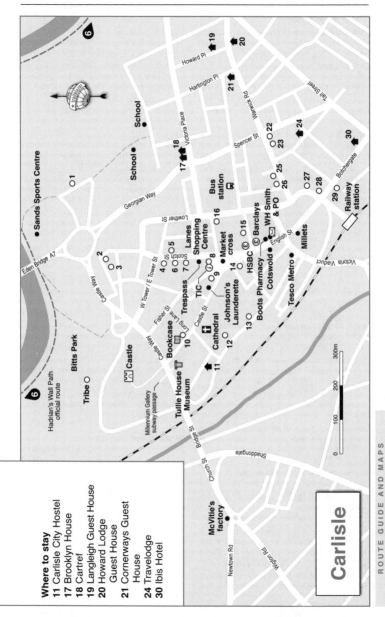

Carlisle

Where to stay

11 Carlisle City Hostel
17 Brooklyn House
18 Cartref
19 Langleigh Guest House
20 Howard Lodge Guest House
21 Cornerways Guest House
24 Travelodge
30 Ibis Hotel

Pubs & restaurants Very close to the path is *Turf Tavern* (☎ 01228-515367; food daily 9am-10pm), one of the Hungry Horse chain offering basic but filling, good-value pub fare and with lots of special deals. For cheap and reliable pub grub there's *William Rufus* (☎ 01228-633160, 🖥 jdwetherspoon .com; food daily 8am-9pm), with excellent value food served all day from breakfast onwards. Do remember, however, that dogs aren't allowed in any Wetherspoons outlet. Thankfully, the pub chain Greene King have emulated the Weatherspoon business model and also provide large plates dirt cheap and delicious grub that you can feast on while watching the football...and *they* allow dogs. In central Carlisle the main Greene King pub is *The Apple Tree* (☎ 01228-521435, 🖥 greeneking-pubs.co.uk; food daily 10am-9pm; 🐾), where most main meals, including a plate of *two* gammon steaks with fried eggs and chips, are just £7.79.

For fish & chips, it's hard to beat *Mamma's Fish Restaurant* (☎ 01228-533056, 🖥 mammasfishrestaurant.com; daily 5-9pm), a super-friendly, down-to-earth chippy that has a café/restaurant area too. You can get fish & chips here for as little as £5.90, but they also do pies, chip butties, burgers and jacket potatoes.

For more upmarket dining there's *Davids* (☎ 01228-523578, 🖥 davidsrestaurant.co.uk, **fb**; Tue-Sat noon-1.30pm & 6-9pm), a cracking little place on Warwick Rd, which serves quality British cuisine and sources much of its food locally. The menu changes regularly, but rarely disappoints. Evening á la carte mains (available Fri & Sat only) cost around £19-29, while the lunch-time set menus are £21 for two courses and £25 for three, and there's set evening menus on Tue-Thur for £27-33 for two/three courses.

Just two doors down, *Alexandros* (see Cafés; Tue-Sat noon-1.30pm & 5-9pm) is a wonderfully authentic Greek eatery, where evening mains cost £13.95-17.95. Their souvlaki, (chicken skewer marinated with herbs, olive oil and lemon juice, wrapped in bacon and served with rice and vegetables) is £15.95.

On the same street is *Royal Outpost* (☎ 01228-818448, 🖥 royaloutpost .co.uk, **fb**; Tue-Thur 2-10pm, Fri-Sun noon-10pm), a superior Thai restaurant with an excellent coconut and coriander fish curry (£14).

There are several good Italian places including *Franco's* (☎ 01228-512305, 🖥 francoscarlisle.com; Mon-Fri 11.30am-2.30pm & 5.30-10pm, Sat 11.30am-10.30pm, Sun noon-2.30pm & 6-9pm) near Market Cross, behind the TIC; this is Carlisle's oldest Italian restaurant, founded here in 1974, and is housed in one of the city's oldest buildings built in about 1407. Pizza or pasta dishes cost from £11.50, with most main-course meat dishes around £16.95. They also run *Adriano's* (yes, it is named after Hadrian; ☎ 01228-599007, 🖥 ristoranteadriano.co.uk; Tue-Sat 11.30am-1.30pm & 5.30-9.30pm, Mon 11.30am-1.30pm & 5.30-9pm, Sun 5-9pm), a slightly cheaper Italian option on Rickergate.

Takeaways The railway station area is the best place to go for takeaways. You'll find plenty of places around there with late opening hours including *Home & Away* (☎ 01228-512615; Sun-Thur 11am-midnight, Fri & Sat 11am-3am), a chippy with some seating on bar stools; and *La Mezzaluna* (☎ 01228-534472, 🖥 lamezzalunacarlisle co .uk, **fb**; Tue-Sat noon-10pm), an Italian restaurant which also offers takeaway.

Not too far away, *Yummy's* (☎ 01228-598800, **fb**; Thur-Tue 5pm-10pm) does Chinese takeaway.

What to see and do
The only must-see Wall-related sight is housed in one of Carlisle's most historic buildings, the Jacobean **Tullie House Museum** (☎ 01228-618718, 🖥 tulliehouse .co.uk; Apr-Oct Mon-Sat 10am-5pm, Sun 11am-5pm, Nov-Mar Mon-Sat 10am-4pm, Sun noon-4pm; £12) on Castle St. But as interesting as the 16th-century townhouse museum building (for which it is named) may be, the main reason for calling in is the chance to see their Roman Frontier Gallery. It's a wonderful run-through of the Roman story in this area and includes many interactive touch-screen displays and some

gorgeous, original Roman items from belt buckles to brooches, tombstones to trinkets. One display recreates a murder case; the victim, with severe skull injuries, was found covered with rubbish at the bottom of an old well within the city of Carlisle.

The rest of the museum shouldn't be ignored though, with absorbing displays on the reivers (see box p96). Even more excitingly, head down to the underground gallery, don a pair of white gloves and you can actually hold some genuine Roman artefacts, such as coins and hairpins. It's all really rather thrilling! And after you've left the building, check out the walkway on the museum's eastern side on Castle St, where you'll see a representation of the entire Wall rendered in brick and paving slab.

From Tullie House a subway passage (the Millennium Gallery) leads under the road to Carlisle's other main attraction: its large **castle** (☎ 01228-591922, 🖳 english-heritage.org.uk/visit/places/carlisle-castle/; Apr-Oct daily 10am-5pm, winter hours vary; £11.60). A castle was originally built on this site by William Rufus in 1092, though that earth-and-timber construction was replaced in 1122 under orders of Henry I by the impressive and imposing stone structure you see today.

A reader also emailed to recommend the modern **henge** (stone circle) in Rickerby Park (see Map 6), erected in 2011 to highlight the diversity of rock types in the Eden valley.

E → CARLISLE TO WALTON [MAPS 6-11]

One stage in, 14 miles done and, apart from a few loose Roman stones in Carlisle's Bitts Park (stones, which, if we're being honest, you were probably too tired to divert off the path to see anyway), there's still very little sign of anything resembling a Roman Wall. And I'm afraid you're going to have a wait a few miles more yet, for it's not until the latter half of this second stage that the Wall makes any attempt to reveal itself (and even then, you probably wouldn't know it was evidence of a Roman wall unless somebody told you). So I'm afraid you're just going to have to put up with some pleasant riverside strolling, a sizeable chunk of walking on mercifully quiet roads and some lengthy roaming among ruminants.

Nevertheless, the path does follow the line of the Wall where it can, and just occasionally you do get proof of this: the unusual, Wall-shaped bump in the ground at Bleatarn Farm, for example (one of the very, very few places where you actually walk on a section of the Wall, albeit one buried deep beneath the turf) and the strip of Vallum and defensive ditch between Oldwall and Newtown. But it is these meagre offerings that you'll have to survive on until after the village of Walton, **11½ miles (18.5km; 4hrs)** away.

Rickerby Park This park (Map 6, p113) has been open to the public since the 1920s. At its heart (and visible from the trail), lies a Cenotaph, and indeed the whole park is dedicated to the memory of the fallen from the Great War. The bridge you cross is also officially called the Memorial Bridge, though locals universally – and incorrectly – call it the suspension bridge.

❏ IMPORTANT NOTE – WALKING TIMES
All times in this book refer only to the time spent walking. You will need to add 20-30% to allow for rests, photography, checking the map, drinking water etc.

RICKERBY [Map 6]

The cycle route here takes you round the back of **Rickerby**, an entire village that, with all its towers and turrets, resembles one enormous Victorian folly. There's even a tower to the north of the trail in a field often planted with oilseed-rape. This eccentric architecture was the work of the eccentrically named George Head Head (1795-1876), a 19th-century mayor, magistrate, banker and mine owner. His estate is now home to a very upmarket spa and restaurant, *Rickerby Retreat* (☎ 01228 544200, 🖥 www.rickerby retreat.co.uk; food Tue & Wed 9.30am-5pm, Thur-Sat 9.30am-9pm, Sun 10am-5pm) with lunchtime mains including deli sharing boards (cured meats & cheeses) for £22.50.

The limited BR1 **bus service** stops here; see pp48-51 for details.

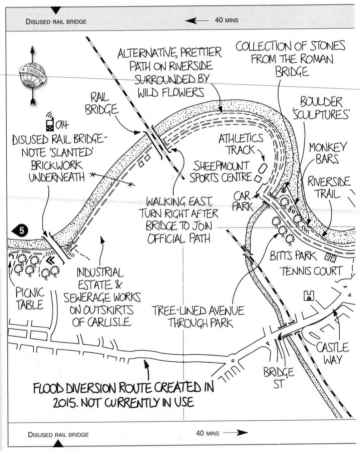

DISUSED RAIL BRIDGE ← 40 MINS

ALTERNATIVE, PRETTIER PATH ON RIVERSIDE SURROUNDED BY WILD FLOWERS

COLLECTION OF STONES FROM THE ROMAN BRIDGE

RAIL BRIDGE

BOULDER 'SCULPTURES'

014

DISUSED RAIL BRIDGE - NOTE 'SLANTED' BRICKWORK UNDERNEATH ✳

ATHLETICS TRACK

SHEEPMOUNT SPORTS CENTRE

MONKEY BARS

RIVERSIDE TRAIL

5

WALKING EAST, TURN RIGHT AFTER BRIDGE TO JOIN OFFICIAL PATH

CAR PARK

INDUSTRIAL ESTATE & SEWERAGE WORKS ON OUTSKIRTS OF CARLISLE

BITTS PARK TENNIS COURT

PICNIC TABLE

TREE-LINED AVENUE THROUGH PARK

CASTLE WAY

FLOOD DIVERSION ROUTE CREATED IN 2015. NOT CURRENTLY IN USE

BRIDGE ST

DISUSED RAIL BRIDGE 40 MINS →

Linstock The path diverts from the line of the Wall temporarily to cross the M6 via the fairly low-key village of Linstock (Map 7, p114). The main highlight for walkers may well be Linstock Cottage's **walkers' shelter and honesty box**, set up in their carport. At the eastern end of the village is Linstock Castle, a fortified house and pele tower now incorporated into a modern farm. The limited BR1 **bus service** stops in Linstock; see pp48-9 for details.

Whichever way you're heading, after Linstock the path then takes its own sweet time meandering back to the Wall.

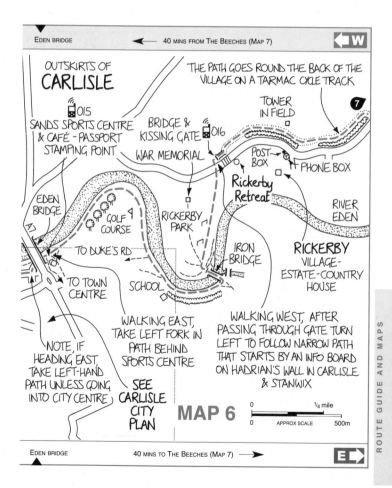

EDEN BRIDGE ◄─── 40 MINS FROM THE BEECHES (MAP 7) ◄W

OUTSKIRTS OF
CARLISLE

THE PATH GOES ROUND THE BACK OF THE VILLAGE ON A TARMAC CYCLE TRACK

TOWER IN FIELD

7

O15

SANDS SPORTS CENTRE & CAFÉ - PASSPORT STAMPING POINT

BRIDGE & KISSING GATE O16

WAR MEMORIAL

POST BOX

PHONE BOX

Rickerby Retreat

EDEN BRIDGE

RIVER EDEN

GOLF COURSE

RICKERBY PARK

A7

TO DUKE'S RD

IRON BRIDGE

RICKERBY
VILLAGE - ESTATE - COUNTRY HOUSE

TO TOWN CENTRE

SCHOOL

WALKING EAST, TAKE LEFT FORK IN PATH BEHIND SPORTS CENTRE

WALKING WEST, AFTER PASSING THROUGH GATE TURN LEFT TO FOLLOW NARROW PATH THAT STARTS BY AN INFO BOARD ON HADRIAN'S WALL IN CARLISLE & STANWIX

NOTE, IF HEADING EAST, TAKE LEFT-HAND PATH UNLESS GOING INTO CITY CENTRE

SEE CARLISLE CITY PLAN

MAP 6

0   1/4 mile
0   APPROX SCALE   500m

EDEN BRIDGE   40 MINS TO THE BEECHES (MAP 7) ───►   E

ROUTE GUIDE AND MAPS

CROSBY-ON-EDEN & LOW CROSBY
[Map 8]

A village split into two parts, **Crosby-on-Eden** lies an hour or two from Carlisle on the trail. As with many of the minor villages encountered in this western half of the walk, Crosby is built around, and consists of little more than the main road (which actually follows the line of the old Roman Stanegate — see p52). It's here on this road you'll find **St John's Church** in **Low**

Crosby village, erected in 1864 on the site of a much older edifice.

As for facilities, where the Path joins/leaves the village at its eastern end you'll find a long-established **refreshment stall** with hot and cold drinks and snacks. Don't forget to use the honesty box! The same people run *Crosby Camping* (☎ 01228-573000; ﹐; from £8pp), a simple site with shower and toilet. They have also

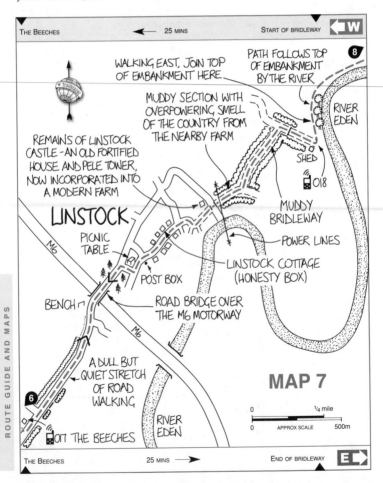

THE BEECHES ← 25 MINS → START OF BRIDLEWAY ◀W

WALKING EAST, JOIN TOP OF EMBANKMENT HERE

PATH FOLLOWS TOP OF EMBANKMENT BY THE RIVER ❽

MUDDY SECTION WITH OVERPOWERING SMELL OF THE COUNTRY FROM THE NEARBY FARM

RIVER EDEN

REMAINS OF LINSTOCK CASTLE - AN OLD FORTIFIED HOUSE AND PELE TOWER, NOW INCORPORATED INTO A MODERN FARM

SHED

018

LINSTOCK

MUDDY BRIDLEWAY

PICNIC TABLE

POWER LINES

POST BOX

LINSTOCK COTTAGE (HONESTY BOX)

BENCH

ROAD BRIDGE OVER THE M6 MOTORWAY

M6

A DULL BUT QUIET STRETCH OF ROAD WALKING

MAP 7

❻

0   ¼ mile

0   500m
APPROX SCALE

RIVER EDEN

017 THE BEECHES

THE BEECHES   25 MINS →   END OF BRIDLEWAY ◼▶

ROUTE GUIDE AND MAPS

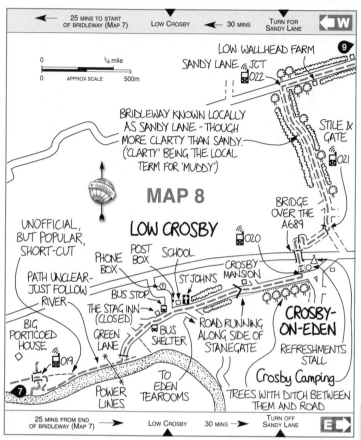

LOW WALLHEAD FARM
SANDY LANE JCT
022

BRIDLEWAY KNOWN LOCALLY AS SANDY LANE - THOUGH MORE CLARTY THAN SANDY. ('CLARTY' BEING THE LOCAL TERM FOR 'MUDDY')

STILE & GATE
021

MAP 8

LOW CROSBY

020

BRIDGE OVER THE A689

UNOFFICIAL, BUT POPULAR, SHORT-CUT

POST BOX
PHONE BOX
SCHOOL
CROSBY MANSION

PATH UNCLEAR - JUST FOLLOW RIVER

ST JOHN'S

BUS STOP

THE STAG INN (CLOSED)

BIG PORTICOED HOUSE
019

GREEN LANE

BUS SHELTER

ROAD RUNNING ALONG SIDE OF STANEGATE

CROSBY-ON-EDEN

REFRESHMENTS STALL

Crosby Camping

POWER LINES

TO EDEN TEAROOMS

TREES WITH DITCH BETWEEN THEM AND ROAD

0   ¼ mile
0   APPROX SCALE   500m

now taken delivery of four wooden camping pods, each sleeping two and with electricity supply (check with them for rates).

Since the closure of the 17th-century Stag Inn, the only dedicated eatery in or near the village is *Eden Tea Room, Restaurant & Bar* (off Map 8; ☎ 01228-573003, 🖳 edengolf.co.uk; daily 8am-9pm). It's a fine place and reasonably priced (sandwiches from £5.95) but it's about 25 minutes off the trail if you take the turning opposite St John's church in Low Crosby, or a bit less if you take the lane south from the centre of Crosby-on-Eden and, as a result, most people prefer to snack on whatever they can find in the honesty boxes en route.

Buses no longer call here so if you need transport, the chances are you'll be relying on the taxi companies of Carlisle; see p106.

Sandy Lane Junction It may be an unmemorable meeting between one very muddy, overgrown track (a bridleway that's been dignified with the name Sandy

Lane) and a slightly less muddy one, but this junction (Map 8, p115) is significant for trail walkers, for it's here that, if you're walking eastwards, the path joins the line of the Wall – and sticks to it (with only four minor diversions) until Heddon-on-the-Wall, and Map 28, almost 45 miles further on.

BLEATARN FARM [Map 9]

Bleatarn Farm Caravan & Campsite (☎ 07795-490579; 🐕; mid Mar to mid Nov) is a small campsite with facilities **for campers only**. They charge £10 per person. The farm is actually one of the more interesting on the path, as the info board attests. Indeed, the farm is believed to sit on what was a Roman quarry, from where they got the stones to make this end of the Wall.

As for the blea ('blue') tarn after which the farm is named, this may once have been filled with fish to feed the soldiers who manned the Wall, and lies to the south of the trail. Note how the trail here is both slightly raised and arrow-straight. As you've probably guessed, this is actually both the Roman Military Way and the base of the Wall that you are walking upon.

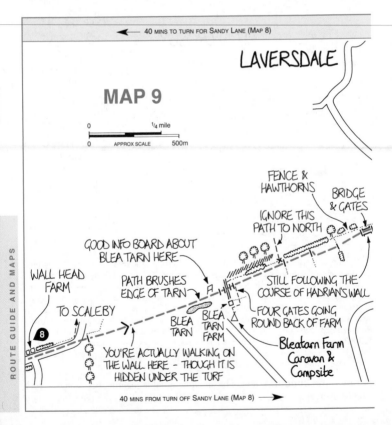

Oldwall There isn't much more to this hamlet (Map 9) than its three houses, though the 17th-century Old Wall Cottage is one of the cutest houses on the trail. (The other two houses here, by the way, are called Romanway Old Wall and Romanside.) There is a bus stop here though (the limited BR1 & BR3 **bus** services call here; see pp48-9 for details).

IRTHINGTON   [off Map 10, p118]

About a mile off the trail, Irthington would not perhaps normally merit a mention in this guide were it not for the paucity of dining options on this stretch of Path; that, and the fact that the village plays host to an excellent pub, *The Sally* (☎ 016977-42956, 🖥 thesallyirthington.co.uk, **fb**; 2D/3D or T en suite; food Mon-Sat noon-8.45pm,

Sun to 7.45pm; advance booking essential). Note that it gets very busy at weekends. They also have five smart **B&B** rooms (from £45pp room only, £55pp with breakfast).

Irthington is a stop on the infrequent BR1 & BR3 **bus services**; see pp48-51 for details.

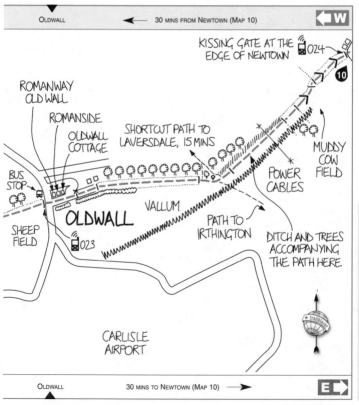

ROUTE GUIDE AND MAPS

NEWTOWN [Map 10]

For quite a large settlement **Newtown** has disappointingly little to tempt the weary trekker. Thankfully, a couple of the locals have tried to change that. One of them has done so by providing an honesty-box **snack shed** in their front garden; they even have a picnic table for walkers to rest up at – just be sure to buy something if you use it. The owners have also converted their garage into B&B accommodation: *Hadrian's Wall Studio* (book through ⌨ airbnb.com, **fb**; 1D or T; Ⓛ) is a self-contained studio including kitchen area with microwave, kettle and toaster; rates are from £41pp.

Another enterprising local runs the highly-regarded *Orchard House Bed and Breakfast* (☎ 016977-42637, ⌨ orchard

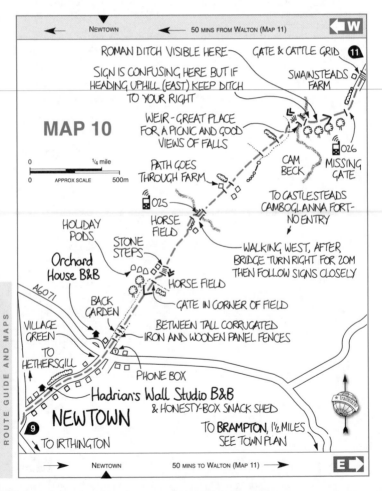

ROUTE GUIDE AND MAPS

← NEWTOWN ← 50 MINS FROM WALTON (MAP 11) ◄W

MAP 10

0 ¼ mile
0 APPROX SCALE 500m

ROMAN DITCH VISIBLE HERE

GATE & CATTLE GRID ⑪

SIGN IS CONFUSING HERE BUT IF HEADING UPHILL (EAST) KEEP DITCH TO YOUR RIGHT

SWAINSTEADS FARM

WEIR - GREAT PLACE FOR A PICNIC AND GOOD VIEWS OF FALLS

CAM BECK

☎026 MISSING GATE

PATH GOES THROUGH FARM

☎025

TO CASTLESTEADS CAMBOGLANNA FORT-NO ENTRY

HOLIDAY PODS

HORSE FIELD

STONE STEPS

WALKING WEST, AFTER BRIDGE TURN RIGHT FOR 20M THEN FOLLOW SIGNS CLOSELY

Orchard House B&B

A6071

BACK GARDEN

HORSE FIELD

GATE IN CORNER OF FIELD

VILLAGE GREEN

BETWEEN TALL CORRUGATED IRON AND WOODEN PANEL FENCES

TO HETHERSGILL

PHONE BOX

Hadrian's Wall Studio B&B & HONESTY-BOX SNACK SHED

NEWTOWN ⑨

TO IRTHINGTON

TO BRAMPTON, 1½ MILES SEE TOWN PLAN

← NEWTOWN 50 MINS TO WALTON (MAP 11) → E►

housebednb.co.uk; 1D en suite, 1D/1T share bathroom if both rooms booked; ☞; (Ⓛ), charging from £45pp (sgl occ £70). Wonderfully, the owner will run guests to The Sally pub and back for their evening meal (though you do need to book your table in advance).

Newtown is a stop on the infrequent BR1 & BR3 **bus services**; see pp48-51 for details. If you head down the A6071, aka Longtown Rd, you'll reach **Brampton**, 2½ miles to the south-east.

BRAMPTON   [map p120]

Brampton is a lovely little market town sitting snugly in the Irthing Valley, reasonably convenient for the trail and with virtually every second building either a pub, hotel or tearoom. Granted a Market Charter in 1252, the main market day is Wednesday. The main sight is **St Martin's Church** (🖳 st martinsbrampton.org.uk; usually open during the day), the only church designed by architect Philip Webb, with some wonderful stained-glass windows by his fellow pre-Raphaelite Edward Burne-Jones. There's also a **statue of Emperor Hadrian** on the western approach into town.

Services

The **visitor centre** (☎ 016977-3433; summer Thur-Fri 10am-2pm, Sat 11am-3pm; phone for winter opening hours) is housed in the cute, octagonal clocktower known as Moot Hall, built in 1817 and located at the eastern end of Front St, the main street in the town. The office is run by volunteers after the funding for the old tourist office was cut; consequently the opening times tend to change quite frequently. There's a Co-op **supermarket** (daily 6am-10pm) behind Market Place, with a Spar (Mon-Sat 7am-10pm, Sun 8am-10pm) across the road from the visitor centre. Just a couple of doors down is H Jobson **pharmacy** (Mon-Fri 9am-6pm, Sat to 1pm). The town no longer has a bank but it does have **ATMs** at both supermarkets as well as the Cumberland Building Society. Brampton also still has its own **post office** (Mon-Fri 8am-5.30pm, Sat 10am-4.30pm).

Transport

[See pp48-51] Arriva's/Stagecoach's No 685 **bus** calls in here as well as the limited BR1 & BR3 services. Note that, while Brampton does boast a **railway station** on the main Newcastle-to-Carlisle line, it's 1½ miles east of town. A branch line connecting the station with the town centre closed in 1923, and is now a pleasant public footpath.

Where to stay

There isn't much choice for those looking to stay in Brampton but the gap left by the 'official' accommodation options is, apparently, more than adequately filled by Airbnb (see p21).

Oakwood Park (☎ 016977-2436, 🖳 oakwoodparkhotel.co.uk; 1S/1D or Tr/2T, all en suite; ☞; Ⓛ; Mar-Nov), Longtown Rd, is a sumptuous Victorian house set in 10 acres of grounds about a mile north of town on the way to the Wall. Full of class and character, it's a wonderful place to stay. B&B costs from £40pp (sgl/sgl occ £45); afternoon teas and evening meals can be arranged with prior notice and there are usually several vegetarian options.

More central, *Scotch Arms Mews* (☎ 016977-41409, ☎ 07786 115621, 🖳 the scotcharmsmews.co.uk; 7D or T, all en suite; ☞; Ⓛ) is a Grade II-listed former coaching inn turned B&B with stylish rooms (from £55pp, sgl occ £85 if booked direct), a guest lounge (with its own well!), parking, laundry facilities and a drying room. The rate includes a buffet breakfast.

Back in the town centre, *Howard Arms Hotel* (☎ 016977-42758, 🖳 howard armsbrampton.co.uk; 1S/6D or T/1Tr, all en suite; ☞; 🐾) is a pub that has a selection of B&B rooms (from £52.50pp, sgl/sgl occ from £85) and does food.

Where to eat and drink

Dominating the centre of town, by the bus stop, is an old Victorian bank building that now houses *Cranston's Brampton Food*

ROUTE GUIDE AND MAPS

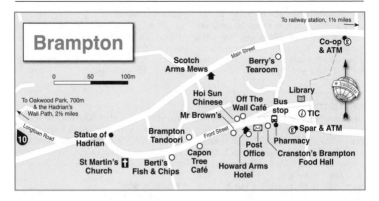

Hall (☎ 016977-2362, 🖥 cranstons.net; Mon-Sat 7.30am-6pm), which is largely a deli but does have hot food to take away.

Nearby, Brampton's longest-running café, *Capon Tree Café* (☎ 016977-3649, **fb**; Tue-Sat 9am-4pm, Mon to 4.30pm; 🐾), does good-value home-cooked fare such as soups, quiches and scones and is still very popular. Between the two, *Mr Brown's* (**fb**; Mon-Sat 9am-5pm, Sun 9.30am-4pm) is smart place with sandwiches (from £5), jacket spuds (from £5.95), soups and breakfasts (from £4.95).

On the opposite side of the road, *Off The Wall Café* (☎ 016977-41600, **fb**; Mon-Wed & Fri 10am-3.30pm, Sat 9am-2.30pm; 🐾) is a lovely, family-run business, serving homemade cakes, scones and soups, plus freshly prepared sandwiches, toasties and paninis. They also exhibit the work of local artists.

Moving round the corner, *Berry's Tearoom* (☎ 016974-51732, **fb**; Wed-Fri 10am-4.30pm, Sat 9am-3pm) is another very friendly café, much loved for its 'freak shakes' (£2.95-3.95); devilishly creamy fruit-filled milk-shakes served in huge jam-jar-type jugs. Don't worry; they do healthy food too.

Howard Arms Hotel (see Where to stay; Mon-Sat 8am-8.30pm, Sun to 8pm) also does pub food and is *the* place for **evening meals** with a wide-ranging menu including plenty of pub classics (£12.95-15.95).

Takeaways in Brampton include *Brampton Tandoori* (☎ 016977-2600/1; Sun-Mon & Wed-Fri 6-11pm, Sat 4-11pm); *Hoi Sun Chinese* (☎ 016977-2090; Tue-Thur 4.30-10.30pm, Fri-Sun 4.30-11pm); and *Berti's Fish & Chips* (Wed-Sat 5-9.30pm).

Cam Beck With its pretty weir, bridge and surrounding woodland, Cam Beck (see Map 10, p118) is a lovely spot to pause for a picnic and, conveniently, there's a bench here to prompt you to do just that.

A 3¾-acre (1.5-hectare) Roman fort, **Castlesteads**, lies just a few hundred metres to the south. Unfortunately it's out of bounds. Unusually, **Camboglanna** (as the Romans knew it; the name means 'Crooked Glen') lay between the Wall and the Vallum and not actually on the Wall. At different times it was garrisoned by troops from Spain, Gaul and Tungria. In his book, *A Walk along the Wall,* Hunter Davies (see p42) mentions visiting the house (built in the late 18th century) that now occupies the site, and finding Roman altars lying around in the summerhouse.

W ← WALTON TO CARLISLE   [MAPS 11-6]

Prepare yourself to say a tearful goodbye to the last remnants of the Wall itself. Sure, there'll still be the odd trace of Vallum and ditch, and even a stretch of Wall, albeit one hiding under the turf. But compared to the Bacchanalian feast of the past couple of days, this is small beer indeed. The depredations of man on this side of the Pennines have served to destroy the Wall completely; odd, considering that Newcastle, the largest of all settlements on the route, still manages to muster two or three remaining sections of its own. But though central Carlisle, at the end of this stage, has much olde-worlde charm, there is nothing left of Roman Britain outside the museums, save for some huge stones that are the remnants of an old Roman bridge that were dredged up from the bottom of the River Eden.

Do not despair, though, for the walking is no less pleasant on this **11½-mile (18.5km; 4hr)** stage, and the scenery, in places at least, is superb. And occasionally, just occasionally, you do get proof that the trail is still following the line of the Wall and its associated defences. [*Next route overview p105*]

WALTON   [Map 11, p122]

With a lovely café, two great little bunkhouses, a brewery and some back-garden camping with magical views of the Pennines, the cute village of Walton is a great place for Wall walkers to rest up. There's even a pop-up **post office** in the village hall (Mon & Wed 10am-noon) where you can take out money. However, it should be emphasised: you must make sure you have pre-arranged your evening meal before you arrive in the village – or you're facing a long walk (or a taxi ride) down to Brampton and back! If you're here when it's open, *The Reading Room* (☎ 07794 388408, **fb**; Wed-Sun 10am-4pm; ⚘) next to the village hall, is a very friendly café with super food and they are happy to refill water bottles for walkers.

For **accommodation**, walking east the first place you'll reach is *Sandysike* (☎ 01697-507067, ⌨ sandysike@gmx.com), just outside the village, a working farm with a gorgeous Georgian farmhouse. The owners allow **camping** (£10pp inc excellent shower facilities; ⚘) in their well-sheltered, flower-filled back garden, which has fantastic views over the Pennines and the north-eastern edge of the Lake District. There's also a charming 8-bed **bunkhouse** (☎ 077256 45929, ⌨ dicconsutcliffe@hot

mail.com; from £20pp, bedding hire £5pp; WI-FI) with kitchen and shower facilities. If arranged in advance campers and bunkhouse guests can order breakfast (bacon rolls £3.50), and evening meals can also be provided. Debit/credit cards are accepted. Overall, a cracking place.

Right on the trail, and in the heart of the village, *Florries on the Wall* (☎ 016977-41704, ⌨ florriesonthewall.co.uk) is an extremely welcoming, family-friendly **bunkhouse** (4 x 4-bed dorms, 1 private room sleeps 5, all en suite; ⚘; ⓛ; Mar-Oct, group bookings in winter) with spotless rooms, all with underfloor heating, and with more electricity sockets than you'll know what to do with. Rates (from £25pp in a dorm) include bedding and a tasty breakfast; the owners also offer evening meals (with booze), including vegetarian and vegan options, if requested in advance. Incidentally, the place is named after the owner's nan, who used to own the house.

For **B&B**, *Low Rigg Farm* (off Map 11; ☎ 016977-3233, ⌨ lowriggfarm.co.uk; 1T/1D shared facilities, 1Qd en suite; ☞; ⓛ; Apr-Sep), a 5-minute walk beyond the Reading Room café, is a 125-acre (5-hectare) working dairy farm where they make their own bread and preserves and

ROUTE GUIDE AND MAPS

serve them at breakfast. The views across to the Pennines are gorgeous. They charge from £45 per person (sgl occ from £90).

In addition to this old favourite are two new options. Behind the village hall is *Greenacres* (☎ 07747-463233, 🖳 greenacreswalton.co.uk; 1T; 🐾, (L)) which has only one room but it's a good one, with its own sitting room and patio doors facing the hills beyond. It's good value starting from £42.50pp (sgl occ £60). The owners also offer **dinner** for residents (£10 two courses). It's a welcoming place, and it's heartening to see it thriving even though it first opened just before the pandemic, as did the *Old Vicarage Brewery* (☎ 01697-543 002; 07948-431031, 🖳 oldvicarage brewery.co

.uk, **fb**; 1D or Tr/1D, T or Tr; en suite; 🐾; (L)), a lovely place tucked away at the end of the drive by the side of the church. The rooms are in the coach-house opposite the main house. Rates are from £40pp in a double (£70 sgl occ), with a third person in the room charged at £15 extra. They also offer home-cooked **evening meals** every night for just £12pp for one course (booking essential) – the perfect accompaniment to their beers (including one named after local Milecastle 56)

Note that Walton has **no regular bus service** so you'll be relying on **taxis** around here; try Brampton's Airbus 2000 (☎ 016977-3735), Atkinsons (☎ 07810 460982) or Brampton Cars (☎ 016977-3386).

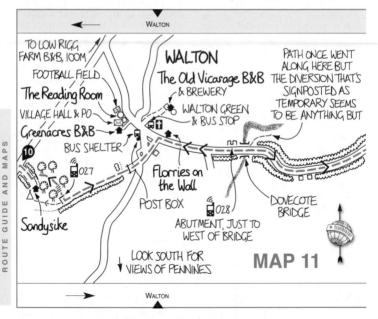

E → WALTON TO STEEL RIGG (FOR ONCE BREWED) [Maps 11-17]

At last! Twenty-six miles in, two stages done, and finally the Wall puts in an appearance. And not just a brief one either, for this stage is packed with both good Wall and good walking too. Proving the old adage that good things come to those who wait, by the end of this **15-mile (24.2km; 6hrs 40 mins)** stretch you'll have encountered milecastles, turrets, a watchtower, a castle made from Roman stones, two Wall forts, the remains of a Roman bridge and a highly informative museum – all directly along the line of both the Wall and the trail. You'll also have encountered both the highest reconstructed and unreconstructed parts of the Wall (at Hare Hill and Walltown respectively), as well as two of the longest remaining continuous stretches of Wall (at Birdoswald and, again, at Walltown).

This stage is significant in other ways, too, particularly for those interested in the evolution of the Wall itself, as you'll see a section of turf Wall – the only bit visible on the trail.

It's also on this stage that you pass the so-called Red Rock Fault, where the building material used to make the Wall changed from sandstone to limestone. And it is at this point that the narrow foundations that have held up the Wall so far are changed for the broad foundations that you'll see from now on.

But even if you have no interest in the actual Wall itself, this is still a red-letter day. Not only do you cross counties, from Cumbria to Northumberland,

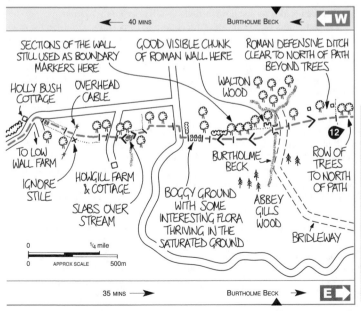

❏ **MILECASTLE NUMBERS**

The **milecastles** built by the Romans along the Wall have each been assigned their own unique number – whether the milecastles can actually be seen today or not. The order runs from east to west, so if you're walking eastwards the first milecastle you encounter (or at least you would have encountered if it still existed) is Milecastle 80 at Bowness-on-Solway, and the last one on the trail, which would have been near Segedunum in Newcastle, is called Milecastle 1.

In addition to this designation, some of the more famous have been given their own name, such as the Grindon Milecastle (aka Milecastle 34). The Wall's **turrets** also have their own special number, each derived from the milecastle immediately to their east, with the turret closest to that milecastle given the letter A, and the next one to the west labelled B. So, for example, the turret immediately to the west of Milecastle 38 is known as Turret 38A, the next one to the west Turret 38B.

Note that a number of these milecastles were destroyed soon after they were built: when it was decided to move the forts up to the Wall from the Stanegate (see p52), many were built on top of old milecastles or turrets. Cilurnum (Chesters) Fort, for example, was built on Turret 27A and remains of the turret can still be seen.

---

but you also pass the watershed; from Gap Farm onwards, all rivers you encounter head east towards the North Sea, not west. And it's on this stage that you pass the trail's highest point, at breezy Green Slack, 345m above sea level.

Aesthetically, too, this is a great stage. One of the advantages of starting in the west is that you get better views of the Whin Sill, and as a consequence have a much better idea of just how formidable a barrier it is.

Then there is Once Brewed, which, despite its position alongside the often busy B6318, manages to somehow maintain a feeling of isolation and remoteness (at least in the evening, after the crowds have gone) that makes it feel rather special. It's an essential stop for most Wall walkers, and a great place to spend the night, contemplate the wonders you have seen – and prepare yourself for an equally invigorating stage the next day.

Indeed, perhaps the only criticism of this section is that it is rather long. Fifteen miles of fairly rigorous walking represents a full day for most people, and that's before you include the fort of Birdoswald, the museum at Walltown and, at the day's end, the must-see treasures of Vindolanda, all of which merit at least an hour of your time (and, in Vindolanda's case, quite a bit more!). You may choose not to see all of these sights, of course, or indeed any of them, but if you do then you might want to consider breaking this stage into two days. It's easily done, with accommodation options at Banks, Gilsland and Greenhead, as well as off the trail at Haltwhistle.

Dovecote Bridge Once upon a time the Roman bridge abutment by the 'modern' Dovecote Bridge (Map 11, p122) would have been the first proper bit of Roman masonry that walkers who started in Bowness would come across. Unfortunately, being made of sandstone, the abutment and the 20m-long section of Wall which once led up to it have been backfilled and covered with turf since

1983 to prevent them eroding away completely, though you can find a description of them in Hunter Davies's travelogue *A Walk along the Wall*.

Burtholme Beck   Near the beck here (Map 11, p122), you can see an original piece of Wall, unaltered and unreconstructed, save for some restoration work that was carefully carried out on it in 2014, beneath the trees to the north of the path. This is the most westerly chunk of Wall visible on the trail.

Haytongate   Haytongate Farm (Map 12, p126) has actually become something of a landmark on the Wall – mention it to a fellow Wall walker and they'll probably know where you're talking about. This is thanks in large part to the '**snack hut**' (daily 7am-11pm) that sits by the path. As with all such huts – and you'll find many on the Cumbrian side of the trail – the owners are relying on your honesty to pay for anything you consume; please don't betray their trust. The hut also sells some neat Hadrian's Wall themed T-shirts. There's a picnic bench and, about 150m along the driveway, a public **toilet**. Incidentally, the farm stands just to the west of the site of Turret 53B, one of the most significant on the trail, for it was here that the building material used changed from sandstone, to the west, to limestone, present to the east of the turret.

Hare Hill   This hill (Map 12, p126) was once thought to have the highest remaining piece of Wall left on the trail, though it is now widely believed to be little more than a 19th-century reconstruction that used original Roman stones. That's not to dismiss it altogether, however, for if you walk around the side of the Wall facing away from the road you might just be able to find, at approximately head height, a small Roman inscription indicating that Primus Pilus, a senior centurion of the First Cohort, built it. In fact, this stone was taken from a site called Moneyholes, some distance to the west. To be honest, though we have located the inscription once before, on subsequent visits we've failed – leading us to deduce that the inscription may possibly have worn away altogether now.

❏ **LANERCOST PRIORY**   **[MAP 12, p126]**
The enchanting Lanercost Priory (☎ 01697-73030, 🖳 www.english-heritage.org.uk; Apr-Sep daily 10am-5pm, Nov to mid-Feb weekends only 10am-4pm; check winter opening days/times before visiting; £6) was founded in 1166 by Sir Robert de Vaux and built, like so much else round here, from masonry taken from the Wall; masonry which has been combined with the local sandstone. The mortally ill Edward I (see p101) rested here for five months as he headed north to fight the Scots. A wealth of Roman stones and remains are housed within, including one of the 19 altars found at Birdoswald.
    Nearby is the excellent *Lanercost Tearoom* (☎ 016977-41267, 🖳 www.cafelan ercost.co.uk, **fb**; daily 9.30am-4.30pm; 🐾) serving good value food including sausage rolls (£2.50) and freshly prepared hot and cold sandwiches, toasties and paninies (from £3.50) plus a great range of cakes. There is also a **Hadrian's Wall Visitor Centre** (same hours).

BANKS [Map 12]

A semi-circular huddle of houses, there's not much to Banks at all, though there is a post box, phone box and a **campsite**, *Camping at Banks* (☎ 07838 225108, 🖥 campingatbanks.com, **fb**; 🐾; Ⓛ) on the west side of the semi-circle. They have 25 pitches and charge just £5, which makes it one of the cheapest sites on the trail. The site has toilet and washing-up facilities, but no showers. There's now a **shepherd's hut**

on the site too (sleeps 3; £50-60), with mattresses (bring your own sleeping bag or hire one for £5 per night), and a stove for warmth and heating water.

If you happen to be here on a Wednesday the BR3 **bus service** calls here; see pp48-51. If you need a lift, try the taxi firms in Brampton: Airbus 2000 (☎ 016977-3735), Atkinsons (☎ 016977-3929) or Brampton Cars (☎ 016977-3386).

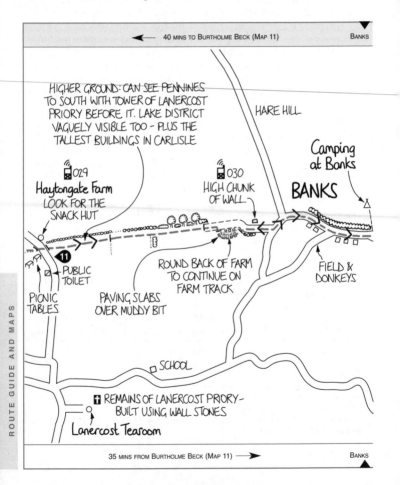

▼ BANKS

← 40 MINS TO BURTHOLME BECK (MAP 11)

HIGHER GROUND: CAN SEE PENNINES TO SOUTH WITH TOWER OF LANERCOST PRIORY BEFORE IT. LAKE DISTRICT VAGUELY VISIBLE TOO - PLUS THE TALLEST BUILDINGS IN CARLISLE

HARE HILL

📶 029
Haytongate Farm
LOOK FOR THE SNACK HUT

📶 030
HIGH CHUNK OF WALL

Camping at Banks

BANKS

⓫

→ PUBLIC TOILET

ROUND BACK OF FARM TO CONTINUE ON FARM TRACK

FIELD & DONKEYS

PICNIC TABLES

PAVING SLABS OVER MUDDY BIT

SCHOOL

✝ REMAINS OF LANERCOST PRIORY - BUILT USING WALL STONES

Lanercost Tearoom

35 MINS FROM BURTHOLME BECK (MAP 11) →

BANKS ▲

Pike Hill Signal Tower There are several turrets along the road and the trail to the east of Banks – **Banks East**, **Turret 51B** and **Piper Sike** (No 51A). More significantly, between the last two is **Pike Hill Signal Tower** (Map 12), the only signal tower on the Wall. A pre-Hadrian construction, the tower was possibly built for the Roman campaigns in Scotland under Agricola, where other such towers have been found, to give early warning of any movements by the Caledones. As these campaigns came to an end and the Wall was built, the tower was integrated into the Wall defences. Note how the Wall kinks to incorporate the tower – proof that the tower came first. The ruined remains of the tower's

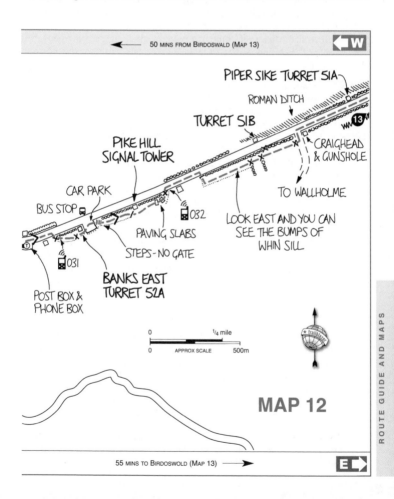

50 MINS FROM BIRDOSWALD (MAP 13) ◄ W

PIPER SIKE TURRET 51A

ROMAN DITCH

TURRET 51B

13

PIKE HILL
SIGNAL TOWER

CRAIGHEAD
& GUNSHOLE

CAR PARK

BUS STOP

032

TO WALLHOLME

PAVING SLABS

LOOK EAST AND YOU CAN
SEE THE BUMPS OF
WHIN SILL

031

STEPS - NO GATE

BANKS EAST
TURRET 52A

POST BOX &
PHONE BOX

0   ¼ mile

0   APPROX SCALE   500m

MAP 12

55 MINS TO BIRDOSWOLD (MAP 13) ⟶

E

ROUTE GUIDE AND MAPS

structure only rise a few feet above the ground these days, but the views from here, as you'd expect from a signal tower, are pretty good.

Coombe Crag   At Coombe Crag the path leaves the road to Birdoswald for the final time, heading south down the slope to enter a small patch of woodland. On the way down you'll run into one of the more organised honesty boxes on the trail, *Matthew's Snack Shed*, which has a fridge, kettle and microwave. The same folk also run *Coombe Crag Camping* (Map 13, p130; ☎ 07969 834808, 🖳 coombecragcamping.co.uk, **fb**; 🐾; Apr-Sep). The facilities are basic, with cold water tap only, no shower, and the only toilet being a Portaloo. But the people who run it are lovely, it's only £5, and you can buy goods (including hot & cold drinks and snacks such as pot noodles) from Matthew's Snack Shed. And besides, in an age when every other campsite is sprouting camping pods, bell tents, shepherd's huts and the like, I feel rather nostalgic for these down-to-earth old-school places.

The Turf Wall   Between Matthew's Snack Shed and Birdoswald, the trail deserts the road to follow what appears to be either the line of the Vallum or the ditch, a clear topographical feature for a couple of miles. But it's a little more complicated than that. Remember, west of the Irthing the Wall was originally built of turf (see p53) and these clear, steep undulations in the earth are the remnants of this, the turf Wall. It is the only obvious turf section left on the entire trail. The turf Wall would later be replaced by one made of stone and this is the only place along the Wall where the replacement stone Wall deviated from the line of the turf Wall. This was necessary in order that the new Wall meet up with the north-western corner of Birdoswald. So what you are actually following in this series of fields is, immediately to the south of the path, the ditch and the Vallum, with the two separated by the remains of the turf Wall.

There's one other point of interest about this stretch: unusually, neither the turf Wall nor the stone Wall near Birdoswald have particularly good views to the north. Why this is the case is unclear, though a popular theory is that the local Brigante tribe in this area were more trouble than the Caledones to the north, so the Romans decided to locate the Wall with good views to the south rather than north.

BIRDOSWALD   **[Map 13, p131]**
(☎ 016977-47602, 🖳 www.english-heritage.org.uk; Apr-Oct daily 10am-5pm, winter hours check website; £10 if booked online)

The Roman name for Birdoswald was **Banna**, meaning 'Spur' and the fort does indeed sit on a spur above the River Irthing. It's a lovely position up here, with views in every direction. Unfortunately, the ruins themselves fail to live up to their setting. But no matter, for the beauty of Birdoswald lies mainly in the details. There's the pleasant **farmhouse** which dominates the site, with Roman stones clearly visible in the fabric of its walls which actually date back to the early 17th century; the remains of a **granary**, the only visible extensive set of ruins that have thus far been excavated in this fort that once held a thousand soldiers; and the **excavated Roman gates**, one of which, on the east side, is among the best preserved on the Wall, with the *voussoir* (arch stone) and the impost stone (the stone that supported the arch) still extant. Perhaps the most remarkable discoveries, however, were the 19 or so religious altars, all but one dedicated to Jupiter, that were found in the same area to the east of the fort. The theory is that these altars were deliberately buried there as part of some elaborate ritual, possibly on Jupiter's day on January 1 after the annual parade. (The only altar not dedicated to Jupiter was dedicated instead to the Cumbrian war god, Codicus.)

The **exhibition centre** is one of the most family-friendly on the trail – you even have the chance of recreating the Wall in Lego if you so desire! – and deals not only with the Roman occupation of the site but with the location's entire history. There is also a **café** (same hours, WI-FI possibly coming soon) here, as well as a souvenir **shop** and **toilets**.

If you are not visiting **Birdoswald Fort** remember to **stamp your Hadrian's Wall Passport** before you continue onwards. The stamp is on the fort's perimeter wall near the bus stop.

Transport-wise, the BR3 **bus** calls in at Birdoswald on Wednesdays all year round (plus Thursdays in summer), while the No 681 stops in the car park at the bottom of the hill.

The Wall east of Birdoswald East of Birdoswald is a lovely stretch of Wall, built before AD138 to replace the turf Wall that was originally put up here. Take your time on this section: there are estimated to be half a dozen or so engravings on this section of the Wall. They say that walls have ears; well, this one's got a penis too. There's a great phallic symbol just 30m or so down from the north-eastern corner of the fort. To find it, look for where a 'modern' stone wall hits Hadrian's Wall at a 90° angle on its northern side, not long before you enter into Birdoswald itself. You'll notice that at this point there is a hole in the foot of the Wall – presumably a culvert to allow the water to drain properly. As you face this hole from the trail, look to the left of it and a few metres away you'll see a second, smaller hole in the foot of the Wall. Almost directly above this, at about chest height, is the symbol. Though it can't compare with one by the bridge at Chollerford (see p167) for size or definition, it's undoubtedly the best on the Wall itself.

Further east, just over halfway between the milecastle and the fort, the eagle-eyed will also spot a centurial stone of Julius Primus: look for the large brown stone near the top of the Wall.

Harrows Scar The beautiful Wall east of Birdoswald terminates at **Milecastle 49** (Map 13), also known as Harrows Scar Milecastle. In its day, this fortification must have been strategically vital, overlooking as it does the Irthing River and the Roman bridge. Much later, with its importance as a military stronghold long since extinguished, a cottage and garden were built on the same spot using stone from the ruins – the outline of which is still visible today.

Incidentally, it was to the **west of Milecastle 49 that the Wall was originally made of turf,** and was only converted to stone much later.

Irthing Bridge Fashioned from weathered steel, Irthing Bridge (Map 13) is one of the most beautiful on the trail. Only 100m or so from it, set back from the Irthing's eastern banks, lie some impressive Roman ruins. This is all that remains of the **Roman bridge abutment**, where the Wall and Military Way once crossed the river. Note how the river has changed its course down the centuries, for this abutment would once have been on the riverbank. There were a number of bridges at this spot, the first being built around the same time as the Wall in AD122-8. The Willowford crossing also holds quite an important place in the history of Hadrian's Wall. It was here that the stone Wall, which the

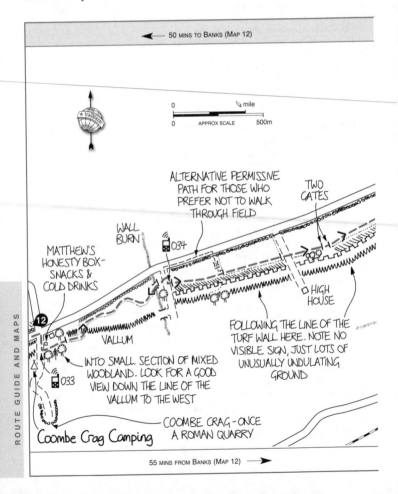

0   ¼ mile
0   APPROX SCALE   500m

ALTERNATIVE PERMISSIVE
PATH FOR THOSE WHO
PREFER NOT TO WALK
THROUGH FIELD

TWO
GATES

WALL
BURN

📻 034

MATTHEW'S
HONESTY BOX-
SNACKS &
COLD DRINKS

□ HIGH
HOUSE

12

VALLUM

FOLLOWING THE LINE OF THE
TURF WALL HERE. NOTE NO
VISIBLE SIGN, JUST LOTS OF
UNUSUALLY UNDULATING
GROUND

INTO SMALL SECTION OF MIXED
WOODLAND. LOOK FOR A GOOD
VIEW DOWN THE LINE OF THE
VALLUM TO THE WEST

📻 033

COOMBE CRAG - ONCE
A ROMAN QUARRY

Coombe Crag Camping

Romans started to construct in Newcastle and extended westwards, finally met up with the turf Wall from Bowness-on-Solway. In other words, this was the last section of Wall to have been built; once they had constructed this stretch and joined the two sections together, their ambition to build a barrier across Britain had been realised. Any construction done after this – moving the forts up to the Wall, for example, or converting the turf Wall into a stone one – were mere refinements carried out when their infrastructure improved and allowed them to transport limestone this far west. It was also here that the **broad Wall foundations** ran out. Presumably, by the time the stone Wall to the west of the Irthing

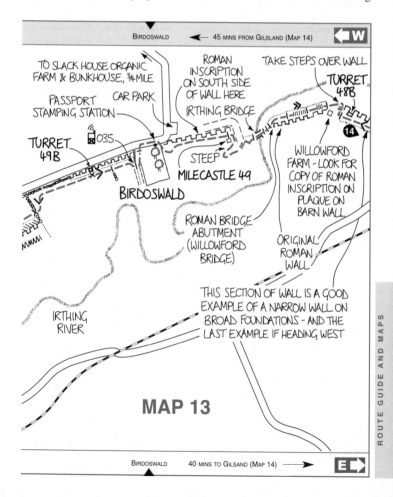

BIRDOSWALD ← 45 MINS FROM GILSLAND (MAP 14) W

TO SLACK HOUSE ORGANIC FARM & BUNKHOUSE, ¾ MILE

ROMAN INSCRIPTION ON SOUTH SIDE OF WALL HERE

TAKE STEPS OVER WALL

TURRET 48B

PASSPORT STAMPING STATION

CAR PARK

IRTHING BRIDGE

035

TURRET 49B

STEEP

MILECASTLE 49

WILLOWFORD FARM - LOOK FOR COPY OF ROMAN INSCRIPTION ON PLAQUE ON BARN WALL

BIRDOSWALD

ROMAN BRIDGE ABUTMENT (WILLOWFORD BRIDGE)

ORIGINAL ROMAN WALL

IRTHING RIVER

THIS SECTION OF WALL IS A GOOD EXAMPLE OF A NARROW WALL ON BROAD FOUNDATIONS - AND THE LAST EXAMPLE IF HEADING WEST

MAP 13

BIRDOSWALD 40 MINS TO GILSLAND (MAP 14) →

was being constructed, in order to replace the original turf and timber one, the Romans had settled on a narrow Wall and so built narrow foundations to suit it.

Willowford Farm Overlooking the impressive Irthing Bridge, and with a hefty chunk of Wall, complete with two turrets, running alongside their driveway and right outside their front door, Willowford Farm (Map 13) boasts one of the most enviable locations on the walk. Their section of Wall has its own turrets too – Nos **48A** and **48B**. Look between the two turrets and, given that the Romans built their turrets at equal intervals between their milecastles, you get an idea of what one-third of a Roman mile looked like – and thus can imagine roughly what one Roman mile looked like.

One of the farm buildings even has its own **Roman inscription** etched into the wall facing the trail, which the owners have kindly translated on a plaque that hangs underneath it.

GILSLAND [Map 14, p134]

Gilsland is an important place on the walk. It is here that you reach the border between Northumberland and Cumbria; Gilsland is actually the first Northumbrian settlement that you visit if coming from the west. Here, too, you cross the watershed and the Red Rock Fault.

Despite its relatively large size, Gilsland is a quiet place. The **post office** is now run on a pop-up basis by volunteers in the Village Hall. Even the railway station has been closed, though there is a campaign to reopen it again, something that would be of great benefit to walkers, particularly as this stretch between Walton and Greenhead is so poorly served by public transport. However, Gilsland does still have a tearoom, a decent pub, a great bunk/ camping barn nearby and a bus service too. Oh, and some of the most impressive Roman ruins on the whole trail as well, for it is here that you will find **Poltross Burn Milecastle** (No 48), one of the most important on the Wall.

In excellent nick, these ruins include a series of steps in their north-east corner; by estimating their direction, archaeologists were able to determine the height of the walkway on the Wall at 12ft (3.66m). It is also one of the first Roman milecastles you come to (when walking eastwards), providing further evidence that you are leaving the rural, cosy scenery of Cumbria, where the land has been ploughed and cultivated

for centuries, destroying much of the Wall in the process, to enter the wild, windswept lands of Northumberland.

Services

The outreach 'pop-up' **post office** (Tue 1-4pm, Thur & Fri 9.30am-12.30pm) has **cash-withdrawal facilities** and sells a very small selection of drinks and snacks.

The limited BR3 **bus** service calls here and Go North East's No 681 (see pp48-51) stops by Bridge Inn.

Where to stay and eat

Originally a 17th century coaching inn, *Samson Inn* (☎ 016977-47880, 016977-47962, 🖳 thesamson.co.uk, **fb**; 2D/1D or T/1D, T or Tr, all en suite; ⓛ) is now a real-ale gastro-pub that also offers **B&B** (from £45-50pp, sgl occ £70) in rooms above the pub. The **food** (daily noon-2.30pm & 6-8.30pm; 🐾) is great with an excellent selection of vegetarian dishes; mains cost around £12-17.

At the other end of town, *Brookside Villa* (☎ 016977-47300, 🖳 brooksidevilla .com; 3D or T/2Qd, all en suite; 🦮; ⓛ; 🐾) also offers good-quality accommodation. They are fully licensed. They charge from £55pp (sgl occ £100); if staying for more than one night they can provide transport to and from the trail. They also have a laundry service and drying room.

Nearby, *Hill on the Wall* (☎ 016977-

47214, ⌨ hillonthewall.co.uk; 1D/1T both en suite, 1T private bathroom; ☎; Ⓛ; Mar-Oct; from £47.50pp, sgl occ full room rate) is an award-winning B&B housed in a fortified 16th-century house, or bastle). It's a beautiful place on the outside – perhaps the best-looking accommodation on the entire trail – and some of the old furniture, including a large pine table hewn from the wood of a 17th-century mill, is interesting too. It's a fair way from the Wall, however – ask the owner about the short cut across the fields to reach it.

A little north out of town but very much part of its history, **Gilsland Spa Hotel** (off Map 14; 85 rooms) dates back to the 1740s, when it was called The Shaw's Hotel, and was a popular spa resort during the 19th and 20th centuries when it was

known as Gilsland Hall Hotel. The remains of the original Spa Well, which dates back to Roman times, and a Victorian swimming pool can be found within the 140-acre grounds. At the time of going to press it was undergoing major refurbishment and plans for reopening were unclear, so check online for further information.

Even further out west of town, past Hill on the Wall B&B (although perhaps best reached from Birdoswald, which stares it in the eye across the valley), *Slack House Organic Farm* (off Map 13 & 14; ☎ 016977-47351, ⌨ slackhousefarm.co.uk/ accommodation; 🐾 by arrangement) is a former B&B turned **bunkhouse** that's deservedly been receiving great reviews since opening in 2012. Run by the friendly and knowledgeable Diane, a former

---

❏ THE TWO ROUTES THROUGH GILSLAND

For the last couple of years a diversion has been established that takes walkers through the centre of Gilsland rather than along the line of the Wall. It is one of a number of diversions on the trail that are advertised as temporary – but which actually show no signs of being temporary at all.

In fact, the route has had to be moved a couple of times over the past two decades. Initially, from Willowford Farm you turned left and then, after a few metres, turned right down a path that ran down along an **extensive and well-preserved piece of Roman Wall**. However, the owners of the dilapidated house through which the Wall ran complained, and so the path was moved west to the other side of the school – meaning walkers now had to turn right after leaving Willowford Farm. But this path, too, became unusable when a bridge fell into disuse across a stream, and the authorities decided that the sleepers that were put in its place were too precarious, particularly for those with backpacks.

That being said, it's actually not too difficult for more nimble walkers to jump across the stream (or simply ford it) and carry on following this 'second' Path. Do so, and you'll still be able to see that section of **Roman Wall** which clearly goes into, and under, the dilapidated but still occupied old house. By the way, this house was once the Romanway Guest House (aka the Old Vicarage), mentioned by Hunter Davies (see p42) and others, which used to have two Roman altars on its porch. There's even a clip on YouTube of Davies visiting the property to look at the antiquities that the owner has found down the years. Unfortunately, they don't accept guests these days – perhaps that's no bad thing, given the state of the roof – and the Wall is out of bounds.

Following the 'temporary' diversion also means you'll miss out on **Milecastle 48** (see opposite), aka the **Poltross Burn Milecastle**, which lies on the original trail. But the diversion does have the advantage of going through the centre of Gilsland, right past the café and close to the pub and post office. And besides, the milecastle is only a few metres from where the two routes reunite at the eastern end of the village so there's nothing to stop you visiting it.

teacher, this independent farmhouse hostel is immaculate and features a wood burner in the downstairs lounge area, an adjacent kitchen area, as well as laundry and drying facilities. For accommodation, there's a 5-bed bunk room, a 10-bed camp-loft and a 3-bed family room. It's £15 per bed in any of the rooms. They provide provisions for guests from their farm shop (though phone in advance to make sure they're aware that you want this), from which they sell the cheeses that they make on site at the Birdoswald Dairy, along with other organic farm produce. Hot drinks and cakes are also available. It's about 20 minutes' walk from the main trail.

For **food** during the day, your best bet is the delightful, and very friendly *House of Meg* (☎ 016977-47777, 🖥 houseofmeg .co.uk, **fb**; Easter-Oct Thur-Tue 10am-3pm). One of the main beneficiaries of the diversion that takes walkers through the village centre, this is a smart little café serving baguettes and sandwiches (from £3.95), coffee and cakes. They also stock a limited supply of groceries. Dogs aren't allowed inside but they've recently set up a pleasant seating area in the garden, with a rain shelter for dog owners and their charges. The name of the café, incidentally, comes from a character from Walter Scott's *Waverley*, which was set around here.

Gap Farm This farm (see Map 14) is named after the Tyne Gap which runs nearby and which marks the watershed of Britain. Between Gilsland and here the Path follows the line of the Wall past the undulations of the Vallum, Military Way and the Wall itself.

GREENCROFT & CHAPEL HOUSE FARM [Map 14]

Right on the trail, there's *Green Croft Arts* (☎ 016977-47828, 🖥 greencroftonthewall com, **fb**), a gallery and yoga/dance studio with **glamping** accommodation in a bell tent (Apr-Sep; sleeps 2, from £85 including bedding) with two single beds and cooking facilities.

Just over the river, *Chapel House Farm* offers 'nearly wild' **camping** (☎ 07717-700049, 🖥 chapelhousefarmgils land.com) to backpackers for £10 (no booking required). Facilities are limited to the farmyard toilet and handbasin, but dogs on lead are permitted at no extra charge and it's very pretty.

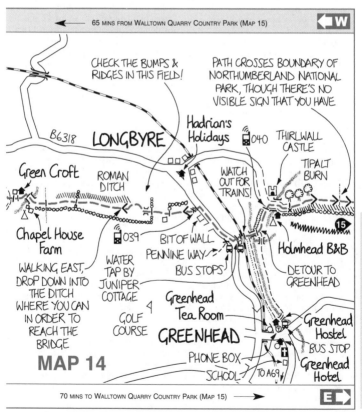

65 MINS FROM WALLTOWN QUARRY COUNTRY PARK (MAP 15) ◄ W

CHECK THE BUMPS & RIDGES IN THIS FIELD!

PATH CROSSES BOUNDARY OF NORTHUMBERLAND NATIONAL PARK, THOUGH THERE'S NO VISIBLE SIGN THAT YOU HAVE

Hadrian's Holidays

040 THIRLWALL CASTLE

B6318 LONGBYRE

TIPALT BURN

Green Croft ROMAN DITCH

WATCH OUT FOR TRAINS!

Chapel House Farm

039 BIT OF WALL

15

Holmhead B&B

WALKING EAST, DROP DOWN INTO THE DITCH WHERE YOU CAN IN ORDER TO REACH THE BRIDGE

WATER TAP BY JUNIPER COTTAGE

PENNINE WAY

BUS STOPS

DETOUR TO GREENHEAD

GOLF COURSE

Greenhead Tea Room

GREENHEAD

Greenhead Hostel

BUS STOP

MAP 14

PHONE BOX

SCHOOL

TO A69

Greenhead Hotel

70 MINS TO WALLTOWN QUARRY COUNTRY PARK (MAP 15) ➤ E ▶

ROUTE GUIDE AND MAPS

LONGBYRE [Map 14, p135]

There's a **B&B** in the quiet hamlet of **Longbyre**; simply head north on the B6318 then turn right down the slip road. There, located in a house called Four Wynds, you'll find the very welcoming *Hadrian's Holidays* (☎ 016977-47972, 💻 hadrians holidays.com). Guests stay in two self-contained lodges (1D/1T; en suite; Ⓛ; 🐾) in the garden. Each has underfloor heating, and breakfast is served in your lodge. A laundry and drying service is available (charge may apply), and the owners have a 'roam and stay' service, whereby they will drop you off and pick you up at further sections of the Wall if you use their B&B as a base for two or more days. Their rates are from £52.50pp (sgl occ £85).

The owner also conducts tours of the forts and other sites along the Wall (see the website for details).

GREENHEAD [Map 14, p135]

Though small, Greenhead is well-known to Wall walkers thanks to its proximity to the trail and its facilities: there's a school, a church, a café, a hostel and a pub with accommodation.

Greenhead Hotel (☎ 016977-47411, 💻 greenheadbrampton.co.uk; 4D/1T/1Tr/1Qd, all en suite; 🍺; 🐾; Ⓛ) is a pub with newly refurbished rooms (from £50pp, sgl occ £70) and a restaurant, and is the focal point of the village. **Food** is served daily (7-10am & noon-8.30pm, Fri & Sat to 9pm), with mains in the evening starting at £14 and rising to £28 for the steak. Under the same ownership is *Greenhead Hostel* (💻 green headhostel.co.uk; sleeps 47 in a mix of dorms & private rooms; from £18pp), housed in a converted Methodist church dating from 1885. Separate toilet/shower facilities are available for men and women. Breakfast is available in the pub if booked the night before.

The only alternative to the pub for food is *Greenhead Tea Room* (☎ 016977-

---

❑ NORTHUMBERLAND NATIONAL PARK AND THE DARK SKY PARK

Walking along the trail from the west, as you climb the hill towards the Roman Army Museum, you actually cross a boundary into Britain's most northerly national park. Covering 1048sq km (404.6 sq miles), or about a quarter of the entire county after which it is named, Northumberland National Park stretches from Hadrian's Wall all the way up to the Scottish border; indeed, if you continue east along the Hadrian's Wall Path, you'll find you don't actually leave the park until you pass round the back of Walwick Hall (see Map 22, p168), almost 20 miles (32km) later.

The park is famous not only for what it has – including several rare species such as black grouse, pipistrelle bats, water voles and bog orchids – but also, beautifully, for what it lacks. The absence of any significant light pollution here means that visitors to the park are able to witness some of the clearest views of the night sky anywhere in the country. Indeed, such is the area's reputation in this respect that in 2013 the International Dark-Sky Association (the leading international organisation combating light pollution worldwide) awarded Dark Sky Park status to the entire area of Northumberland National Park and the adjacent Kielder Water and Forest Park, thus making it the largest protected Dark Sky Park in the UK. In giving the award the Association described the park as 'a wild and remote place that demonstrates an ability to conserve the dark skies above and a commitment to providing opportunities for the public to enjoy them'. The award was not only deserved but necessary, conferring as it does 'protection' on the clarity of the night sky, with controls in place to prevent light pollution from nearby sources.

❏ **THE ELIZABETHAN WALL THAT NEVER WAS**
Much of the period between the departure of the Romans and the ordination of the Wall as a UNESCO World Heritage Site was characterised by the practice of border reiving, where gangs would attack their rivals and neighbours to raid, rustle and rape.

While these days this 'hidden history' of the Wall receives scant attention, there is no doubt that at the time the problem was a serious one; serious enough for a protection racket to be established and a new word, 'blackmail', to be coined. Indeed, the raiding reached such a height in Elizabethan times that in 1587 a proposal was made to revive and rebuild the Wall in order to keep some semblance of order. If that wasn't practical, the proposal declared, a new wall, constructed on similar lines to the Roman version, should be built, with *sconces* (castles) at every mile. Alas, the cost was estimated to be a prohibitive £30,000 and was never taken up.

47400; 🖳 greenheadtearoom.co.uk; Mon-Sat 10am-4pm). Under new management, it's a bright, airy café with large windows and a good choice of teas, coffee, cakes and fresh fruit as well as sandwiches, soups and jacket potatoes.

GNE's No 681 **bus** stops by the hotel/village hall and if you walk to the road end (A69), a few minutes away, you can catch Stagecoach's No 685 service; see pp48-51 for further information. Greenhead is also on the AD122 route.

THIRLWALL CASTLE [Map 14, p135]
Thirlwall means 'Gap in the Wall' in the local dialect and Thirlwall Castle was built in the 14th century in a gap in the Wall where it was crossed by the Tipalt Burn. A typically strong, defensible home, Thirlwall was built to protect the owners from the cross-border reiving raids (see box p96) that were rife at this time.

The Thirlwall family (they adopted the name when they bought the land) had made their fortune in military campaigns in France. It is one thing to earn a fortune, however, and quite another to keep it, particularly in this part of the world in the 14th century. Hence the extravagant fortifications to their family home, built using whatever material lay close at hand – which, of course, meant the Wall.

The castle lasted for 300 years before the family moved to Hexham and it was sold to the Earl of Carlisle for £4000. Already in possession of one large country pile, the earl was interested only in Thirlwall's land and allowed the castle to fall into disrepair and, eventually, ruin. There's little to see today except the shell of the keep, but it remains an atmospheric

and charmingly dilapidated place.

Separated from the castle by a small footbridge is *Holmhead* (☎ 016977-47402, 🖳 bandb-hadrianswall.co.uk; Easter-Oct), a popular place with a delightful location. Almost directly in the shadow of the enigmatic Thirlwall Castle, right on the line of the Wall, and actually *built* from Hadrian's Wall stones (which, with delicious irony, were nicked from Thirlwall Castle, which had stolen them from the Wall in the first place) this fabulous farmhouse, surrounded on two sides by pretty streams, provides accommodation for all budgets. As well as **B&B** (1S/2D, all en suite; Ⓛ; from £37.50pp, sgl occ £70), there is a **camping barn** available for private hire only (from £30 if solo trekker, £10 each extra person) which sleeps up to six people and has a kitchenette with hob, microwave, fridge and toaster as well as decent shower/toilet facilities. The owners also allow hikers to **camp** in their back garden (£7pp). Camping facilities are limited, though, to a picnic table in the garden, a water tap and a small outhouse with toilet and shower combined.

ROUTE GUIDE AND MAPS

Carvoran/The Roman Army Museum A visit to the **Roman Army Museum** (Map 15; ☎ 016977-47485, 🖥 vindolanda.com; daily Apr-Sep 10am-6pm, Feb-Mar & Oct-mid Nov to 5pm; £8; combined entry with Vindolanda £14) is a diverting way to spend an hour or two. The museum is situated by the site of the Roman fort, Magna ('Rocks'), at **Carvoran**. As the name suggests, the focus of the museum is more about the men who manned the Wall than the Wall itself, a subject it explores both through original Roman exhibits and modern recreations. The fort lay to the south of the Vallum by the Stanegate so, presumably, was not a Wall fort, despite its proximity to the Wall. The museum itself has a reasonable collection, though it comes a distant second compared to its sister museum at Vindolanda (see pp148-9). But then, doesn't everything? Besides, it does have a wonderful **video** featuring a bird's-eye view of the Wall, including

WALLTOWN QUARRY COUNTRY PARK

PATH NOT VERY CLEAR HERE, PARTICULARLY IF WALKING WEST BUT STICK TO THE TOP OF THE RIDGE

SECTION KNOWN AS THE NINE NICKS OF THIRLWALL

TURRET 44B (KING ARTHUR'S TURRET)

TARN → WALLTOWN CRAGS

PAVING SLABS

WALKING EAST IT'S EASIER/SAFER TO TAKE THE MORE SOUTHERLY PATH

PATH KEEPS TO THE NORTH OF THE ROMAN DITCH

FANTASTIC BIT OF WALL UP TO 13 COURSES HIGH

🖳043

AD122 BUS STOP

OUTLINE OF MILECASTLE 45 IN GROUND

WALLTOWN FARM

PAVING SLABS OVER MUDDY BIT

PATH ROUND CRAGS

BENCH TURRET 45A

14

NOTE HOW THE VALLUM IS FAR FROM THE WALL HERE, BEYOND THE ROAD

CP

WALLTOWN QUARRY-NOW A POND

IGNORE STILE 🖳04

CARVORAN (MAGNA)

WALLTOWN LODGE

PICNIC TABLES

PICNIC TABLES

WALLTOWN VISITOR CENTRE & 24 HR TOILETS 🖳042

ROMAN ARMY MUSEUM; REMAINS OF ROMAN FORT & TEAROOMS

B6318

WALLTOWN QUARRY COUNTRY PARK

ROUTE GUIDE AND MAPS

computer-generated reconstructions of how the Wall must have looked almost 2000 years ago. Note that **the café here is for museum visitors only.**

The Roman Army Museum is a stop for the AD122 **bus** and GNE's No 681 also calls in here on its way between Haltwhistle and Gilsland. See pp48-51 for further information.

Walltown Quarry Across the road from the Roman Army Museum is the Walltown Quarry (see Map 15, below). Once a working quarry, the land is now a country park and plays host to a variety of ducks and other birdlife. This is where you'll also find the **Walltown Visitor Centre** (Easter to end Sept daily 10am-5pm; contact The Sill – see p147 – for opening times outside this period), which sells hot drinks, snacks, ice-creams and Wall-related souvenirs. The picnic benches outside make this a pleasant place to hang out and soak up the sun.

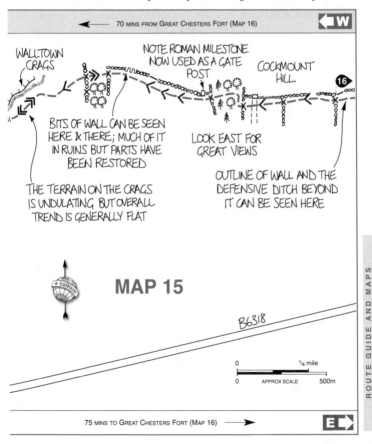

← 70 MINS FROM GREAT CHESTERS FORT (MAP 16)

WALLTOWN CRAGS

NOTE ROMAN MILESTONE NOW USED AS A GATE POST

COCKMOUNT HILL

16

BITS OF WALL CAN BE SEEN HERE & THERE; MUCH OF IT IN RUINS BUT PARTS HAVE BEEN RESTORED

LOOK EAST FOR GREAT VIEWS

THE TERRAIN ON THE CRAGS IS UNDULATING BUT OVERALL TREND IS GENERALLY FLAT

OUTLINE OF WALL AND THE DEFENSIVE DITCH BEYOND IT CAN BE SEEN HERE

MAP 15

B6318

0   ¼ mile

0   APPROX SCALE   500m

75 MINS TO GREAT CHESTERS FORT (MAP 16) →

ROUTE GUIDE AND MAPS

The Walltown Crags   There is an impressive section of Wall near the Walltown Crags (Map 15). In places it's up to 13 courses high, making it the highest part of the Wall that hasn't been restored or rebuilt by well-meaning 19th-century archaeologists. This section of Wall also has two turrets, **Turret 44B** (also known as King Arthur's Turret) and the excellently preserved **Turret 45A**. The latter pre-dates the Wall. Built as an observation tower, it's not surprising there are some great views from here.

The Nine Nicks of Thirlwall   East of Walltown Crags to the no-longer existent Turret 44A is a bumpy section of the Whin Sill known as the Nine Nicks of Thirlwall (see Map 15), the 'nicks' referring, of course, to the undulations in the crags. Thanks largely to all the quarrying activity there are actually only about five nicks left.

The Roman milestone   The only Roman milestone on the line of the Wall lies at the western end of a small patch of woodland (Map 15). Unloved and anonymous, the milestone today has been compelled to act as a gatepost though its large size and cylindrical shape give away its original identity.

The only other sign of Roman construction is the **defensive ditch** which appears intermittently along this section; the Wall itself has disappeared for the time being, while the Vallum lies some way to the south.

Great Chesters Fort   Round the back of a working farm and usually presided over by a pair of somnolent horses lies the buried remains of Great Chesters Fort (Map 16). Not to be confused with Chesters Fort in Chollerford (see p165), Great Chesters Fort was known to the Romans as **Aesica**. The Dalmatae from the Yugoslav mountains were garrisoned here during Hadrian's reign and later the Hamii from Syria, who were famous archers.

There have been some important finds at Great Chesters. One of the few tombstones of a legionary soldier (as opposed to an auxiliary) was found here. Archaeologists also found evidence of an aqueduct that once supplied the fort – bringing water from the head of Haltwhistle Burn, some six miles away. What's more, before the fort, which was built to guard Caw Gap, this farmyard was the home of Milecastle 43. This is yet further evidence that the Wall and its accompanying defences were built in two stages, with the decision to move the forts up to the Wall taken only after the Wall itself and its accompanying milecastles and turrets had already been built; see p55 for details. Indeed, where Haltwhistle Burn crosses the Stanegate the remains of an early Roman fort have been discovered – presumably the one that was abandoned when Aesica was built, its garrison moved to the new premises.

Alas, there's little remaining of small, three-acre (1.2-hectare) Aesica except for some outer walls and an **altar** to the east of its south gate; heavily eroded, it is nevertheless the only original altar remaining in situ on the Wall and still inspires many a hiker to leave a small fiscal donation on its top, presumably for luck. The path to Haltwhistle leaves from near the altar, heading down the slopes.

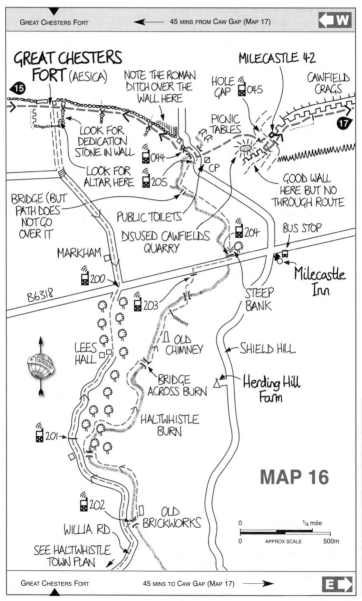

GREAT CHESTERS FORT (AESICA)

15

NOTE THE ROMAN DITCH OVER THE WALL HERE

LOOK FOR DEDICATION STONE IN WALL

📱 044

LOOK FOR ALTAR HERE

📱 205

HOLE GAP 📱 045

MILECASTLE 42

CAWFIELD CRAGS

17

PICNIC TABLES

CP

GOOD WALL HERE BUT NO THROUGH ROUTE

BRIDGE (BUT PATH DOES NOT GO OVER IT)

PUBLIC TOILETS

DISUSED CAWFIELDS QUARRY

📱 204

BUS STOP

Milecastle Inn

MARKHAM

📱 200

B6318

📱 203

STEEP BANK

SHIELD HILL

Herding Hill Farm

LEES HALL

OLD CHIMNEY

BRIDGE ACROSS BURN

HALTWHISTLE BURN

📱 201

MAP 16

📱 202

OLD BRICKWORKS

0 — 1/4 mile

0 — 500m
APPROX SCALE

WILLIA RD

SEE HALTWHISTLE TOWN PLAN

Walking to and from Haltwhistle (1hr)   **[Map 16, p141]**

Those heading to Haltwhistle have a couple of places where they can leave the trail, either at Great Chesters Fort or along the road to the east. For either path, see Map 16, p141, and the route below.

Of the two, the latter is the best option, being both easy and lovely. The trail shadows Haltwhistle Burn and you hike in woods under the shade of trees for much of the path – a stark contrast to the more exposed, wind-blasted walking along much of the Wall.

If you're in need of a hot meal or a pint, there's *Milecastle Inn* (☎ 01434-321372, 🖥 milecastle-inn.co.uk; food daily noon-2.30pm & 6-8.30pm; takeaway available) with a menu of standard – but good quality – pub fare. Note, however, that dogs are not allowed inside. If you continue for 10 minutes or so along Shield Hill (the road running south from Milecastle Inn) you'll reach *Herding Hill Farm* (☎ 01434-320175, 🖥 www.herdinghillfarm.co.uk; 🐾), a very well equipped **campsite** with **tent pitches** (from £20-36 tent & 2 people). They also have 17 **wooden wigwams** (sleep 2-5; min 2 nights if booking online, call for 1-night availability; £40-135 for 2 adults, extra adults £20). Rates depend on the time of year and the size and spec of the wigwams – some have hot tubs. If it's luxury glamping you're after they also have en-suite 'castle' **pods** (2 adults only, min 3 nights, from £375). There is a small **shop** (summer daily 8-10am & 2.30-6pm) with camping essentials plus beer and wine, and they offer homemade pizza for campers (Fridays, Easter to Oct). Check the website for details of when the site is closed.

The AD122 **bus** service (see p50) calls both here and at Milecastle Inn.

For the **return journey**, you can take the same path back or, for a bit of variety, stick to the road up to **Lees Hall**.

HALTWHISTLE

Though not on the trail itself, Haltwhistle is an important place for hikers. Good bus and train connections (Haltwhistle is on the Newcastle–Carlisle line), a variety of accommodation, plenty of shops, restaurants and tearooms and a location almost exactly halfway along the Wall ensures that many a Wall walker calls in for the night. The town is not backward in celebrating its position, either: not only is there a plaque in the ground of the market square that celebrates Haltwhistle being at the midpoint of mainland Britain, but there's also a hotel, launderette, sweet shop and even an army surplus store that are all called 'The Centre of Britain'.

It's also a particularly historic town, with bastle houses lined up along Main St and an even earlier pele tower now forming part of the Centre of Britain Hotel. These buildings were, of course, built as defensive fortifications during the long-running skirmishes between the English and the Scots, a time when much of the border region was

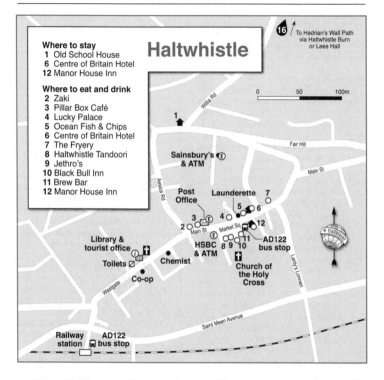

Where to stay
1 Old School House
6 Centre of Britain Hotel
12 Manor House Inn

Where to eat and drink
2 Zaki
3 Pillar Box Café
4 Lucky Palace
5 Ocean Fish & Chips
6 Centre of Britain Hotel
7 The Fryery
8 Haltwhistle Tandoori
9 Jethro's
10 Black Bull Inn
11 Brew Bar
12 Manor House Inn

Haltwhistle

16 To Hadrian's Wall Path
via Haltwhistle Burn
or Lees Hall

Willia Rd

0   50   100m

Fair Hill

Main St

Sainsbury's
& ATM

Aesica Rd

Post
Office   Launderette   7

3   4   5   6

2   12
Main St   Market Sq

Library &
tourist office   HSBC   8 9 10 11   AD122
                          & ATM   bus stop

Toilets   Chemist

Larry's Lonnen

Church of
the Holy
Cross

Co-op

Westgate

Saint Meen Avenue

Railway   AD122
station   bus stop

considered bandit country. Such was the fear and enmity between both sides that a plaque in Market Square recounts the sad tale of a young local girl who had attempted to run away and marry a Scot. Her reward for this act of 'treason' was to be the last person executed in Market Square – along with her fiancé – in 1597.

Today Haltwhistle is a genteel sort of place with a pretty main street and a plethora of tearooms and eateries, many of which display notices saying that 'Walkers are welcome here' – a nice touch.

Services
The **tourist information centre** (☎ 01434 321863; Mon-Fri 10am-1pm & 1.30-4.30pm, Sat 10am-1pm), in the **library**, is perhaps the office most dedicated to the Hadrian's Wall Path.

There is a Barclays Bank with **ATM** on Main St and another outside the **post office** (Mon-Fri 9am-12.30pm & 1.30-5.30pm, Sat 9am-12.30pm only), while a little further up you'll find a self-service **launderette**, a rarity on this walk (£6 per load). There's also a Boots the **chemist** (Mon-Fri 9am-6pm, Sat to 1pm).

For **provisions**, there's a Co-op (daily 7am-10pm) on Main St and a large Sainsbury's (Mon-Sat 8am-9pm, Sun 10am-4pm) just to the north of Main St behind the shops; there is a path to it between Lucky Palace and the launderette. Sainsbury's also has an **ATM**.

Transport
[See pp48-51] The AD122 **bus** stops at Market Sq and at the railway station. Arriva's No 685 and GNE's No 681 also

call in Haltwhistle.

There are **trains** approximately every hour to Newcastle (journey time around an hour) and Carlisle (just over 30 mins).

Where to stay

The first place you reach if walking down from the Wall is *Old School House* (☎ 01434-312013, ☐ oldschoolhousehaltwhistle.com; 1S private facilities, 1D/2T/1D or T en suite; ⓛ), a super-smart place chock full of features including laundry facilities, drying room with heated racks, and smart TVs in the bedrooms. Rates are from £45pp (sgl £65, sgl occ £70-75) including what they call 'a full border breakfast' (like a full English but with added haggis).

Manor House Inn (☎ 01434-322588, ☐ manorhousehaltwhistle.com; 1D/7D or T/1F, all en suite; ✆; ⓛ; ✖) is a friendly pub with basic but neat and tidy rooms above it. B&B is from £45pp (sgl occ £80).

Just across the road – but a few steps up in terms of quality – *Centre of Britain Hotel* (☎ 01434-322422, ☐ centreofbritain.co.uk; 5T/6D/1Qd, all en suite; ✆; ✖; ⓛ), part-housed in a 15th-century pele tower, is the pick of the hotels on Main St. One room also has pull-out beds for children and two rooms have their own sauna. Rates are £45-75pp (sgl occ £75-95).

Where to eat and drink

Our favourite café in Haltwhistle, and very popular with the locals too, is the *Brew Bar* (☎ 01434-321370, **fb**; Mon, Tue & Thur 9am-5pm, Wed 9am-9pm, Fri & Sat to 11pm; food served daily 9am-3pm), in an ideal location right on Market Square. A regular café by day, in the evenings at weekends it becomes a bar. The food itself is fair value, with a fish-and-chip butty £7. Although they don't serve food in the evening, on Wednesdays and Saturdays **food trucks** turn up outside serving a range of delicious street food from barbecues to Asian fusion. Check their Facebook page to find out what will be on offer.

Nearby, *Jethro's* (**fb**; Mon-Sat 8.30am-2.30/3pm) is a friendly sandwich deli with some seating out back, overlooking the historic Black Bull Inn. Next to the post office is the quirkily named but down-to-earth *Pillar Box Café* (**fb**; Mon, Thur & Fri 9.30am-4pm Sat to 2pm), a cheap, no-frills place that's popular with Haltwhistle's older locals.

There are a couple of Indian places in town: *Zaki* (☎ 01434-341174, ☐ zakihaltwhistle.co.uk; daily 5-10.30pm) and the takeaway-only *Haltwhistle Tandoori* (☎ 01434-321388; Wed-Mon 5-11pm). Other takeaways include *Oceans Fish & Chips* (☎ 01434-321024; Mon-Wed 5-8pm, Thur-Sat 11.30am-1.30pm & 5-8pm), the Chinese *Lucky Palace* (☎ 01434-322330; Tue-Sun 5-11pm), and the kebab-pizza-chippy outlet *The Fryery* (☐ haltwhistlefryery.co.uk, **fb**; Tue-Thur 11.30am- 9pm, Fri & Sat to 10pm, Sun 1.30-9pm).

There are a few options for **pub food** too, the stand-out choice being the historic *Black Bull Inn* (☎ 01434-320463, ☐ the blackbullhaltwhistle.co.uk, **fb**; food summer Mon-Fri 5-8pm, Sat noon-3pm & 5-8pm, Sun noon-3pm, winter hours vary; ✖), a traditional, cosy, dog-friendly timber-and-horse-brass sort of place; a real ale pub with pub-grub mains that won't break the bank.

You could also try *Manor House Inn* (see Where to stay; food daily noon-9pm; ✖ in bar only), or the more expensive but good quality *Centre of Britain* (see Where to stay; daily 6.30-9pm) where a one-/two-/three-course meal in the evening costs £15/20/26.

Cawfield Quarry and Crags

The former quarry at **Cawfields** (see Map 16, p141) is a peaceful spot that now plays host to a pond, a toilet block and a few picnic tables. It also marks the western end of an unbroken half-mile stretch of magnificent Wall. Look out for the swastika etched by the Romans into one of the Wall stones – another symbol of prosperity – near **Milecastle 42**, which originally had an entrance in the north Wall until, presumably, the builders saw the steep drop beneath, realised such a door was unnecessary and blocked it up.

Turret 41a This turret (Map 17) marks the eastern end of one of the finest bits of unspoilt Wall. The land around here has been uninhabited since the Romans retreated, though the names printed on the maps – Bogle Hole, Caw Gap, Bloody Gap, Thorny Doors – only serve to add to the sense that you're in a land of folklore and myth.

Green Slack At 345m above sea level, **Green Slack**, on Winshields Crags (Map 17), is the highest point on the trail. Whichever direction you're coming from it's quite a schlep to get to it, with the hills particularly, well, hilly at this point. A decent section of Roman Wall, to the east of the trig point, helps to detract your brain from the screaming coming from your calf muscles. Just comfort yourself with the thought that, no matter how hard the walking is at the moment, for the rest of the trip, there'll be more downhill than uphill!

If you feel like taking a breather while you're up here, according to scientists there's no better place in England to take it: the lichen that grows on Winshields Crags requires extremely pure air and, apart from Dartmoor, this is the only place in the entire country where the air is clean enough for this lichen to thrive.

W ← STEEL RIGG TO WALTON   [Maps 17-11]

[Route section begins on Map 17, p147] While this **15-mile (24.2km; 6hrs 40mins)** stage may not be quite as spectacular as the one that preceded it (though that's debatable), it is arguably the most interesting. It's also something of a red-letter day, for it is on this stage that you climb to the highest point of the entire trail. It is on this stage, too, that you cross from Northumberland into Cumbria and the scenery changes from the windswept slopes and crags that provided the previous stage's backdrop to the more gentle, rolling, cultivated landscape of England's far north-west.

You also cross the watershed on this stage, so that by the end of it any river you encounter from now on flows west to the Irish Sea, not east to the North Sea as had previously been the case.

The limestone runs out on this stage, too, near Banks where the Red Rock Fault splits the country. Moreover, to the west of Gilsland, at Willowford Bridge, the Wall was originally made of turf (possibly because of the lack of limestone) and rebuilt in stone only later. Also at Willowford, the broad foundations that have held up the Wall so far are reduced; from now on it is narrow wall on *narrow* foundations. And, at the River Irthing, the remains of the third Roman bridge on your walk can be seen; a bridge which once would have carried both the Wall and the Military Way. Quite a stage indeed. And that's before any mention has been made of all the turrets, forts and milecastles – and even, uniquely, a Roman watchtower – that are encountered along the way.

One word of warning, however, before you set off: though this section has been written so that it ends in Walton, it does make for a very long stage. Furthermore, if you visit one of the forts and museums en route (which we urge you to do) then you probably won't have enough time to complete the stage in a day. We suggest you stay somewhere before Walton – for example at Greenhead (see p136), Gilsland (pp132-4) or Banks (p126). Off the trail there are some more B&Bs at Haltwhistle (p144) which provide further options. *[Next route overview p121]*

Steel Rigg A car park lies hidden away behind trees at the top of the hill. This is known as Steel Rigg (Map 17). There's not much here for walkers now the coffee van has stopped coming, but if you've been canny, you will have booked yourself in for the night at one of the accommodation options in Once Brewed, which you can reach either by the road or via the short-cut round the back of Peel Bothy.

CAW GAP ← 45 MINS ←

0 ¼ mile
0 APPROX SCALE 500m

★ Trailblazer

WELL-MADE WALL - RESEMBLES HADRIAN'S WALL AND USES ROMAN STONES

THORNY DOORS - A GATE IN THE WALL

CAW GAP
NATIONAL TRUST SIGN: SHIELD ON THE WALL

TURRET 41A

UNDULATING GROUND BUT GENERAL TREND IS UPWARDS, IF WALKING EAST

16

BLOODY GAP

BOGLE HOLE
046

LOOK FOR THE VALLUM AND ROMAN MILITARY WAY DOWN THE SLOPE TO THE SOUTH

MILITARY ROAD B6318

MAP 17

→ CAW GAP   45 MINS →

ROUTE GUIDE AND MAPS

ONCE BREWED [Map 17]

A popular overnight spot with Wall walkers, Once Brewed is tiny but, nevertheless, boasts a decent pub, a brewery, an excellent campsite and bunkhouse and a state-of-the-art visitor centre and YHA hostel. It also sports a curious name... and a legend: according to the story, General Wade, he of Military Road fame and bane of Bonnie Prince Charlie, once stayed at an inn here and, unhappy with the quality of the beer, ordered it to be brewed again. Hence the pub name, or at least that's how one story has it.

At the eastern end of the hamlet stands the country's first **National Landscape Discovery Centre** (☎ 01434 341200, 💻 www.thesill.org.uk; Easter-Oct 10am-5pm, Nov-Easter 10am-4pm), aka **The Sill**. The idea behind the centre is to help open up the area's rich history and fabulous landscape to families, children and people with disabilities who might otherwise not have the confidence or the ability to explore the region. Its modern, all-glass design is covered by a fully accessible 'living roof' with sweeping views of the surrounding countryside and

STEEL RIGG CAR PARK ← ⬅W

ROMAN SWASTIKA CARVED INTO WALL

'CLAYTON WALL'

STEEL RIGG

PEEL CRAGS

WINSHIELDS CRAGS

CP

18

📱047

ROMAN DITCH & WOOD OVER WALL

📱049

SHORTCUT TO ONCE BREWED

LOOK SOUTH AS YOU GO THROUGH GATE TO SEE A SMALL BIT OF WALL

PEEL BOTHY

📱048

GREEN SLACK, 345M- THE HIGHEST POINT ON THE PATH

ONCE BREWED

PEEL GAP TOWER (TURRET; UNNUMBERED)

TALL TREES

Vallum Lodge

Twice Brewed Inn

BUS STOPS

Winshields Farm Campsite & Bunkhouse

The Sill NATIONAL LANDSCAPE DISCOVERY CENTRE, YHA HOSTEL CAFÉ & TOILETS

18

TO VINDOLANDA →

STEEL RIGG CAR PARK → E▶

the Wall. There's also a large **café** (same opening hours) with some decent offers on the menu (eg mug of soup and any half sandwich or panini for £5.95) that is licensed and serves beer from Haltwhistle's Muckle Brewery, a **tourist information centre**, a souvenir shop and exhibitions on national parks and the landscape.

Regarding **accommodation**, for **campers** the ***Winshields Campsite*** (☎ 07968-102780, 🖳 winshieldscampsite.co.uk; 🐕; Apr-Oct) is a smashing and friendly place. They charge £10pp to camp, with facilities including showers and toilet and a covered sitting area – a godsend on a rainy day. They also have a very comfortable five-bed **camping barn** (from £20pp) with kitchen and smart shower blocks. All in all, this is a great place, and perhaps a more walker-friendly option than the YHA.

YHA The Sill at Hadrian's Wall (🖳 yha.org.uk/hostel/yha-the-sill-at-hadrians-wall; 8 x 2-, 2 x 3-, 8 x 4-bed rooms, all en suite, 8 x 4-bed room separate facilities). is part of The Sill complex. This brand new hostel has 86 beds, is licensed and meals are provided. There's a shop, self-catering and laundry facilities, a drying room and 24hr access. Beds can go for as little as £16 in a shared room, or £14.50 in a private room for two people; but, more realistically, in summer prices are nearer £30 for a bed (£30pp for a private room). Be warned: we find it's often swamped with school groups.

For B&B, ***Vallum Lodge*** (☎ 01434-344248, 🖳 vallum-lodge.co.uk; 2D/2T/1D or T/1D, T or F, all en suite; ▼; Ⓛ; Mar-Oct) charges from £50pp (sgl occ £90). To save you the trudge to the pub, they can do an evening meal (£20 for three courses plus a glass of wine). There are also plenty of rooms at the local pub. The ***Twice Brewed Inn*** (☎ 01434-344534, 🖳 twicebrewedinn.co.uk; 7D/11D or T/1Qd, all en suite; ▼; Ⓛ; 🐕), whilst not *quite* so accommodating as to rebrew your beer, still does its best to please and provides many a happy hiker with a meal, a pint, and a bed for the night. B&B here costs from £59.50pp (sgl occ £105). They serve good-quality pub **food** (daily noon-8.30pm; mains £11-14) and a decent selection of real ales, mainly from their own **brew house** next door. It's possible to book yourself on a tour of the brewery (£15pp; contact ☎ 01434-344534 or visit the website 🖳 twicebrewedbrewhouse.co.uk); tours last 60-90 minutes and you get the chance to try three of their ales. They also regularly hold **Dark Skies stargazing nights** (from £30), using their own on-site observatory and local expert astronomers, and taking advantage of their location in the Northumberland National Park.

The **AD122 bus** calls in at the National Landscape Discovery Centre in the summer months; See pp48-51 for details. For a **taxi** call Sprouls Taxis (☎ 07712-321064).

VINDOLANDA [Map 18, p153]

(☎ 01434-344277, 🖳 vindolanda.com; daily Apr-Sep 10am-6pm, Mar & Oct 10am-5pm, Nov 10am-4pm, Dec-Feb check website; Vindolanda ticket £9.25, joint saver ticket with entrance to Carvoran Roman Army Museum (see p138) £14)

According to a panel of experts at the British Museum, the artefacts found at the fort at Vindolanda are collectively the single most important historic find on these shores, beating even such treasures as the Anglo-Saxon hoard at the Sutton Hoo burial, the Roman Mildenhall Treasure and the Lewis Chessmen.

Upon first arriving at Vindolanda, you may well wonder what all the fuss is about. Sure, the **1½-mile (2km) walk or bus ride** (see above) from Once Brewed is nice enough, with some decent views of Sycamore Gap. But once through the gates you'll find none of the impressive, near-complete ruins found at nearby Housesteads, for example. Here at Vindolanda the remains rise only just above foundation level, and the only impressive structures on the site are the 1970s' mock-ups of Hadrian's Wall – one in timber-and-turf and one in stone – that overlook the ongoing archaeological work from the south.

Nevertheless, as those experts at the British Museum tell us, this is *the* most important site along the whole of the Wall. Indeed, it's *the* most important site in Roman Britain, and when the excavation is finally finished – a job that, according to some estimates, could take at least another two hundred years – it could even turn out to be the most important Roman site in *the entire world*. And the reason why can be seen in the **museum** at the rear of the site, where you'll find an incredible array of artefacts that have lain preserved in the earth for almost 2000 years, providing us with a hitherto unrivalled glimpse into the everyday life of the Roman Empire.

Most famously, this is where, in 1973, Robin Birley discovered the **Vindolanda tablets** – paper-thin, wooden writing sheets used by the Romans for everything from official reports to shopping lists and school homework to love letters. Many of the 2500 or so tablets that have so far been discovered are now in the care of the British Museum, though the museum in Vindolanda has kept several on display. Examples include a letter from a concerned mother promising to send her son more underwear to protect him from the bitter British winter and the icy northern wind that blows up the toga at certain times of the year. Then we have a misquote from Virgil's *Aeneid* written in a schoolchild's hand, after which someone else – presumably the teacher – has written 'seg', short for *segnis* or 'sloppy work'. One of the more famous tablets is a birthday invitation, the oldest example of female handwriting in Western Europe. There's also the tablet with the famous reference to the 'Britunculli', or 'wretched Britons'. Humdrum, mundane and everyday, these tablets nevertheless add much colour to our understanding of life in the Roman Empire.

So how have these items been so well preserved? Well this is due to a lucky combination of the soil here, which acts as a natural preservative, and the unique way in which the Romans who lived at the site renovated their buildings. The fort at Vindolanda was actually built around AD85, thus predating both the Wall and the reign of Hadrian – though it is believed he did visit the fort, and archaeologists believe they've found the remains of the building where he stayed too. It was eventually abandoned sometime in the 4th century, but in the intervening years the buildings within the fort were regularly dismantled and new ones put up in their place. Indeed, there are said to be nine forts, each constructed on top of the previous one, at the site. The first six of these forts were made of wood and when they needed to be replaced – which they would probably need to be around every 6-8 years – the fort's inhabitants would just cut the building's supporting timbers at ground level, throw some clay on the floor, then start work on their new building. But by covering the ground with clay, the Romans were unwittingly sealing the ground beneath – thus preserving everything that lay below ground level by preventing air from getting in. The anaerobic conditions under the floor of the fort were so good at preserving whatever lay there that even something as delicate as a hair net has survived, as well as a lady's wig made out of locally-grown hair moss. Plenty of other objects amaze as well. Take the beautifully intricate leather sandals, for example, discarded casually by the last owner into a ditch when they broke, but immaculately preserved to this day. Indeed, this footwear, together with other leather items such as clothing and even a pair of boxing gloves, form the largest cache of Roman leatherware found anywhere in the world, with about 4000 items in total. There are also keys, cutlery, combs, pottery, weapons and some exquisitely delicate jewellery. Over 2500 coins have also been discovered, dating from the earliest years of the fort to the end of the 4th century and the final days of the Romans in Britain. There's also a whole new gallery devoted to the wooden items – from hair combs to work tables – that have been preserved in the soil for the last 1600 years.

Most beautiful of all, perhaps, are the fragments of glass with a gladiatorial scene painted upon them, in colours that are still as vibrant today as they must have been nearly 2000 years ago. When the first edition of this guide was written only one piece had been found; since then, however, several other pieces have been unearthed and pieced together, showing just how the archaeological dig at Vindolanda is still very much a work-in-progress. (Indeed, according to their website they estimate that only 24% of Vindolanda has so far been excavated – meaning that, at current rates, they have about 150 years worth of digging still to go!) Digging currently takes place Mon-Fri in summer, and you're welcome to watch the archaeologists at work.

Overall, the museum is a fascinating, absorbing, mind-boggling collection that will ruin your planned schedule for the day. But it also brings home just what life on the Wall during the Roman era was like more than any other attraction on the walk. Don't miss it, or it will haunt you for the rest of your trek.

The **AD122 bus** calls at Vindolanda; see p50 for further information.

E → STEEL RIGG TO CHOLLERFORD [Maps 17-22]

It's a toss-up whether this **13-mile (21km; 5hrs 15mins)** trek is the most rewarding day's walking on the entire trail, or the previous one. We think that yesterday perhaps shades it in terms of thrills and the variety of Roman ruins that you can see, while today has the best scenery, particularly when you're walking atop the blustery Whin Sill. This day also has the most complete Wall fort on the entire trail – the wonderful Housesteads, which you'll encounter just a few miles into your day's walk.

Other highlights include a genuine Roman quarry, where they would collect material for making the Wall, a quarry that also happens to mark the northernmost point of the entire Roman Empire; a mysterious and enigmatic Roman temple; and perhaps the most famous point of the entire Wall, made famous by a 1991 blockbuster movie, which also boasts the winner of the 2016 English Tree of the Year award.

A word of warning: Other than snacks and a hot drinks machine at Housesteads, and a coffee van at Brocolitia, **there aren't any places en route where you can buy food today**. If you stayed at Once Brewed then perhaps have breakfast there, preferably at the lovely café at the Sill, and then ask them to pack you a lunch; you've got a long way to go before Chollerford.

Note, too, that accommodation is thin on the ground at Chollerford, though there is a campsite, a hotel and a couple of B&Bs. If you can't find anywhere to stay there or in neighbouring **Humshaugh**, don't despair (as long as you aren't here on a Sunday), for Go North East's No 680 bus service (see pp48-51) stops near the main roundabout and goes down to Hexham.

❏ THE BIRLEYS – AN ARCHAEOLOGICAL DYNASTY
For the past century or so most of the major advances in our understanding of the Wall have come about as a result of the work of one family: the Birleys. The association between the family and the archaeology of Roman Britain started with **Eric Birley** (1906-1995), who began excavating at Hadrian's Wall – at Birdoswald Fort – while still an undergraduate at Oxford. His interest in all-things Roman suitably piqued, and having graduated from Oxford with a double first, Eric bought the Clayton Estate at Chesterholm (ie Vindolanda) that had previously belonged to Anthony Hedley, the 19th century antiquary, and, before him, John Clayton (see p64).

Eric Birley owned Vindolanda until 1950, when his job as a professor at Durham University (he founded the department of Archaeology there) forced him to sell it. Nevertheless, he continued to excavate both there and at Housesteads. He died in 1995 in his bed at his last family home, Carvoran, next to where the Roman Army Museum now stands, and his ashes are buried, perhaps unsurprisingly, at Vindolanda.

His work was taken up by his sons, **Robin** and **Anthony**, who had both lived with their father at Vindolanda (their family home now houses the museum) and who had started excavating there while still teenagers. It was Robin (1935-2018) who was central to the discovery of the site's most significant treasure, the so-called Vindolanda tablets, in 1973. The following year his son, **Andrew**, was born, and in 2012 Andrew unearthed more of the aqueduct and piping system – used to supply the site with fresh water during Roman times – that had first been found by his grandfather 80 years before. They also found the original spring which would once have fed the whole site.

Peel Crags There are some odd features to the Wall around here. Firstly, at Peel Gap there are the remains of a turret. There's nothing unusual about that, of course, except that this is an *extra* turret, ie a third turret in the mile between milecastles 39 and 40 where normally, of course, there would only be two. Presumably it was built to watch over Peel Gap, which is all but invisible from the two turrets on either side. The distance between these two neighbouring turrets, 39B and 39A, that would have stood either side (but are no longer there) is also the greatest known distance between any two turrets on the Wall. And because it is an 'extra' turret, it hasn't been included as part of the numbering system – it is the only turret without this designation on the Wall – and is instead usually known simply as Peel Gap Tower (see Map 17, p147).

Cat Stairs and the swastika Between Turret 39A (which exists merely as a bump in the ground these days) and the Cat Stairs (see Map 18, p153) the truly eagle-eyed will be able to spot a Roman **swastika symbol** carved into the Wall. It's on the second course of stones on the Wall's southern side, and, according to one reference I've read, about 37m east of where Turret 39A once stood. This is actually a fragment of a funerary inscription and is in fact Roman shorthand for 'To the spirits of the departed'.

Milecastle 39 & Sycamore Gap Another unique feature of the Wall around here are the remains of what have been called by some the **Officer's Quarters**, near Milecastle 39 (which is also known as Castle Nick; Map 18). These are the only such ruins along the length of the Wall. The truth is, of course, that nobody is really sure what these buildings were for, though they are widely regarded today as just more examples of *shielings* – simple farm huts usually used by herdsmen.

Just below is the famous **Sycamore Gap**, named after the solitary tree growing in the dip, which gained fame when it featured alongside Kevin Costner in the 1991 film *Robin Hood: Prince of Thieves*.

Crag Lough There is nothing particularly significant or historical about Crag Lough (Map 18), but if the sun's shining it's a delightful spot even if you can't actually get that close to the water and are limited to distant views between the trees as you amble along the northern side of the Wall.

The wood itself is just delightful too – though the drop down to the north can be very steep.

Hotbank Farm Hotbank Farm (Map 18) is owned by the National Trust and is built by the **site of Milecastle 38**. The trail circumvents this milecastle to avoid further damage to the site; it was this stretch of Wall that suffered so much from the group of 800 bankers who walked on top of it in 2004 (see p67).

It was also near here that part of an inscribed stone was found that stated the second legion built this milecastle under the governorship of Aulus Platorius Nepos. As Aulus was governor during Hadrian's time, it provided archaeologists with almost irrefutable proof that this was Hadrian's Wall and not, as had previously been believed, Severus's (see box on p54).

Whin Sill and Cuddy's Crags Milecastle 37 (see Map 19, p156) is one of the best preserved and perhaps the most important on the Wall. It was excavated by Clayton in 1853. Note the start of an archway over the north gate, from which the experts were able to extrapolate the height of the arch and from this the height of the milecastle. Why a north gate was deemed necessary here but not at Milecastle 35 is unclear, for they both have steep drops to the north. You can also see holes in the floor by the southern entrance – postholes for the wooden door.

This whole ridge that you are walking across is called the **Whin Sill**, while the section on which Milecastle 37 sits is known locally as **Cuddy's Crags**, after St Cuthbert.

The Clayton Wall To the west of Housesteads is one of the finest sections of Wall (see Maps 18 and 19, p156). It is known as 'Clayton Wall' after the archaeologist John Clayton who bought and rebuilt this section. You can tell a bit of Clayton Wall – as opposed to regular, unreconstructed Roman Wall – because Clayton's method of rebuilding differed from the original Roman style, with no mortar and a turf top. This section of Clayton Wall runs through the wooded Housesteads Plantation.

The National Trust owns the Wall for three miles west of Housesteads; it owns the grand on which the fort is built too, though the day-to-day maintenance of it remains in the hands of English Heritage.

MAP 18

GREAT STRETCH OF WALL. STICK TO IT AND IGNORE OTHER PATHS. BETWEEN HERE AND HOUSESTEADS (MAP 19) IS 'CLAYTON WALL', I.E. WAS REBUILT BY JOHN CLAYTON IN THE 1800s

19

WALL HERE HIDDEN BY TURF

HIGHSHIELD CRAGS

HOTBANK FARM

SLABS AROUND MILECASTLE

050
MILECASTLE 39 (CASTLE NICK)

CRAG LOUGH

SITE OF MILECASTLE 38

CAT STAIRS

17

ORIGINAL WALL

ROMAN MILITARY WAY WEST TO STEEL RIGG VERY CLOSE TO WALL

MILKING GAP

SYCAMORE GAP - NOTE YOU CROSS TO THE OTHER SIDE OF THE WALL HERE

IGNORE THIS LADDER STILE TO SOUTH OVER FENCE

MILITARY ROAD B6318

0   ¼ mile
0   APPROX SCALE   500m

'OFFICERS' QUARTERS' ABOVE MILECASTLE 39 - PROBABLY JUST SHIELINGS

VINDOLANDA FORT

MILESTONE

STANEGATE

CAR PARK

Don't forget to occasionally walk up to the Wall to savour the magical views stretching away to the north. This is Northumberland's version of the Lake District, with **Bromlee Lough** (Map 19), immediately to the north, and **Greenlee Lough** beyond.

HOUSESTEADS   [Map 19, p156]
(☎ 01434-344363, 🖳 english-heritage.org.uk or 🖳 nationaltrust.org.uk; Easter-Sep daily 10am-5pm, Oct-Easter 10am-4pm, winter days/hours subject to change, check website; £9)

Visiting the fort
Those who wish to visit Housesteads should turn off the trail at the fort's north-western corner and head south down the slope to the ticket office. Note that this office has a **Hadrian's Wall passport stamping station** (just outside its entrance). They also sell hot drinks and snacks but have no seating save for a couple of chairs in the museum. You can also saunter downhill to the car park, where there's a National Trust Café (daily 10am-5pm), though it's a ten-minute walk from the trail. The AD122 **bus** calls in at the car park here; see p50 for further information.

The site
'The grandest station in the whole line – in some stations the antiquary feeds upon shells, but here upon kernels'   **William Hutton**, 1802 (see p64)

This quote pretty much sums up Housesteads. For if you visit only one Wall fort (ie a fort that actually lies on the line of the Wall, as opposed to Corbridge, Vindolanda or Aesica that all lie away from it), make it this one. Housesteads is the one place where you can really get a feel for how a Wall fort would have looked. Where the ruins of most other sites are rather fragmentary and barely break the surface of the earth, here the walls in places run to six courses or more – up to 10ft (almost 3m) high – with only the roof apparently missing to complete the structure. For this, as usual, considerable thanks must go to John Clayton, who bought the site in 1838 to protect and excavate it.

By positioning yourself up near the Wall at the top of the hill near the North Gate, you get a great overview of the fort as well as some incomparable views north and south, which is presumably why the Romans built it here in the first place. Known to them as **Vercovicium**, Housesteads was constructed around AD122, making it one of the first to be built along the Wall, and housed around 800 men on its five acres. The First Cohort of Tungrians from Belgium is the auxiliary unit most associated with Housesteads, having been based here in the 3rd and 4th centuries AD.

While the fort has the usual playing-card shape, its layout is not entirely typical. For one thing, you'll notice as you approach the fort from the trail that the *whole* of Housesteads lies south of the Wall, unlike Chesters, Segedunum and other sites which protrude north beyond the line of the Wall. Furthermore, Housesteads is elongated west–east (with the **Military Way** forming its central axis), where the longest axis of other forts runs north–south. The central core of the fort is familiar, with the **headquarters** at the centre and the Commander's House or **praetorium** next door. However, on this occasion, the latter lies to the south of the HQ, not to the east as is more typical, probably because the whole fort is on a ridge and slope. As is usual, the **granaries** and the **hospital** are nearby, with the near-complete ruins of the **communal latrines** in the south-eastern corner of the fort. To the south, in the extensive civilian settlement outside the fort walls, stands the **Murder House**, so-called because the skeleton of a man with a knife stuck between his ribs was discovered during excavations. The ticket office by the ruins at Housesteads doubles up as the **museum**, where, via the medium of scale models, film, Roman finds and CGI recreations of Roman buildings, you get a good idea of what the place may have looked like 2000 years ago.

❑ THE LAYOUT OF THE WALL FORTS

The fort at Housesteads is pretty typical of the design of all Wall forts along the trail. Often described as '**playing-card shaped**' (ie rectangular with rounded corners), the layout varied little from one to the next. At its centre were the **headquarters (HQ)**, the *Principia*, the heart and brains of the fort. It was here that justice was dispensed, plans formulated, men paid and ceremonies, both secular and religious, performed. Sometimes, as with Housesteads, a **shrine** was housed within this building under which, in a small safe-room, the money to pay the soldiers' wages would be stashed. The **commanding officer's house**, or *praetorium*, where he lived with his family and servants, stood next door, usually to the east of the *Principia* (though at Housesteads it's to the south), while the **hospital** and other public buildings sat to its west. Often you'd find the fort's **granary** here too, one of the most interesting buildings, architecturally, of the whole fort. The granary's sides were buttressed to help the walls withstand the pressure created by all that grain being housed within it, while the floor itself was raised to allow air to circulate, thus preventing the grain at the bottom of the heap from going mouldy. The granary would have had a porch, too, to stop the grain getting wet when it was being unloaded from the carts. There's a particularly good granary, complete with the porch pillars, at Corbridge.

Flanking these buildings to north and south were the barracks. **Cavalry barracks** are distinguishable from the infantry barracks by a recess or ditch hewn into the floor – dug to collect the horse's urine and prevent it from seeping into the cavalry officers' quarters next door. Segedunum and Aesica, both in Newcastle, have fine recreations of these. Usually, three men and three horses would share one of these 'apartments' and there would be about nine apartments to each barrack. **Infantry barracks** were much simpler affairs, housing about five to eight men to a room. At the end of each barrack were the living quarters of the *decurian*, or possibly a centurion – the man in charge of each barrack. The fort at Arbeia has recreated a block of infantry barracks to show what the living conditions were like (it's fair to say, they were cramped!). Scattered amongst these buildings were others, such as the **public latrines**, of which Housesteads has a particularly fine example.

Sometimes, as with Segedunum, the whole fort would lie on both sides of the Wall, with its northern end extending beyond the Wall's line into 'barbarian' territory, though at Housesteads, of course, the Wall marks the northern limit of the fort. There would usually be more gates on the northern side than the southern side, too, to allow the soldiers to charge out quickly to meet their barbarian foes.

Other buildings associated with the fort would lie outside its walls, including religious buildings such as **temples** (witness the Mithraeum outside Brocolitia, for example; see p164), and **public baths** (the ruins at Chesters have a great example of these). A **civilian settlement**, or *vicus*, would often grow up around the Wall, too, peopled with retired soldiers from the fort, their children (who automatically became Roman citizens when their father did), wives (who *didn't*) and traders and locals.

ROUTE GUIDE AND MAPS

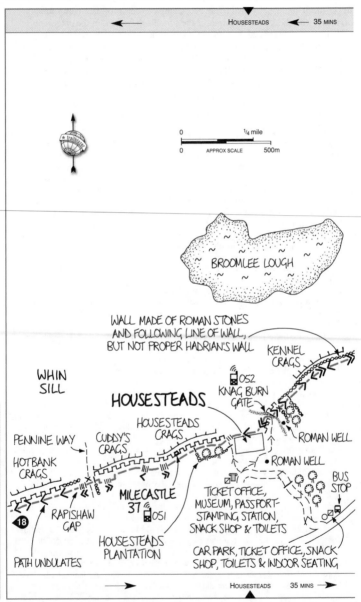

0   ¼ mile
0   APPROX SCALE   500m

BROOMLEE LOUGH

WALL MADE OF ROMAN STONES
AND FOLLOWING LINE OF WALL,
BUT NOT PROPER HADRIAN'S WALL

KENNEL CRAGS

WHIN SILL

HOUSESTEADS

052
KNAG BURN GATE

HOUSESTEADS CRAGS

PENNINE WAY   CUDDY'S CRAGS

HOTBANK CRAGS

ROMAN WELL

• ROMAN WELL

BUS STOP

18

RAPISHAW GAP

MILECASTLE 37   051

TICKET OFFICE,
MUSEUM, PASSPORT-
STAMPING STATION,
SNACK SHOP & TOILETS

PATH UNDULATES

HOUSESTEADS PLANTATION

CAR PARK, TICKET OFFICE, SNACK
SHOP, TOILETS & INDOOR SEATING

HOUSESTEADS   35 MINS →

ROUTE GUIDE AND MAPS

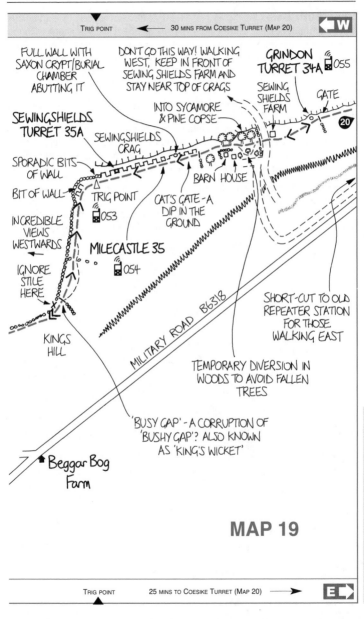

FULL WALL WITH SAXON CRYPT/BURIAL CHAMBER ABUTTING IT

DON'T GO THIS WAY! WALKING WEST, KEEP IN FRONT OF SEWING SHIELDS FARM AND STAY NEAR TOP OF CRAGS

GRINDON TURRET 34A 📱055

SEWING SHIELDS FARM

GATE

🔵 20

SEWINGSHIELDS TURRET 35A

SEWINGSHIELDS CRAG

INTO SYCAMORE & PINE COPSE

SPORADIC BITS OF WALL

BIT OF WALL

TRIG POINT 📱053

BARN HOUSE

CAT'S GATE - A DIP IN THE GROUND

INCREDIBLE VIEWS WESTWARDS

MILECASTLE 35 📱054

IGNORE STILE HERE

KINGS HILL

MILITARY ROAD B6318

SHORT-CUT TO OLD REPEATER STATION FOR THOSE WALKING EAST

TEMPORARY DIVERSION IN WOODS TO AVOID FALLEN TREES

'BUSY GAP' - A CORRUPTION OF 'BUSHY GAP'? ALSO KNOWN AS 'KING'S WICKET'

↗ ▲ Beggar Bog Farm

MAP 19

Knag Burn Gate To the east of Housesteads, surrounded by particularly boggy ground, is Knag Burn Gate (Map 19, p156). This was another Roman gateway through the Wall, similar in that respect to Port Gate to the east. This gate, however, was introduced into the Wall only in the 4th century AD, presumably to allow the considerable number of locals who lived around the fort to move between the northern and southern sides of the Wall with greater ease.

Beggar Bog Farm For those who have had enough for the day *Beggar Bog Farm* (Map 19; ☎ 01434-344652, 🖥 www.beggarbog.co.uk; 1D/1T, both en suite; 🐾 allowed in a separate building by prior arrangement; Ⓛ; Mar-Nov) lies a few hundred metres east of the turn-off to Housesteads fort on the Military Road. A traditional stone-built farmhouse offering **B&B** from £40pp (sgl occ room rate), Beggar Bog also offers evening meals subject to prior arrangement.

Trig Point The trail round the trig point (see Map 19, p157) is amongst the most splendid parts of your entire journey along the Hadrian's Wall Path, with great views, wonderful walking and some really fine bits of Wall. In truth, the wall to the west of the Trig Point is actually not Roman at all but something far

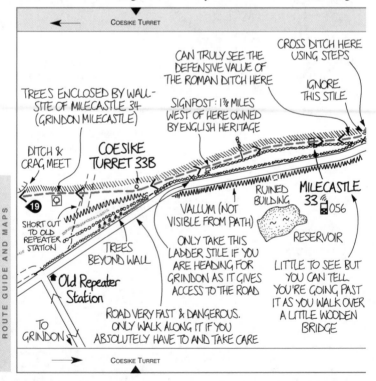

more modern. Nevertheless, it does follow the line that the Wall would have taken, and is clearly made, at least in part, from Roman stones, and thus performs rather well the task of simulating what the Wall would have looked like here.

Sewingshields Crags This is a **fine stretch of Wall**. To the south of the trail the land slopes away gently down to the Military Road but to the north a 200ft/60m drop awaits those who cross the Wall. These are **Sewingshields Crags** (see Map 19, p157), a wild and rugged land that, perhaps unsurprisingly, has become the setting of a number of myths and legends, many concerning those stalwarts of British folktales, King Arthur and his knights. Sewingshields Castle, which used to stand at the foot of the crags, was also used by Walter Scott as the setting for his story *Harold the Dauntless*. Whatever the truth or otherwise of the stories surrounding Sewingshields, there's no doubt that the Romans clearly saw no need to construct a defensive ditch to the north of the Wall here. Coming to **Milecastle 35**, you see that, with such a large drop to the north, there's no northern gate here either, presumably for the same reason. Note, too, that the Vallum is now quite a way south of the Wall, where the ground is less stony.

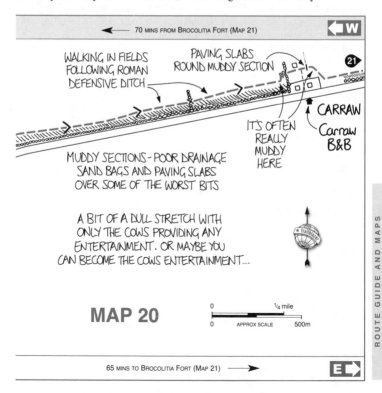

70 MINS FROM BROCOLITIA FORT (MAP 21)

W

WALKING IN FIELDS FOLLOWING ROMAN DEFENSIVE DITCH

PAVING SLABS ROUND MUDDY SECTION

21

CARRAW
Carraw B&B

IT'S OFTEN REALLY MUDDY HERE

MUDDY SECTIONS - POOR DRAINAGE SAND BAGS AND PAVING SLABS OVER SOME OF THE WORST BITS

A BIT OF A DULL STRETCH WITH ONLY THE COWS PROVIDING ANY ENTERTAINMENT. OR MAYBE YOU CAN BECOME THE COWS ENTERTAINMENT....

MAP 20

0 ¼ mile
0 APPROX SCALE 500m

65 MINS TO BROCOLITIA FORT (MAP 21)

E

ROUTE GUIDE AND MAPS

Grindon and Coesike Turrets There is a small flurry of turrets and other defensive buildings east of Sewingshields. **Grindon Turret** (Map 19, p157) or, more prosaically, **Turret 34A**, hides in the corner of a cow field and trekkers are usually too concerned about the field's occupants to give the turret the time it deserves – even though the cows are usually very docile. Both it and **Coesike Turret** (see Map 20, p158), also known as **Turret 33B**, were probably abandoned less than a century after they were built, before the end of the 2nd century AD, as the Wall forts were established. But unlike other turrets which suffered the same fate, after the Romans had gone both these turrets had *shielings* (herdsmen's huts) built into their remains, from which we get the name Sewingshields. Between the two turrets is a small copse surrounded by a wall that marks the site of **Milecastle 34** – more popularly known as **Grindon Milecastle**. Note how the ditch meets crag here. The Roman ditch that runs through the fields east of here was clearly deemed unnecessary by the Romans to the west of this point, as the crags were considered a formidable enough barrier.

Grindon On the junction with the B6318 and the road down to Grindon you'll come to the wonderful **B&B** that is the *Old Repeater Station* (Map 20; ☎ 01434-688668, 🖳 hadrians-wall-bedandbreakfast.co.uk; 1S/1D/1T, all en suite; 🐾 by arrangement) which charges from £42.50 (sgl/sgl occ £70) including breakfast. A lovely converted stone-and-slate building that makes extensive use of eco-technology (including boreholes, biowaste systems, solar panels and the like), this one-man operation is run by the affable, laconic Les, a man never less

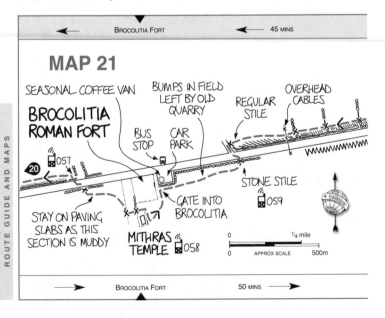

ROUTE GUIDE AND MAPS

than generous with his teapot, and a great cook to boot. Call in advance if you want an evening meal (they are licensed too) or accommodation out of the main season. **Internet access** (charity donation welcome) is available all day (including to non-residents), and Les will even sometimes let you **camp** (£8) in the garden if he's full and you're stuck, and food can be purchased. A repeater station, by the way, was a building located roughly halfway between telephone exchanges and was where the signals on telephone cables were amplified to compensate for the loss of electricity which made speech fainter and led to a loss of clarity.

Carraw The path goes on the northern side of the road to follow the **Roman ditch**, continuing through **Northumberland National Park**. Across the road is *Carraw B&B* (Map 20; ☎ 01434-689857, ☐ carraw.co.uk, **fb**; 2D/1D or T, all en suite; ☞; (Ⓛ), a high-quality place (from £55pp, sgl occ £98-110) on the main road right by the trail. They have very comfortable rooms in the Farmhouse and, while not serving dinner as such, they do offer a 'Carraw supper', namely a bowl of homemade soup and a ploughman's platter (£13.50) served at 6.30pm every day except Sundays. They are also licensed to sell alcohol.

Brocolitia Fort Also known as Carrawburgh (pronounced 'Carrawbruff'), **Brocolitia** (see Map 21) remains unexcavated. It is, however, an unusual fort, clearly built some time after the Wall, for Brocolitia actually lies over the infilled Vallum. It was around this site in 1876 that John Clayton opened up

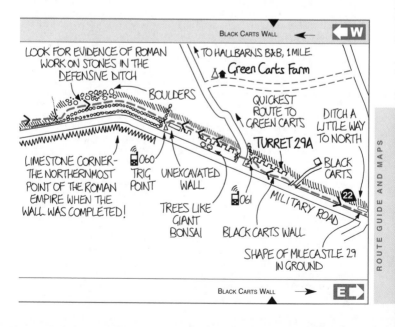

Coventina's Well and discovered 13,487 coins (4 gold, 184 silver and the rest bronze) which would have been tossed into the water for good luck – just as we throw money into wishing wells today. Three hundred of these coins commem-

❏ THE MYSTERIOUS RELIGION OF MITHRAISM

Mithraism was a mysterious religion centred around the worship of the god Mithras, and was practised throughout the Roman Empire from about the 1st to the 4th century AD. There are several reasons why you may not have heard of the faith, and why we know so little about it today. The distant era in which it enjoyed its greatest popularity is clearly a factor, as is the secrecy with which it was practised and the attempts that various people made down the centuries to suppress it. Another factor is that much of the written information we do have for the faith comes not from its adherents – the secrecy surrounding the faith was both strict and all-encompassing – but from its detractors, such as the early Church fathers who were probably not the most reliable of sources. However, although the followers themselves were silent about their faith, their iconography, by comparison, speaks volumes; and this iconography, found in every Mithraeum (Mithraic temple) throughout the Roman Empire, including those discovered at Hadrian's Wall, has taught us most of what we know about this most clandestine of religions.

The origins of the faith are still uncertain, with one school of thought believing it to be Persian, dating back as far as 1400BC, while another suggests it was a near-contemporary of Christianity. Plutarch mentions it in 67BC, while the earliest physical remains date from the 1st century AD. Whatever its genesis, we do know that the Mithraic faith quickly gathered a huge following. One of the likely reasons for this popularity was its adoption as the unofficial faith of Roman soldiers. Though originally appealing to slaves and freedmen, the Mithraic emphasis on truth, honour, bravery and discipline would have appealed to the Roman army who would probably have proselytised the faith wherever they were stationed.

Mithraism enjoyed its heyday in the 2nd century AD; by the 5th century it had all but disappeared. The first blow came with the *sole* accession of Theodosius to the imperial throne in AD392 (prior to this he had ruled with two other 'emperors'). The last emperor of a united Roman Empire (following his demise the split between the empire's western and eastern halves, which first appeared at the beginning of the 4th century AD, became permanent), Theodosius was also the first emperor to make Christianity the official religion and went out of his way to promote his chosen faith, issuing edicts and encouraging Christian subjects to attack pagan buildings. One edict in particular, issued in AD91 before he became sole ruler, banned the worship of pagan gods, and many Mithraic temples were destroyed at this time.

The Mithraic organisation

The faith was a complicated one. Its followers were organised into a strict **hierarchy** of seven grades, or levels. An initiate new to the faith would have been known as a *Corax*, or 'Raven', the first and lowest level in the Mithraic hierarchy. At the other end of the spectrum was the rank of '*Pater*', or 'Father', the seventh and highest level. Their clothes, such as the colour of their tunic or the mask they wore at Mithraic rituals, indicated their status in the religious community.

Rising through the ranks was no easy matter. Near to many Mithraic temples, including Carrawburgh, an 'ordeal' pit has been found, with a bench very close to what would have been a large fire. It is assumed that followers would have undergone some sort of physical trial by fire, cold or fasting in order to climb to the next level.

orated the pacification of northern Britain following disturbances in AD155; Britannia, who may be found on the back of some 50p coins looking regal and serene, appears slumped and forlorn on these Roman coins.

The Mithraic beliefs: one theory

As a reward for rising through the ranks, the faithful were given revelations into the secrets and mysteries of the faith (similar to the way that the modern cult of scientology, so it is said, works today). According to their beliefs, the god Mithras was born either from the living rock or from a tree. An early life filled with pain and hardship culminated in the **defeat and slaughter of the primeval bull**. This killing allowed the life force of the bull to be released for the benefit of humanity: plants and herbs came from the bull's body, while wine came from the bull's blood and all livestock came from the slayed bull's semen. This victory over the primeval bull, known as the **tauroctony**, would have been depicted in every Mithraeum and each time the same few characters appear in the picture, namely a dog, scorpion, snake and raven, as well as Mithras's torchbearers, Cautes and Cautopates.

As for the Mithraeum itself, it would originally have been quite a dark and gloomy place. Indeed, the temples were usually constructed underground in order to simulate the cave in which Mithras was supposed to have killed the primeval bull. Entering via a door in the south-west corner, a worshipper would have first found himself in a small antechamber with a bench and what would have been a large fire, originally the ordeal pit. Beyond a wickerwork screen at the end lay the nave, with benches arranged along the side to allow the faithful to recline when partaking of ritual meals. Four small altars lay at the end of these benches. It is estimated that the average temple would have been able to hold between 30 and 50 men.

Mithraic beliefs: an alternative theory

For 70 years or so, this interpretation of Mithraism was held to be the definitive one. There was, however, one small problem. The whole reason it was believed that Mithraism came from the east is because the name 'Mithras' is the Latin form of the Iranian god Mithra; that, and the fact that the Roman authors themselves believed it to have come from Persia. But if Mithraism did have its origins in Persia and the Indian subcontinent, why have there never been any discoveries of Mithraism in Iran or any parallels in the folklore and mythologies of that region?

Thus, recently, a new interpretation has been suggested. This postulates that the depiction of Mithras slaying the bull, with the dog, raven, snake and scorpion as onlookers, and the torchbearers, Cautes and Cautopates, in attendance, is in fact a symbolic depiction of the cosmos, with the *dramatis personae* symbols of the zodiac. For example, the dog is in fact a representation of the constellation Canis Minor, and Cautes and Cautopates are the sun and moon respectively.

In this theory, therefore, the reason these temples were 'built' underground is because this subterranean chamber represents the night sky. This new theory may sound far-fetched at first but gathers credence when we look at the remains of Mithraea on the Wall. In particular, at Housesteads they discovered a carved stone relief of Mithras emerging from what has been called a Cosmic Egg – a depiction of the cosmos in an oval frame (the image is now preserved in Newcastle's Great North Museum: Hancock). Could it be that this singular sculpture, found in a remote fort in a far-flung corner of Rome's conquered territories, holds the key to our understanding of this empire-wide faith?

In addition to the money, Clayton also found carved stones, altars, jars, pearls, brooches and incense burners – the religious stuff having been deliberately placed here for safe keeping following the Theodosian Edict banning pagan temples in AD391 (see box p162). Much of this can be seen at Chesters Museum (see opposite). Coventina, by the way, was a local goddess associated with water; the Roman Empire was largely tolerant of other religions and beliefs and even assimilated certain local gods into their pantheon, in much the same way that Hinduism has done with both Christianity and Buddhism.

While Brocolitia is once more underground, the nearby **Mithras Temple** is open to both the skies and the public, though the altars are mere copies of the originals now housed in Newcastle's Great North Museum: Hancock (p208). The temple was rediscovered by John Gillam in 1949 when a particularly dry summer 'shrank' the surrounding peat to reveal the stones. Mithraism was one of the more popular religions on the Wall and other Mithraeums, such as at Rudchester, have been unearthed.

During high season (Mar-Oct), and maybe at weekends outside this time, lucky hikers should find Corbridge Coffee Company's **coffee van** (daily 10am-4pm) parked in the car park at Brocolitia. Over the past decade or so this stop has become as much a part of the trail as any milecastle or turret. As well as good strong coffee he serves tea, hot chocolate, cold drinks, snacks (usually one savoury snack, such as sausage rolls, and one sweet, such as muffins) and all accompanied by decent conversation.

Limestone Corner As Limestone Corner (Map 21, p161) is the northernmost point of the trail, the Wall here would have been the northernmost point of the entire Roman Empire. Here you'll find some large boulders lying in the Wall ditch that clearly display evidence of having been worked on by workmen – and specifically Roman workmen. The rock here is whinstone, a super-hard basalt stone, and it appears the Romans soon realised that trying to hack through this rock was pointless; so they left the blocks where they were and moved on. This is one theory, anyway, and it's interesting that the ditch does stop here (though it's worth noting that the Vallum continues unbroken on the other side of the road). Incidentally, the grand house you can see to the north is Chipchase Castle, a medieval tower house with Jacobean and later additions.

Black Carts & Green Carts Farm This handsome stretch at **Black Carts** (Map 21) is a cracking bit of Wall that has its own **turret** (No 29A) and is even joined, along its length, by the distinctive 'V' of the **Wall ditch**. At its western end is a country lane, along which, to the north of the Wall, you'll find *Green Carts Farm* (Map 21; ☎ 01434-681320, 🖥 greencarts.co.uk; 🐎). The farm lies about half a mile north of the path and is, for many hikers, the best **campsite** (£10pp inc use of shower/toilet facilities; coin-operated laundry) on the whole trail; super friendly, and with a great location in a huge grassy field with wonderful countryside views. They also boast a well-equipped **bunkhouse** (2 x 4-bed rooms; from £30pp for 2 or more people sharing, £40 sgl occ) with its own kitchen, toilets and shower. Note that the bunkhouse is rented out per room, rather than per bed, so if you're after just a single bed you may prefer to stay in the basic but delightful **camping barn** (sleeps 13; WI-FI; from £20pp inc pillow & towel), which comes equipped with some cooking facilities (kettle, toaster) and an old TV. If you don't have your own sleeping bag you can hire bedding from £3. If requested in advance, you can also get a takeaway continental breakfast (£7) and packed lunches (£7), while for an evening meal you can order from the local Indian takeaway (ask the owners for a menu).

Hallbarns A local home here called *Hallbarns* (☎ 01434-681419, 🖥 hall-barns-simonburn.co.uk; 2T/1D/1Qd en suite; ▬; (L)) is a pleasant **B&B** (from £40pp if booked direct, sgl occ £60-80) with drying room. They can also provide an evening meal if booked 48 hours in advance. Note, it's around a mile to the north of the trail – off Map 21.

Walwick The path leaves the line of the B6318 at **Walwick** (Map 22) to go around the back of grand Walwick Hall. You cross the boundary of the **Northumberland National Park** at a stile here.

W ← CHOLLERFORD TO STEEL RIGG (FOR ONCE BREWED)
[Maps 22-17]
Perhaps the most thrilling section of the entire walk, this is a **13-mile (21km; 5hrs 25mins)** stage to be savoured. Encompassing the best-preserved fort on the Wall, the finest views, the most complete sections of the Wall, the northernmost point of the trail and some fabulous if slightly exhausting walking, this is a day for superlatives. So bring plenty of food and water with you (there's nowhere to stock up between Chesters and Housesteads apart from a seasonal café van at Brocolitia car park), bucketloads of stamina, and make sure your camera's fully charged – you'll be taking snaps all day.

[Next route overview pp145-6]

CHESTERS [Map 22, p169]
(☎ 01434-681379, 🖥 english-heritage.org.uk; Apr-Oct daily 10am-5pm, Nov-Mar usually weekends only except Feb half-term – check website; £9 if booked online)

'Jack Bob and self went to Chesters to view the remains of the Roman Fort and Bridge.' Found in the **diary of a militia officer** and dated June 1761, proving that Wall tourism is not a new phenomenon.

In its day, Chesters, or **Cilurnum** (meaning, 'Cauldron Pool') as it would have been known then, was *the* fort in which to be stationed out of all of those on the Wall. Set on a beautiful spot amongst mature trees on a bend in the river, the fort was built to guard the nearby bridge over the North Tyne, covered 5¾ acres, and was inhabited by 500 members of the Roman cavalry – who were better paid than their infantry counterparts and seemed to have enjoyed slightly preferential treatment too. The Asturian Cavalry from Spain is the auxiliary force most associated with Chesters. The fort itself was built around AD130 on land previously occupied by Turret 27A. It was excavated by that one-man preservation society, John Clayton, in the 19th century, undoing the work of his father, Nathaniel Clayton, who had turfed over the fort ruins in order to enjoy a smooth, uninterrupted grassy slope down to the River Tyne. John Clayton inherited the estate in 1832, and continued working on this and other Wall fortifications until his death in 1890.

Today's visitors will not only be able to **stamp their Hadrian's Wall passports** (see box p42) on the wall by the entrance but will also be able to enjoy the beautiful, traditional-style **museum** that Clayton established – full of altars and some fascinating finds from the Coventina Well near Brocolitia. Top billing goes to the fort's **baths**, the highest of all the Roman ruins on the entire trail and located, as is usual, outside the fort itself, in this instance down the hill near the river.

These ruins give a really good idea of how the baths would have looked in their heyday, and how the water was channelled around and heated. Incidentally, during an early excavation of the baths in the 19th century, no fewer than 33 bodies, together with the remains of two horses and a dog, were discovered interred in the bathhouse. Curiously, their whereabouts is something of a mystery today, though at the time it was speculated that they dated back to the Saxon period. From the scattered remains beside the baths you can also make out how the Wall itself would have travelled across the bridge, up to the fort (some Wall remains abutting the fort can be seen), right through the spot where the large country house (Clayton's old home) now stands, and beyond into the hills.

CHOLLERFORD & HUMSHAUGH
[Map 22, p169]

The trail all but bypasses **Chollerford** and its neighbour, Humshaugh. There's no ATM here, but there is a good eatery, *The Riverside Kitchen* (☎ 01434-689850, ☐ theriversidekitchen.co.uk; **fb**; summer Mon-Sat 9am-5pm, Sun 10am-4pm, winter Tue-Sun 10am-4pm), a friendly café serving tasty sandwiches, soups, good coffee and homemade cakes. Behind the café is *Riverside Campsite* (☎ 07747-362231 or ☎ 01434-681325; Easter-Oct; 🐾 on lead) where camping (for walkers only) costs £10pp, including use of the shower/toilet block. Across the roundabout is *The George Hotel* (☎ 01434-681611, ☐ bespokehotels .com/the-george-hotel; 2S/ 25D/20T, all en suite; ☛; 🐾; ⓛ), set in its own landscaped gardens with a pool and gym. B&B costs from £50pp (sgl £80). Food served Mon-Fri noon-2pm & 6-8pm, Sat & Sun noon-8pm). There's also a bar.

Humshaugh is about half a mile north (off Map 22). Just past the church, you'll find *The Crown Inn* (☎ 01434-681231, ☐ crowninnhumshaugh.co.uk; **fb**; food Mon-Fri noon-2pm & 5-8pm; Sat noon-8pm, Sun to 6pm; 🐾 beer garden only), with hearty meals and real ale. There's a pleasant B&B here too: *Orchard View* (☎ 01434-681658, ☐ www.northumberlandbedand breakfast.biz; 2T en suite; ☛; ⓛ; Mar-Oct) charges from £47.50pp (sgl occ £85).

About 100 metres past the pub is the community-run **Humshaugh Village Shop** (☎ 01434-681258, ☐ humshaughshop.co .uk; Mon-Fri 7.30am-1pm, Thur also 6-7pm, Sat 7.30am-noon, Sun 9am-noon, bank hols 9-11am). It's small, but sells milk, bread, snacks and fruit & veg with a smile.

The AD122 **bus** stops outside Chesters Roman fort in summer, while on the road to Humshaugh the 680 to Hexham via Acomb runs year round. see pp48-51.

E → CHOLLERFORD TO HEDDON-ON-THE-WALL   [MAPS 22-28]

This is the day where you truly earn your badge and certificate. This is not because this stage is particularly difficult physically; for the truth is, at **15 miles (24.2km; 7hrs)**, it's not, though there are enough undulations to make sure you arrive at your destination suitably weary and dishevelled. Nor is it especially tricky to find your way; indeed, the good people at the national trails are as diligent in their installation of signposts along this stage as they are with every other part of the trail. And even if they weren't, it would be hard to lose your way given that, for all but the first mile of this stage, you are following the B6318. But that's also, of course, the problem with this stage: because it's hard to get too excited about a path that follows a busy road for over 90% of its length.

Of course, you will already have been following this thoroughfare since the middle of the previous stage – and there's a reason why the path follows the road. As mentioned in Part 2, the B6318 is based on the original Military Road built in the first half of the 18th century; a road which was in turn built on top of the foundations of the Wall. (There was a recent archaeological dig by the turn-off to Albermarle Barracks (see Map 27) where they uncovered some of the Military Way beneath the tarmac, which they have left exposed.)

So what are the highlights? Well, for Roman-o-philes the main wonders of the Wall occur within the first mile. Brunton Turret and Planetrees are both highly significant from a historical point of view, though in all honesty they simply cannot compare as a spectacle to the delights of the previous two stages. After that, there's a fine and incongruous Roman altar behind the red doors of the cute church of St Oswalds, and the Vallum and defensive ditch both make several appearances. However, given the paucity of Roman sights, for some people the highlight of the day will be a break at the welcoming Errington Coffee House at the Port Gate, (which was once a very significant location in Roman times, though any indication of that importance has been obliterated by the modern road network of Northumberland). There, and the two eateries – a café and a pub – at East Wallhouses, are the **only places to find refreshments on this stage**.

In summary, therefore, treat this as a day to put your head down and hurry through, pausing only to enjoy the relatively meagre sights en route, such as Whittledene Reservoir, where the great-crested grebe, tufted duck and dunlin all thrive. But if you really can't face 15 miles of hiking along a highway, consider **the diversion to Hexham and Corbridge** beginning on p213.

Roman phallus You'll want to check out the remains of the **Roman bridge abutment** (Map 22) on the southern side of the river facing Chesters Fort. It's just over half a mile (800m) off the trail but it's a pleasant walk and you'll be rewarded with a sighting of a big fat **phallus** that would make your auntie blush; this is arguably the most impressive example of this Roman symbol of prosperity on the entire trail. The symbol is carved into one of the stones on the eastern abutment's side, suitably enough in its nether regions, often hidden by leaves. Two other piers in the water were also discovered but are visible now only when the water is low. Incidentally, this was the third Roman bridge over the Tyne; the first being Pons Aelius in Newcastle, and the second at Corbridge.

WALL   **[off Map 22]**
It is typical of the sometimes perverse nature of this trail that Wall village doesn't actually lie on the Wall.

The village is perhaps of most interest to hikers because of a highly commendable decision by the local parish council to allow a night's **camping** on the village green, free of charge, as long as you don't stay for more than 24 hours, leave the place exactly as you found it, and request permission beforehand from the local council (✉ clerk@wall-pc.gov.uk). There are **public toilets** nearby but no other facilities to speak of. However, there is a very good pub-cum-B&B at the southern end of town,

about 10 minutes from the trail: *The Hadrian Hotel* (☎ 01434-681232, ☐ hadri anhotel.co.uk; 3D/7D or T/1Qd; ✦; 🐾; Ⓛ) is an 18th-century coaching inn with some very comfortable **rooms** but no food available other than breakfast for its residents. B&B from £60pp (sgl occ £120).

GNE's **680 bus** service stops here; see pp48-51 for further details.

Brunton Turret Only a couple of hundred metres from the trail, **Brunton Turret** (Map 22), officially known as Turret 26B, is said to be the finest turret extant on the Wall. Up to eleven courses high in places, it was excavated by John Clayton in 1876. Note how the Wall is of different widths here, going into

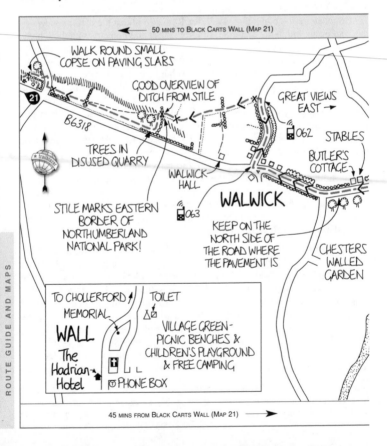

50 MINS TO BLACK CARTS WALL (MAP 21)

WALK ROUND SMALL COPSE ON PAVING SLABS

GOOD OVERVIEW OF DITCH FROM STILE

GREAT VIEWS EAST →

B6318

062 STABLES

TREES IN DISUSED QUARRY

WALWICK HALL

BUTLER'S COTTAGE

WALWICK

STILE MARKS EASTERN BORDER OF NORTHUMBERLAND NATIONAL PARK!

063

KEEP ON THE NORTH SIDE OF THE ROAD WHERE THE PAVEMENT IS

CHESTERS WALLED GARDEN

TO CHOLLERFORD

MEMORIAL

TOILET

WALL

The Hadrian Hotel

PHONE BOX

VILLAGE GREEN - PICNIC BENCHES & CHILDREN'S PLAYGROUND & FREE CAMPING

45 MINS FROM BLACK CARTS WALL (MAP 21) →

ROUTE GUIDE AND MAPS

the turret at one width and coming out the other side at a narrower gauge. As at Planetrees, this kind of chopping and changing with the width of the Wall continues for several miles, though nobody's really sure why. Possibly it was for economic reasons, or maybe it was because the limestone core they used west of here was stronger than the puddled clay used in the eastern section of the Wall, and thus the Romans decided a thinner Wall would suffice.

Planetrees The existence of Planetrees (Map 22) is largely due to the efforts of William Hutton (see p64), who came across some workmen taking stones from the Wall to use for a new farmhouse. Hutton's entreaties to the local landowner responsible for the desecration, Henry Tulip, ensured that this small fragment survived; though 224 yards of the Wall did not, having already been pulled down by Tulip's men before Hutton arrived. However, the portion that has

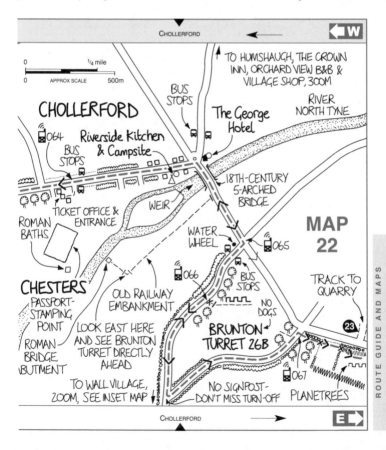

CHOLLERFORD

TO HUMSHAUGH, THE CROWN INN, ORCHARD VIEW B&B & VILLAGE SHOP, 300M

RIVER NORTH TYNE

CHOLLERFORD

0   ¼ mile
0   APPROX SCALE   500m

BUS STOPS

The George Hotel

064   Riverside Kitchen & Campsite

BUS STOPS

18TH-CENTURY 5-ARCHED BRIDGE

TICKET OFFICE & ENTRANCE

WEIR

ROMAN BATHS

WATER WHEEL

MAP 22

065

CHESTERS

PASSPORT-STAMPING POINT

ROMAN BRIDGE ABUTMENT

066

OLD RAILWAY EMBANKMENT

LOOK EAST HERE AND SEE BRUNTON TURRET DIRECTLY AHEAD

BUS STOPS

NO DOGS

TRACK TO QUARRY

23

BRUNTON TURRET 26B

TO WALL VILLAGE, 200M, SEE INSET MAP

NO SIGNPOST-DON'T MISS TURN-OFF

067

PLANETREES

CHOLLERFORD

ROUTE GUIDE AND MAPS

survived is interesting: notice how, near the culvert built into the Wall to prevent water from collecting and weakening the foundations, the Wall changes from being a *broad* Wall on broad foundations, (as seen to the east of here at Heddon, for example), to a *narrow* Wall on broad foundations. A similar pattern can be seen at Brunton Turret (see p169), and suggests that it was around here that the Romans gave up building an all-broad Wall and opted instead for a narrower version that still made use of the original broad foundations.

St Oswald's Hill Head This tiny hamlet (Map 23), with its lovely little church (see box p172) set in a meadow to the north of the trail, sits adjacent to the site of the **Battle of Heavenfield**. Those staying in Acomb or Hexham may wish to turn south off the trail by the large cross in the corner of Heavenfield to join the route of the Acomb–Hexham–Corbridge diversion (see route pp213-24).

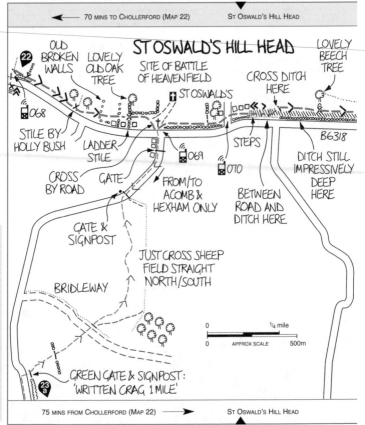

ROUTE GUIDE AND MAPS

Roman earthworks around Milecastle 24 There's not much in the way of Wall on this stage, but there is plenty of other Roman construction that you can discern in the ground. The trail pivots around Milecastle 24 (Map 23), the form of which you can just make out in the ground. Near here, the road crosses the B6318, and in doing so crosses between the **Roman ditch**, that you can appreciate for several hundred yards east of St Oswald's, and the Vallum, that runs (though it's not always visible) between Milecastle 24 and Port Gate.

Port Gate Today, Port Gate (Map 24), also spelt Portgate, is marked by a modern traffic roundabout at the junction of the A68 and the Military Road. This may not seem the most auspicious place to find evidence of Roman occupation. But the A68 to Corbridge was once the old Roman **Dere Street** that ran between the fort (and indeed further on down to York) all the way north to Scotland, making

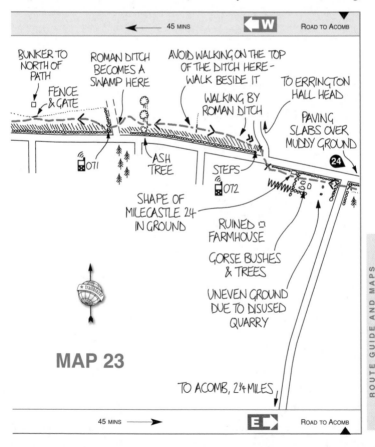

← 45 MINS ◄▌W ROAD TO ACOMB

BUNKER TO NORTH OF PATH

FENCE & GATE

ROMAN DITCH BECOMES A SWAMP HERE

AVOID WALKING ON THE TOP OF THE DITCH HERE – WALK BESIDE IT

WALKING BY ROMAN DITCH

TO ERRINGTON HALL HEAD

PAVING SLABS OVER MUDDY GROUND

📱071

ASH TREE

STEPS 📱072

24

SHAPE OF MILECASTLE 24 IN GROUND

RUINED FARMHOUSE

GORSE BUSHES & TREES

UNEVEN GROUND DUE TO DISUSED QUARRY

MAP 23

TO ACOMB, 2¼ MILES

45 MINS → E▌► ROAD TO ACOMB

ROUTE GUIDE AND MAPS

❏ ST OSWALD'S CHURCH

This was built to commemorate the victory of the eponymous saint over his rivals Cadwallon and Penda at the **Battle of Heavenfield**, which took place in the field in which you are probably now standing. In the 7th century St Oswald, who was merely a king at this stage, was the leader of the Angles following the death of Edwin (after whom Edinburgh is named) in AD633. His defeat of the combined forces of Gwynedd and Mercia, though not quite the victory of Christianity over paganism that the Venerable Bede portrays in his *History*, was nevertheless a significant victory for the Anglo-Saxons over the Celts and, as such, an important moment in English history. Incidentally, at the back of the church by the font there's a large **Roman altar**.

The church also marks one end of **St Oswald's Way** (🖥 stoswaldsway.com) which covers 97 miles of beautiful Northumberland countryside and coastline between here and Lindisfarne, linking places associated with St Oswald.

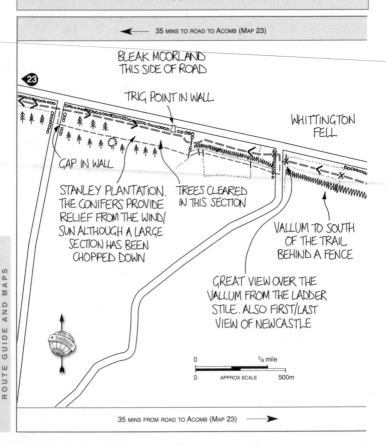

35 MINS TO ROAD TO ACOMB (MAP 23)

BLEAK MOORLAND
THIS SIDE OF ROAD

TRIG POINT IN WALL

WHITTINGTON
FELL

GAP IN WALL

STANLEY PLANTATION.
THE CONIFERS PROVIDE
RELIEF FROM THE WIND/
SUN ALTHOUGH A LARGE
SECTION HAS BEEN
CHOPPED DOWN

TREES CLEARED
IN THIS SECTION

VALLUM TO SOUTH
OF THE TRAIL
BEHIND A FENCE

GREAT VIEW OVER THE
VALLUM FROM THE LADDER
STILE. ALSO FIRST/LAST
VIEW OF NEWCASTLE

0   ¼ mile
0   APPROX SCALE   500m

35 MINS FROM ROAD TO ACOMB (MAP 23) ⟶

Port Gate one of the few gateways the Romans built into the Wall. When the roundabout was built in the '60s it was deliberately moved a little to the north so as not to disturb the unexcavated archaeological remains around here.

Port Gate now has a second claim-to-fame that, for most walkers, is far more significant. For it's here that you'll find *The Errington Coffee House* (Map 24; ☎ 01434-672666, ⌨ erringtoncoffeehouse.com; **fb**; daily 10am-4pm), the only eatery on the trail between Chollerford and Wallhouses. It's a lovely place, a former pub (The Errington Arms) that now packs in the punters with a delicious menu of freshly made sandwiches, scones, cakes, hot drinks and some wonderful puddings too. It has the feeling of a place – like the Twice Brewed Pub near Steel Rigg and the Kings Arms in Bowness – that is set to become an essential stop and an important meeting point for walkers.

Go North East's No 74 **bus service** calls here; see pp48-51 for details.

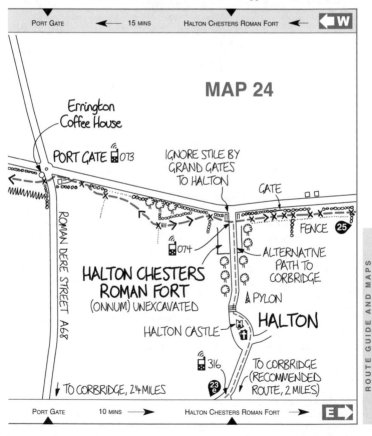

ROUTE GUIDE AND MAPS

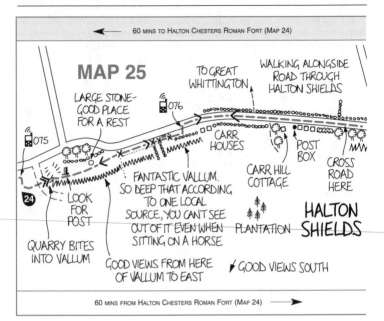

60 MINS TO HALTON CHESTERS ROMAN FORT (MAP 24)

MAP 25

LARGE STONE-
GOOD PLACE
FOR A REST

🕽 076

TO GREAT
WHITTINGTON

WALKING ALONGSIDE
ROAD THROUGH
HALTON SHIELDS

🕽 075

CARR
HOUSES

POST
BOX

CROSS
ROAD
HERE

24

LOOK
FOR
POST

FANTASTIC VALLUM.
SO DEEP THAT ACCORDING
TO ONE LOCAL
SOURCE, YOU CAN'T SEE
OUT OF IT EVEN WHEN
SITTING ON A HORSE

CARR HILL
COTTAGE

PLANTATION

HALTON
SHIELDS

QUARRY BITES
INTO VALLUM

GOOD VIEWS FROM HERE
OF VALLUM TO EAST

GOOD VIEWS SOUTH

60 MINS FROM HALTON CHESTERS ROMAN FORT (MAP 24)

Halton Chesters The incongruous grassy bumps by the monumental gates of Halton Castle are the remains of **Halton Chesters** (also known as Onnum; Map 24), one of two unexcavated Roman forts on this stage. As with Rudchester Fort (Vindobala), to the east, there's little to get too excited about with everything covered by a layer of turf and the undulations, other than the outline of the fort itself, difficult to distinguish from other, later, bumps.

Those wishing to take the Corbridge–Hexham–Acomb diversion (see pp213-24), or who are staying in Corbridge overnight, can head south from here.

Go North East's No 74 **bus service** (see pp48-51 for details) calls at Halton.

The Vallum The Vallum between the fort at Halton Chesters and the row of pretty cottages lining the busy B6318 that is known as **Halton Shields** (Map 25) is perhaps the most 'visible' on the trail, at least at the eastern end; at its western end it's been lost beneath the corrugations caused by medieval ploughing and the depredations of an old quarry. To illustrate how deep the Vallum is, according to one local you could sit on a horse in the middle of it and still not be able to see out! An exaggeration, maybe, but you get the idea.

EAST WALLHOUSES [Map 26, p176]
The *Robin Hood Inn* (☎ 01434-672549, 🖥 robinhoodinnhadrianswall.com; 🐕 bar only), dating back to 1752, is a favourite stop for hikers with some decent **food** (served daily noon-9pm) and a **Hadrian's**

Wall passport stamping point in a box outside the entrance. You can **camp** at the back (Apr-Sep, £12 for 2-person tent) and, if requested in advance, can have breakfast (£9.95) too. There are also **B&B rooms**

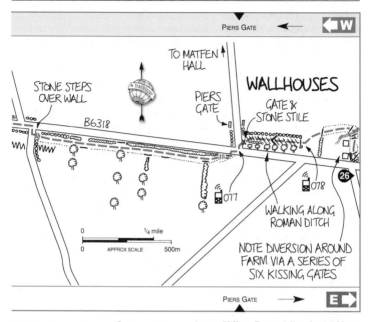

PIERS GATE ◀ ◀W

TO MATFEN
HALL

WALLHOUSES

STONE STEPS
OVER WALL

PIERS
GATE

GATE &
STONE STILE

B6318

🌐 trailblazer

☎077

☎078

26

WALKING ALONG
ROMAN DITCH

NOTE DIVERSION AROUND
FARM VIA A SERIES OF
SIX KISSING GATES

0   ¼ mile
0   APPROX SCALE   500m

PIERS GATE ⟶ E▶

(1D/2T, all en suite; ☕; Ⓛ) from £50pp Sun-Thur, £60pp Fri & Sat (sgl occ £80) and five en suite **log cabins** (sleep 2; from £50pp inc breakfast, sgl occ £100).

The closest alternative to the pub for food is at the nearby Vallum Farm and *Café Aroma* (☎ 01434-672652, **fb** search Cafe Aroma Vallum Farm; daily 10am-4.30pm, last orders for hot food 3pm; 🐾), a very popular, licensed café with a great selection of cakes, breakfasts and lunches.

To the north of East Wallhouses, Matfen is a stop on Go North East's No 74 **bus** service; see pp48-51.

Whittle Dene Reservoir With Welton Burn feeding Whittle Dene Reservoir's **Great Northern Lake**, and Whittle Dene Aqueduct from Hollington Reservoir flowing into **Great Southern Lake** at the southern end, this series of lakes (Map 26) rarely freezes over even in the depths of winter, and as such attracts birdlife year-round. Indeed, over 190 species of birds, as well as red squirrels and deer, have been spotted on or near the lakes. This gigantic series of reservoirs is more than just a nature reserve, however, for the reservoir pumps 25 million gallons of water a day to the treatment works. With picnic tables, a hide that provides invaluable shelter from the rain, and views opening up north and south, it's a highly disciplined hiker who resists taking a break here.

Harlow Hill Harlow Hill (Map 27) is a tiny, lonely little settlement whose most noticeable feature is its old church, now converted into a farmyard barn. A few yards up the hill, many of the buildings in the hamlet have been converted into Harlow Hill MXVI (🖥 harlowhill-mxvi.co.uk), a series of luxury holiday cottages (min 3 nights). The unusual name, by the way, refers to the fact that this was once the site of Milecastle 16. Note that to both the east and west of here the Path takes you into the **Roman defensive ditch**, the fortification that lay to the north of the Wall.

Northside Farm South of the trail, *Northside Farm* (Map 27; ☎ 07904 119 327, 🖵 northsidefarm.co.uk) boasts ten very smart and surprisingly roomy **'wooden wigwams'** (sleep 5; 🐾) in its orchard. They have lighting and heating, a fridge, kettle and microwave (but no bedding or towels provided). There's an outside water tap, though note that the wigwams aren't en suite (the stable block has four bathrooms), nor are there any cooking utensils, cooking equipment, crockery or cutlery. But if you're camping and have all that gear already, and the weather leads you to decide that you would prefer not to spend the night under canvas, then they could be ideal. Rates start at £52 for 1-2 people per wigwam, with each extra person costing £26. The wigwams lie about three-quarters of a mile south of the trail along a farm track; take the signposted turning off the trail to the west of the Albermarle Barracks junction.

Around Ironsign Farm Where the path takes an unexpected detour to the south, around Ironsign Farm, is *Pitch on the Wall* campsite (Map 27; ☎ 07733

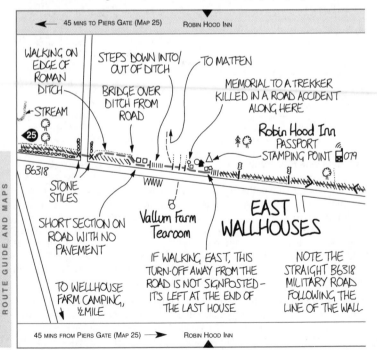

45 MINS TO PIERS GATE (MAP 25) ← ▼ ROBIN HOOD INN

WALKING ON EDGE OF ROMAN DITCH

STEPS DOWN INTO/ OUT OF DITCH

TO MATFEN

MEMORIAL TO A TREKKER KILLED IN A ROAD ACCIDENT ALONG HERE

BRIDGE OVER DITCH FROM ROAD

STREAM

25

Robin Hood Inn
PASSPORT
STAMPING POINT 079

B6318

STONE STILES

WWW

Vallum Farm Tearoom

EAST WALLHOUSES

SHORT SECTION ON ROAD WITH NO PAVEMENT

IF WALKING EAST, THIS TURN-OFF AWAY FROM THE ROAD IS NOT SIGNPOSTED – IT'S LEFT AT THE END OF THE LAST HOUSE

NOTE THE STRAIGHT B6318 MILITARY ROAD FOLLOWING THE LINE OF THE WALL

TO WELLHOUSE FARM CAMPING, ½ MILE

45 MINS FROM PIERS GATE (MAP 25) → ▲ ROBIN HOOD INN

114364; **fb**; 🐎). It's a basic place with no showers, though there is a water tap and portaloos. Walkers are charged £12.50 for a night.

Rudchester Fort The subterranean remains of **Rudchester Fort** (Map 27), or Vindobala, as the Romans knew it, are hard to distinguish. Once heavily pillaged by local farmers and the builders of the Military Road in the 18th century, it now lies undisturbed beneath the soil of Rudchester Farm. (Indeed, it actually stretches north over the other side of the B6318 too.) Now owned by the local county council, there are hopes that this 4½-acre (1.8-hectare) fort will be re-excavated (it was last explored thoroughly in the 1930s) and developed properly one day – though what exactly is left after all these depredations remains to be seen.

Milecastle 13 and the road embankment Don't be too downhearted if you can't make out these two isolated examples of Roman construction (Map 28). Neither is spectacular and, if you're walking west, you won't have had much practice in the art of identifying bits of Roman masonry. But there are **stones from the Roman Wall** lying where they emerged from the road embankment, by the exit/entrance to the field near Heddon. Those with eagle eyes may also be able to make out the platform outline of Milecastle 13, though it's extremely faint. If nothing else, it does at least prove that the trail is adhering to the Wall.

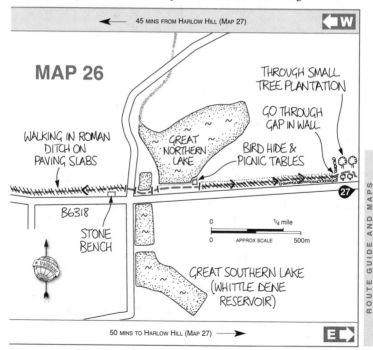

MAP 26

◄— 45 MINS FROM HARLOW HILL (MAP 27)   ◄ W

THROUGH SMALL TREE PLANTATION

GO THROUGH GAP IN WALL

WALKING IN ROMAN DITCH ON PAVING SLABS

GREAT NORTHERN LAKE

BIRD HIDE & PICNIC TABLES

27

B6318

STONE BENCH

★ trailblazer

0   ¼ mile
0 APPROX SCALE 500m

GREAT SOUTHERN LAKE (WHITTLE DENE RESERVOIR)

50 MINS TO HARLOW HILL (MAP 27) —►   E ►

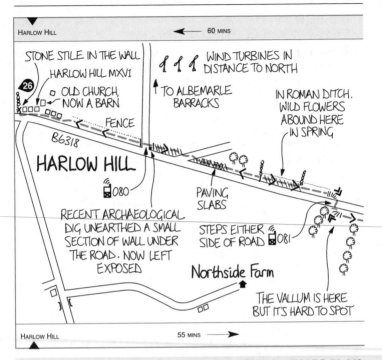

HARLOW HILL ← 60 MINS

STONE STILE IN THE WALL
HARLOW HILL MXVI
OLD CHURCH, NOW A BARN
26
FENCE
B6318
HARLOW HILL
080
RECENT ARCHAEOLOGICAL DIG UNEARTHED A SMALL SECTION OF WALL UNDER THE ROAD. NOW LEFT EXPOSED
PAVING SLABS
STEPS EITHER SIDE OF ROAD 081
Northside Farm
THE VALLUM IS HERE BUT IT'S HARD TO SPOT

WIND TURBINES IN DISTANCE TO NORTH
↑ TO ALBEMARLE BARRACKS
IN ROMAN DITCH. WILD FLOWERS ABOUND HERE IN SPRING

HARLOW HILL 55 MINS →

W ← HEDDON-ON-THE-WALL TO CHOLLERFORD [MAPS 28-22]

Anyone glancing at the maps for this **15-mile (24.2km; 7hrs)** stage will find their heart sinking and probably conclude that this is not a walk that will last long in the memory. Why? Because most of the trail on this stage is owned by Northumberland Highway Department and throughout nearly all of its length this walk is accompanied by one of its most important charges, the thundering B6318. Indeed, based on what the map is telling you, some of you may even decide to take the Corbridge–Hexham–Acomb deviation instead (see pp213-24), and rejoin the official trail again towards the end of the stage at St Oswald's Hill Head.

But don't be so hasty; this stage does have some interest. For one thing, though the road is a constant companion, for most of this stage you'll be hiking slightly away from it in fields with livestock and other, wilder creatures of the British countryside such as hares, rabbits and a superb variety of birdlife including crows, lapwings, finches, swallows and, on the waters of Whittledene Reservoir, the great-crested grebe, tufted duck and dunlin.

Furthermore, permanent presence though it may be, the road is rarely an obtrusive one. (That said, sometimes you'll need to cross or at the very least

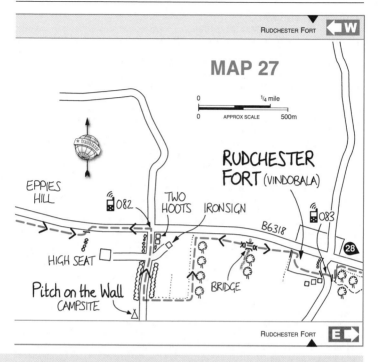

MAP 27

0   ¼ mile

0   APPROX SCALE   500m

EPPIES HILL

📱082

TWO HOOTS

IRONSIGN

RUDCHESTER FORT (VINDOBALA)

📱083

B6318

28

HIGH SEAT

Pitch on the Wall
CAMPSITE

BRIDGE

walk alongside this very straight – and thus very fast – road, and outside Robin Hood Inn there's a memorial to a trekker who was hit and killed by a vehicle on this stage, so you do need to exercise due caution throughout.)

Bear in mind that the reason the trail follows the highway in the first place is because it is built right *upon* the Wall: the B6318 is merely the modern and more mundane moniker for the **Military Road**, built in the 18th century to facilitate the rapid movement of troops across the country in order to ward off incursions by Bonnie Prince Charlie and his followers. And though the Wall itself may not make much of an appearance, at least up until St Oswald's, this allows its accompanying defences – the Vallum and, on the Wall's (and thus the road's) northern side, the Roman ditch – a chance to bask in the spotlight for a change; and it will be these, and the expansive views beyond, that will be occupying your attention for this stretch.

So, by all means, take the **Hexham-Corbridge alternative** if you prefer – it's a cracking walk, which we describe beginning on p224 – but not if your only reason for doing so is because you believe the official trail to be a bit duff. It's not. Perhaps best of all would be to take the detour and *then* come back and do the proper trail, or vice versa. [*Next route overview p165*]

ROUTE GUIDE AND MAPS

HEDDON-ON-THE-WALL
[Map 28, p182]

If you're walking west, Heddon-on-the-Wall is a fine place for your first night. It also marks the point where you actually join the Wall properly and, as if to emphasise that point, there's a **sizeable chunk of Wall** for you to savour, just a minute's walk from the Path. Of course, travelling east, it's the last bit of Wall you'll see until Segedunum and the very end of the trail; from now on, rather than walking the Wall, it's the Tyne where you'll spend your time.

The petrol station doubles up as a Spar **supermarket** (Mon-Sat 7am-9pm, Sun 8am-9pm) and the local **post office** (same hours as shop). Note that there is a charge to use the **ATM** in the Spar, but with a debit card you could withdraw cash without charge at the post office counter instead. Some foreign bank cards are not accepted at this ATM.

Heddon also has a couple of **pubs**. The *Three Tuns* (☎ 01661-852172, **fb**; food served Mon-Sat noon-8pm, Sun noon-4pm; 🐾), on the B6528, is a great old place, really popular with locals; indeed, you get the feeling that this is where the spirit of the village resides. It serves simple but tasty and incredibly good value pub grub. Across the village, *The Swan* (☎ 01661-853161, 🖳 vintageinn.co.uk; food served Mon-Sat noon-10pm, Sun to 9.30pm; 🐾 in bar only) also does standard pub fare (mains £12.50-17.50) as well as sandwiches, and a roast on Sundays.

For **accommodation**, *Heddon Lodge* (☎ 01661-854042 or ☎ 07802-660485, 🖳 heddonlodge.co.uk; 1D/1T en suite/1D private bathroom; ●; Ⓛ; well-behaved 🐾; Mar-Oct), at 38 Heddon Banks, has some splendid accommodation (from £52.50pp, sgl occ from £105) surpassed only by the fantastic breakfasts, with ingredients sourced locally and organic where possible.

On the trail itself is the handy but basic *Hadrian Hideout* (☎ 07786-592634; book through 🖳 airbnb.co.uk, search Hadrian Hideout, 1T or Tr, en suite), a converted garage that sleeps two in bunk beds plus a sofa bed for a third person (from £21pp, sgl occ £37, service fee applies). There are rudimentary cooking facilities including a kettle; ingredients are provided for a make-your-own, fruit-and-porridge type breakfast. Guests can use the garden patio and the owner's home wi-fi.

More comfortable, but about a half-mile's walk from the trail, is *Hadrian's Barn* (☎ 07944-004601, 🖳 hadriansbarn .co.uk), a delightful self-contained cottage (1D/2T or Qd; free Ⓛ) with a living area, which has a sofa bed, and a fully equipped kitchen. Evening meals are available by prior arrangement. The rate (from £52.50pp, 3/4 sharing £145/175) includes ingredients to make your own breakfast (and you can make your own packed lunch, which is an excellent – and novel – bonus). To make sure solo travellers aren't left out, they have also opened up a single room in the main house (from £75).

Slightly further along the B6528 is the large *Houghton North Farm* (☎ 01661-854364, ☎ 07708 419911, 🖳 houghtonnorth farm.co.uk; 1T/3Qd shared facilities, 1Tr /1 rm sleeps 5 en suite; Ⓛ; Mar/Apr-Nov). Previously a luxurious bunkhouse or hostel, they now offer private rooms only, though the kitchen, TV lounge and dining area are still available for guests, as is a power shower to die for – and very high standards of comfort and cleanliness. Rates (from £30pp, sgl occ £35) include a light breakfast.

There are several **bus** services between Heddon and either Newcastle or Hexham, including Arriva's/Stagecoach's No 685 service and Go North East's 684 service; see pp48-51 for details.

E → HEDDON-ON-THE-WALL TO WALLSEND [MAPS 28-33]

In some strange way, you could say that this final **15-mile (24.2km; 5hrs)** march to the end of the Wall and the walk at Wallsend is an uncanny echo of the very first stage. Just like that first walk, from Bowness, there isn't much Wall to see on this day save for the longest section of so-called 'broad Wall' at

Heddon, at the very, very beginning of today's walk. (Indeed, perhaps in recognition of the lack of any proper Roman Wall on today's stage, the authorities don't even mention the Wall on the signposts through Newcastle, but instead you'll see that its name has been changed to 'Hadrian's Way'.)

Just like the first stage, too, you'll find that much of today will be spent ambling alongside a river. For no sooner do you leave Heddon than you're descending down the slopes towards the Tyne, which will be your intermittent companion for much of the stage. *(cont'd on p184)*

❏ GEORGE STEPHENSON AND THE WYLAM WAGGONWAY

Born (on 9 June 1781) and raised on the eastern fringes of Wylam, right by the old Wylam Waggonway, it was perhaps inevitable that George Stephenson – who, as a child, must have watched the progress of those early horse-drawn waggons passing his house – would somehow be drawn into the industry. Indeed, his very first job was working on the waggonway, where he was hired as a boy to keep a neighbour's herd of cows off the tram road. Lacking formal education and unable to read or write, Stephenson joined his father at Killingworth Colliery, though it wasn't long before his fascination for machinery, combined with a single-minded nature and fierce ambition, was leading him in new directions. In 1812 he became enginewright at the colliery and less than a year later he had persuaded his manager to let him try his hand at building a railway engine. The result was *Blucher*, a slow and clumsy beast (it was said to do no more than 4mph) which nevertheless became the first engine to avoid using cog-and-rack pinions – a breakthrough that thrust Stephenson to the very forefront of steam technology at the relatively tender age of 32.

Sixteen locomotives later and in 1819 Stephenson, his reputation for engine building now unmatched, was asked to construct an eight-mile line from Hetton to Sunderland. It was his – and the world's – first major steam railway project. It was also the task that convinced Stephenson that steam railways, if they were to have a future, needed to be constructed on as level a ground as possible; the hilly terrain that separated Hetton from Sunderland meant that his locomotive could not complete the journey without significant help from fixed hauling engines to help it negotiate the steeper parts, which slowed down the engine's progress considerably.

Further success followed; on 27 September 1825 – a date now known as the Birth of the Railways – his invention, *Locomotion*, carried 450 passengers at 15mph (24km/h) between Darlington and Stockton along his own railway line. Several years later, in 1829, an updated version of *Locomotion*, built with the help of his son Robert and called *Rocket*, won a competition to find the fastest locomotive when it travelled at an average speed of 36mph (58km/h) from Liverpool to Manchester, the line for which Stephenson had become chief engineer. It became his most celebrated achievement and firmly established his reputation as 'Father of the Railways'. With his new-found fortune Stephenson bought Tapton House, a grand Georgian manor near Chesterfield, where he kept busy opening coal mines, ironworks and limestone quarries in the nearby area. It was at Tapton that he died, on 12 August 1848, aged 67.

The white-stone cottage that was **Stephenson's childhood home** (🖳 national-trust.org.uk/george-stephensons-birthplace), at Wylam, is now owned by the National Trust. It lies about ten minutes from the trail. At the time of research it had been closed to the public for several years, but the National Trust are aiming to reopen it as part of a guided, ticketed walking tour of Wylam so check the website for updates.

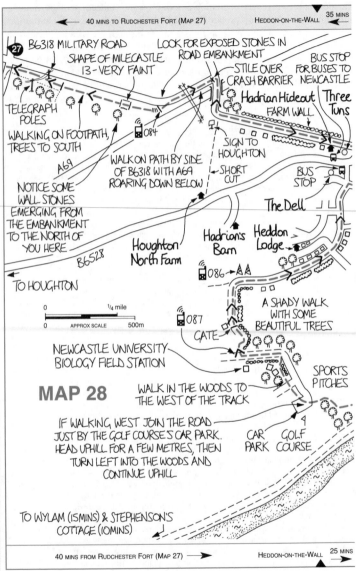

27 B6318 MILITARY ROAD

SHAPE OF MILECASTLE 13 - VERY FAINT

LOOK FOR EXPOSED STONES IN ROAD EMBANKMENT

STILE OVER CRASH BARRIER

BUS STOP FOR BUSES TO NEWCASTLE

TELEGRAPH POLES

Hadrian Hideout   FARM WALL   Three Tuns

WALKING ON FOOTPATH, TREES TO SOUTH

084

A69

WALK ON PATH BY SIDE OF B6318 WITH A69 ROARING DOWN BELOW

SIGN TO HOUGHTON

SHORT CUT

BUS STOP

NOTICE SOME WALL STONES EMERGING FROM THE EMBANKMENT TO THE NORTH OF YOU HERE

B6528

The Dell

TO HOUGHTON

Houghton North Farm

Hadrian's Barn

Heddon Lodge

086 → AA

A SHADY WALK WITH SOME BEAUTIFUL TREES

087

GATE

NEWCASTLE UNIVERSITY BIOLOGY FIELD STATION

MAP 28

WALK IN THE WOODS TO THE WEST OF THE TRACK

SPORTS PITCHES

0   ¼ mile
0   APPROX SCALE   500m

IF WALKING WEST JOIN THE ROAD JUST BY THE GOLF COURSE'S CAR PARK. HEAD UPHILL FOR A FEW METRES, THEN TURN LEFT INTO THE WOODS AND CONTINUE UPHILL

CAR PARK   GOLF COURSE

TO WYLAM (15MINS) & STEPHENSON'S COTTAGE (10MINS)

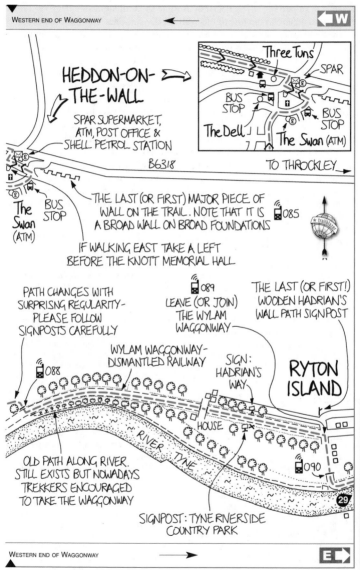

WESTERN END OF WAGGONWAY ← ◀W

HEDDON-ON-THE-WALL

SPAR SUPERMARKET, ATM, POST OFFICE & SHELL PETROL STATION

B6318

TO THROCKLEY →

Three Tuns

SPAR

BUS STOP

BUS STOP

The Dell

The Swan (ATM)

The Swan (ATM)

BUS STOP

THE LAST (OR FIRST) MAJOR PIECE OF WALL ON THE TRAIL. NOTE THAT IT IS A BROAD WALL ON BROAD FOUNDATIONS

☎085

IF WALKING EAST TAKE A LEFT BEFORE THE KNOTT MEMORIAL HALL

PATH CHANGES WITH SURPRISING REGULARITY- PLEASE FOLLOW SIGNPOSTS CAREFULLY

☎089 LEAVE (OR JOIN) THE WYLAM WAGGONWAY

THE LAST (OR FIRST!) WOODEN HADRIAN'S WALL PATH SIGNPOST

WYLAM WAGGONWAY- DISMANTLED RAILWAY

SIGN: HADRIAN'S WAY

RYTON ISLAND

☎088

HOUSE

☎090

RIVER TYNE

OLD PATH ALONG RIVER. STILL EXISTS BUT NOWADAYS TREKKERS ENCOURAGED TO TAKE THE WAGGONWAY

29

SIGNPOST: TYNE RIVERSIDE COUNTRY PARK

(cont'd from p181)   The decision to route the trail alongside the river rather than try to adhere to the line of the Wall is only sensible. Yes, there are sections of the Wall still in existence within the boundaries of metropolitan Newcastle (see pp208-9), but you would have to follow a busy A186 artery to see them, and that's not a walk that many people would choose to do voluntarily. Far better to end your odyssey with a leisurely amble through the city centre itself, the trail authorities obviously concluded – and we heartily agree. Indeed, the path through the city centre is quite a glorious walk as you pass under the series of bridges that cross the Tyne, each one feeling, almost, like a finishing line.

Almost – but not quite. For while your stroll through the city's historic centre may be the most memorable part of today, you still have a few miles to go from the last bridge to the end of the trail itself, which is now marked by a newly installed sculpture of a Roman centurion at Wallsend. It stands by the entrance of the final Wall fort of Segedunum (don't forget to stamp your Hadrian's Wall passport!) and just a few yards away from the final remaining stretch of the Wall itself, which once connected the fort to the river. It's a most fitting and lovely end to a fascinating and lovely trail.

WYLAM [off Map 28, p182]

There is some decent accommodation in the village as well as good places to eat.

There's also a **pharmacy** (Mon-Fri 8.30am-6pm, Sat 9am-noon) and a couple of **supermarkets**, Co-op (daily 7am-10pm) and Spar (daily 6am-8.30pm); the former has a free **ATM**, while the latter houses the **post office** (same hours as shop) where, of course, you can also get money out.

Wylam has a small **railway station** on the Newcastle to Carlisle line. Go North East's No 684 **bus** service also calls here as does their 686 between Hexham and Newcastle; see pp48-51 for further details.

For **B&B** there's *Wormald House* (☎ 07815 903167 or ☎ 07850 322406, ☐ wormaldhouse.co.uk; 1D/1T/1T, all en suite; ✉; Ⓛ). They have drying facilities and, if prearranged, will pick you up at Heddon and drop you off the next morning. B&B costs £47.50-60pp (sgl occ £75).

Further up the hill, the *Black Bull* (☎ 01661-853112, ☐ blackbullrestaurants.com, **fb**; 1S/4D/1Tr/2Qd, all en suite; Ⓛ; 🐾) has rooms starting from £25pp (sgl £35). Note that they don't provide breakfast. **Food** (Mon-Fri 4-9pm, Sat noon-9pm, Sun noon-4pm) is served both in the pub or from their neighbouring takeaway outlet, *Paul's To Go* (☎ 01661-853112, **fb**; Mon-Fri 4-9pm, Sat 9am-9pm, Sun 9am-4pm). By Wormald House is *Wood Oven* (☎ 01661-852552, **fb**; Wed-Sat 5-9pm, Sun 6-8.30pm), a pizza place with some very unusual pizzas (squid & octopus, and wild garlic & courgette being just two examples). Prices start at about £10.

At the other end of the village, just across the river by the railway station, *Boathouse* (☎ 01661-853431, **fb**) is renowned for its award-winning cask ales (it often wins the CAMRA Northumberland Pub of the Year).

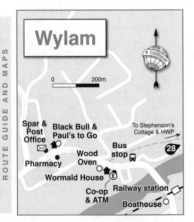

Wylam

0   200m

Spar & Post Office

Black Bull & Paul's to Go

To Stephenson's Cottage & HWP

Bus stop

28

Pharmacy

Wood Oven

Wormald House

Co-op & ATM

Railway station

Boathouse

The Wylam Waggonway Walkers now take the Wylam Waggonway (see Map 28, p183) for a couple of miles. The waggonway is named after the village/suburb at its western end. Although Wylam is about 20 minutes' walk from the trail, thanks to the popularity of the walk, and the relative paucity of accommodation options in Heddon-on-the-Wall, the village still sees a steady stream of hikers looking for somewhere to stay on either their first or last night.

Tyne Riverside Country Park The Tyne Riverside Country Park (Map 28-29) provides a pleasant and peaceful riparian stroll with dog-walkers, joggers, butterflies, swans and the last (or first) truly mature trees on the trail as company. There's also a pleasant café, the *Hedley Riverside Coffee Shop* (Map 29; ☎ 07858 474212, **fb**; summer 10am-4pm, winter 10am-2pm; 🐾), a most welcome spot on an inclement day – and they allow dogs, which is always a bonus.

A few metres further back from the river, those who don't want this stage to end may like to consider calling in at *The Keelman* (Map 29; ☎ 0191-267 1689, 🖥 biglampbrewers.co.uk). It's one of the best pubs on the route; a vast place with real ales, its own micro-brewery, called **Big Lamp Brewery**, and **accommodation** (☎ 0191-267 1689, 🖥 keelmanslodge.co.uk; 8D in Salmon Cottage, 5Tr/1Qd in Keelman's Lodge, all en suite; 👜; Ⓛ; 🐾). They charge from £36pp (sgl occ £56), with breakfast £9.95 extra. The pub serves **food** (Mon-Fri 7-10am & noon-8pm, Sat to 9pm, Sun 8-10am & noon-8pm) including breakfast. Non-residents can also have breakfast if booked in advance.

Lemington & Denton Dene The trail continues to seek out the city's greener elements amidst the noisy urban sprawl, hopping from one green space to the next. Between the country park and the city centre this often means following the disused railway-turned-footpath, particularly through the suburbs of Scotswood, Lemington and Newburn. Though the path threads its way through a spaghetti-like mix of major traffic arteries, factory showrooms and noisy warehouses, the walk itself is pleasant enough, with the worst industrial excesses hidden behind a screen of trees. Sights are few on this stretch but do note the **Lemington Glass Cone** (Map 29). This marvellous late 18th-century cone-shaped brick chimney derives its name from its former purpose as a furnace for making glass. Almost opposite, the **café**, *Maximo's Deli* (☎ 07710-401776; **fb**; Mon-Fri 9am-3pm) in **Lemington Centre** (☎ 0191-264 1959) is a nice (and very cheap) little stop serving snacks and lunches.

Arriva/Stagecoach's 684/685 22 **buses** call at Lemington.

Dunston Coal Staithes The dominant architectural feature of this section lies across the river on the south bank. These are Dunston Coal Staithes (Map 31), which were used to load coal from the collieries onto the colliers – the ships that would transport the cargo south to London and elsewhere.

The glorious walk along the Tyne The walk now takes you past such modern Tyneside icons as **BALTIC** and **Gateshead Millennium Bridge** (Map 31 p191) – the most easterly of the city's seven bridges (see box p207). Keep a look out for seals swimming in this stretch of the Tyne. They have been spotted

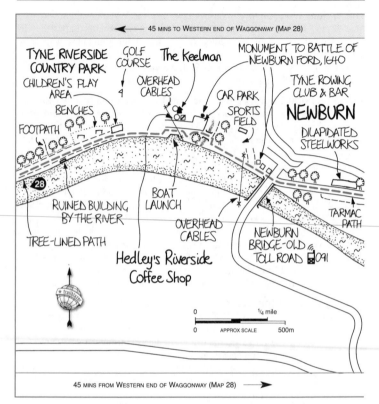

45 MINS TO WESTERN END OF WAGGONWAY (MAP 28)

TYNE RIVERSIDE COUNTRY PARK
GOLF COURSE
The Keelman
MONUMENT TO BATTLE OF NEWBURN FORD, 1640
CHILDREN'S PLAY AREA
OVERHEAD CABLES
CAR PARK
TYNE ROWING CLUB & BAR
BENCHES
SPORTS FIELD
NEWBURN
FOOTPATH
DILAPIDATED STEELWORKS
28
RUINED BUILDING BY THE RIVER
BOAT LAUNCH
OVERHEAD CABLES
TARMAC PATH
TREE-LINED PATH
NEWBURN BRIDGE-OLD TOLL ROAD 091
Hedley's Riverside Coffee Shop

0   1/4 mile
0   APPROX SCALE   500m

45 MINS FROM WESTERN END OF WAGGONWAY (MAP 28)

by hikers close to St Peter's Marina, as well as by the bridge at Wylam. The heart of the city centre is marked by Castle Keep (see p209 and map p201), situated on the site of the Roman fort of Pons Aelius. It may seem curious that one of the Wall's seventeen Roman forts stood here, when a second one lay only a two-hour walk away at Segedunum. There is a very sensible reason for this. Though the milecastles and turrets were evenly spaced out along the Wall, the forts were not, being built instead at strategic points along it – in this case, to overlook one of the two Wall bridges to cross the Tyne. This bridge would have stood where Swing Bridge now stands though, alas, nothing remains today.

Walker Riverside Park This is an appropriate name for a park (Map 32 & 33) near the end (or start) of a national trail. However, it must be said that, though not without interest, this is not the most auspicious part of the trail. It's not the way the trail leads through the industrial heart of the city that disappoints; if you're in the right frame of mind a short walk through an entirely

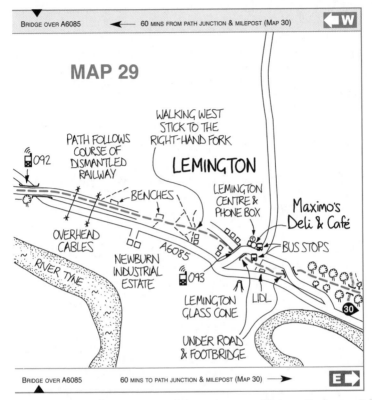

MAP 29

WALKING WEST
STICK TO THE
RIGHT-HAND FORK

LEMINGTON

PATH FOLLOWS
COURSE OF
DISMANTLED
RAILWAY

092

BENCHES

LEMINGTON
CENTRE &
PHONE BOX

Maximo's
Deli & Café

OVERHEAD
CABLES

A6085

BUS STOPS

RIVER TYNE

NEWBURN
INDUSTRIAL
ESTATE

093

LEMINGTON
GLASS CONE

LIDL

30

UNDER ROAD
& FOOTBRIDGE

man-made landscape can be as diverting as any countryside romp. But hemmed in by warehouses and the backs of housing estates, there's little industry, or indeed anything to see. Unfortunately, one or two hikers have also been subjected to insults and threats from local kids on this stretch and have written to say that they felt threatened in these areas. The abuse, as far as we know, has only ever been verbal and seems to be quite rare, but is unpleasant to hear about nonetheless.

The site of the original Roman baths In 2014 the site of the original Roman baths was discovered, and you can now visit them (see Map 33, p194). First discovered by John Hodgson in 1814, his description of the baths' whereabouts was imprecise enough that subsequently nobody could be really sure of their exact location. The closure and destruction of the neighbouring Ship Inn, however, gave archaeologists the opportunity to search the ground beneath. Sure enough, in 2014, exactly 200 years after Hodgson's initial discovery, the baths were excavated once more – providing a valuable illustration on this trip that the history of the Wall, and the study and discovery of it, is still very much alive and ongoing.

The end – or start – of the trail Standing sentinel by the official end of the trail is a sculpture of an invented Roman centurion, called Sentius Tectonicus. The sculpture overlooks the remnants of the fort and that is now the official eastern end of the walk.

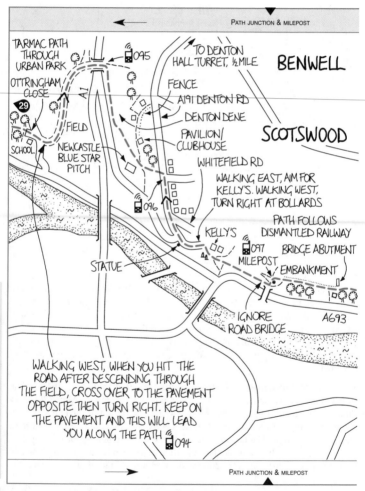

ROUTE GUIDE AND MAPS

Whatever way you're travelling, before you leave Segedunum don't forget to **stamp your Hadrian's Wall passport** at reception or, if they're closed, at the box by the rear entrance to the museum or at Asda across the road. (Segedunum also sell the passport, badge and certificate.)

And if you started your walk in Bowness? Well, that's it. You've made it. It's done.

All done.

Wall: done.

Well done!

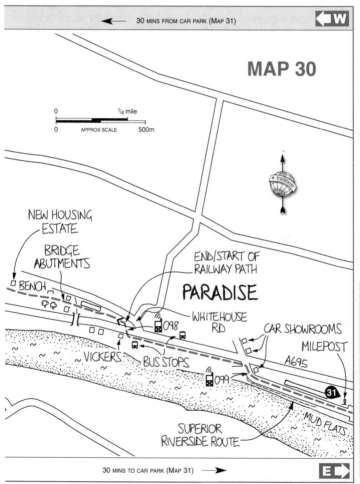

SEGEDUNUM   **[see Map 33, p194]**
(☎ 0191-278 4217; 🖳 segedunumromanfort.org.uk; Apr-Sep daily 10am-5pm,
winter hours check website; £5.95)

Segedunum provides a fitting farewell for those who are finishing the hike; or,
for those just about to embark on their own Roman-themed roaming, a good
introduction to the kind of Wall fort that will become oh-so-familiar as you
progress along the trail.

　　Translating as 'Strong Fort', Segedunum is the last Wall fort heading east;
instead of continuing from here to the sea, the Wall took a sharp turn south at
this point, heading off from the fort's south-eastern corner through the now-
defunct shipyard and down to the water's edge. You can see a little bit of this
Wall poking through the fort's southern fence, just a few metres from the
start/end of the trail.

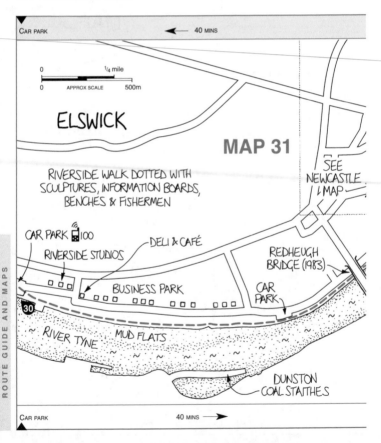

ROUTE GUIDE AND MAPS

At first it seems strange that the Wall doesn't actually cover the entire breadth of the country. After all, what is the point of building a wall right across an island if you're not going to finish the job, thereby allowing the locals to sneak around one end? But with Arbeia Fort (see p212) guarding the river's mouth from the other side of the Tyne and this fort watching over the land to the east on this side, it's fair to say that little could cross undetected from one side – of either the Tyne or the Wall – to the other. In fact, Segedunum was actually something of an afterthought; originally, the Wall terminated at Pons Aelius (see p210) and only later did they decide to extend it a further three miles east to Segedunum.

Today, little remains of the original Roman fort which, in its heyday, would have held 600 men. The Saxons proved pretty efficient at carting off the masonry for their own building projects, such as Bede's monastery at Jarrow.

Newcastle's Great North Museum: Hancock has proved equally efficient at appropriating much of the remainder to fill their display cases.

But what makes the fort here so appealing is not so much what the Romans left behind but the way the little that has survived has been presented. From the 35m-high Panorama Tower, which provides great views over the site to the clear information boards, this fort is a good example of how history should be told. And whilst some may complain at the slightly child-centric **galleries**, with their games and quizzes designed to keep young minds interested (including the opportunity to dress like a Roman emperor!), many will find it stimulating and useful and the reconstructed cavalry barrack (complete with horse!) gives a fair idea of what living conditions were like on the Wall.

Highlights of Segedunum include the aforementioned **Panorama Tower**, where you get a better idea of just how large the fort was (note that the fort originally covered the large paved area to the north of the main road too, which today is outside the official site), as well as the only stone toilet seat surviving from Roman Britain. Sadly, the actual site itself is rather disappointing. As the most pilfered and excavated of all the forts, we perhaps shouldn't be surprised that there's almost nothing left above ground, and as you survey the site from

the Panorama Tower you'll see that the tallest items are actually the interpretation boards dotted around the fort; boards that do their best to provide an explanation of the rows of gravel and pebbles patterning the floor which mark out the footprints of various Roman buildings. Even the reconstructed Roman baths, in the south-western corner of the site, are in a parlous state, have been closed for several years and are unlikely to open again any time soon.

The ticket also includes entry to the 20m-long **reconstructed Wall**, which lies outside the site just to the north-west. Less eye-catching, but of greater historical significance, is the 50m-stretch of **Wall foundations** which lies beside it and which was excavated in 2016. On the other side of the reconstructed Wall are the remains of **Wallsend Colliery B pit**, an old colliery shaft which dates from 1781 and which was rediscovered during the Segedunum excavations.

Travelling between Wallsend and Newcastle There are several ways of travelling between the eastern end of the walk at Wallsend and the centre of Newcastle. Most people choose to use public transport (see p198) and the Wallsend Metro station is conveniently close, as is the adjacent bus station

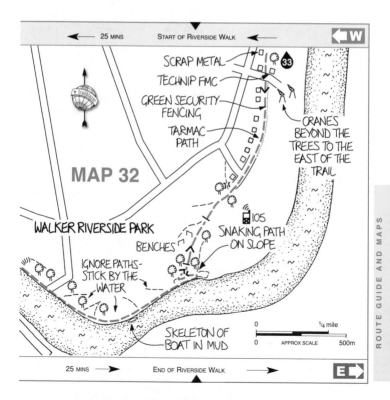

(which is helpfully signed in Latin – *Raedarum Publicarum Statio*. Someone in charge of signage at the city council clearly has a sense of humour, for other examples include *Noli Fumare* – 'No Smoking' – and *Suggestus 1* – 'Platform 1'.) One of the most useful bus services is Stagecoach's No 22 (2-6/hr) which goes from Wallsend Forum (High Street West, near the Metro) to Grainger St (near Central Station).

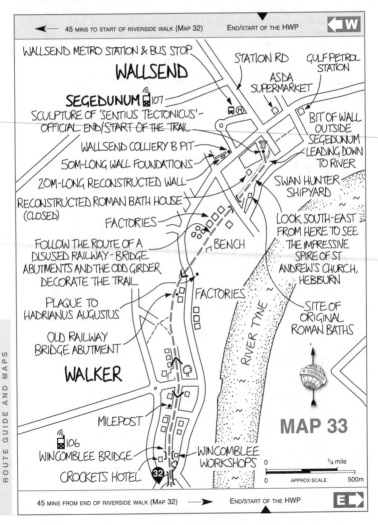

45 MINS TO START OF RIVERSIDE WALK (MAP 32)   END/START OF THE HWP   W

WALLSEND METRO STATION & BUS STOP
WALLSEND
STATION RD   GULF PETROL STATION
ASDA SUPERMARKET
SEGEDUNUM 107
SCULPTURE OF 'SENTIUS TECTONICUS' – OFFICIAL END/START OF THE TRAIL
BIT OF WALL OUTSIDE SEGEDUNUM LEADING DOWN TO RIVER
WALLSEND COLLIERY B PIT
50M-LONG WALL FOUNDATIONS
20M-LONG RECONSTRUCTED WALL
SWAN HUNTER SHIPYARD
RECONSTRUCTED ROMAN BATH HOUSE (CLOSED)
FACTORIES
BENCH
LOOK SOUTH-EAST FROM HERE TO SEE THE IMPRESSIVE SPIRE OF ST ANDREW'S CHURCH, HEBBURN
FOLLOW THE ROUTE OF A DISUSED RAILWAY – BRIDGE ABUTMENTS AND THE ODD GIRDER DECORATE THE TRAIL
FACTORIES
RIVER TYNE
SITE OF ORIGINAL ROMAN BATHS
PLAQUE TO HADRIANUS AUGUSTUS
OLD RAILWAY BRIDGE ABUTMENT
WALKER
trailblazer
MILEPOST
MAP 33
106
WINCOMBLEE BRIDGE
CROCKETS HOTEL   32
WINCOMBLEE WORKSHOPS
0   1/4 mile
0   APPROX SCALE   500m

45 MINS FROM END OF RIVERSIDE WALK (MAP 32)   →   END/START OF THE HWP   E

Starting from Wallsend

Start here if you're walking Hadrian's Wall Path from Wallsend (Newcastle) to Bowness. Look for the **W ←** symbol with shaded **route overview** text (as over-leaf) and follow the **W ←** symbol with the shaded timings text on one edge of each map, working back through the book. The shaded text route overviews describe the trail between significant places and are written for walking the path

❏ SWAN HUNTER SHIPYARD   [see Map 33]

Though not quite as venerable as the nearby Roman ruins of Segedunum, the Swan Hunter Shipyard, with its iconic, multi-coloured cranes puncturing the skyline of north Tyneside, was nevertheless a vital part of the region's history. Unfortunately, it appears that this history has come to an end. In 2007, Swan Hunter's boss Jaap Kroes declared shipbuilding to be an industry with no future, and put the yard – and its cranes – up for sale. Sold to North Tyneside Council and One NorthEast in 2009, by 2013 it was being cleared up in preparation for development, with the council unveil-ing plans in 2015 to turn the 32-acre (13-hectare) site into a centre for the renewable energy, advanced engineering and offshore sectors.

The sale was a huge body blow to both Wallsend and the city of Newcastle as a whole, an area that had suffered from more than its fair share of economic woes through the decades. Though it must be said that on this occasion the decision to close the site permanently wasn't entirely surprising, given its dramatic decline. Between 1993 and 2003 not one new ship was launched from Swan Hunter's yard, and a deci-sion by the Ministry of Defence to hand over the work on an unfinished ship at Swan Hunter to the BAE Systems site at Govan in Glasgow in 2006 resulted in the ship-yard being mothballed. Attempts to secure new contracts or change tack and become a breaking business both failed, and the managers were left with no choice but to lay off all but 10 of Swan Hunter's remaining 260 workers.

All of which seems a long way away from the time when Britain led the world in shipbuilding and the Tyne produced a staggering 25% of the world's ships. Many of the world's most famous and innovative vessels were created at Swan Hunter dur-ing the 20th century, including the Cunard liner *Mauretania*, a revolutionary steamship launched in 1906 that was, for a time, not only the world's largest ocean liner but also its fastest.

In recent years, however, the stories coming out of the Swan Hunter shipyard tended to be about job cuts and industrial disputes as the yard struggled to make its mark in the new globalised market. Jaap Kroes's decision to invest in the shipyard in 1995 brought a glimmer of hope and for a while, as several refurbishment contracts rolled in, it appeared as if the good times were back once more. But when the *Lyme Bay* was taken to Scotland to be fitted out, it was the first time a ship had left Swan Hunter unfinished, and many then saw the writing on the wall.

On a lighter note, there are plans to rejuvenate the site, and the upper floors of the Swan Hunter offices are gradually being transformed into a Centre for Innovation (CFI) in an attempt to give it new purpose for the 21st century.

ROUTE GUIDE AND MAPS

from east to west. For **map profiles** see the colour pages and **overview maps** at the end of the book. For an overview of this information see the 'Itineraries' box on p35 and the 'Village facilities' table on p33.

W ← WALLSEND TO HEDDON-ON-THE-WALL   [MAPS 33-28]

There's nothing wrong with this **15-mile (24.2km; 5hrs 10mins)** first stage, but don't go expecting to see much in the way of the Wall. True, the day is bookended by two significant chunks of it. The first, at Segedunum, is the only remaining piece of the Wall that originally ran down from the fort to the Tyne, and which now stands just over the railings outside the fort grounds. As the easternmost part of the Wall still in existence, this is an appropriate place to begin. And there's another significant slab of Wall at the aptly named Heddon-on-the-Wall at this stage's end. But you won't see any remnants of Wall in between. Indeed, the path makes no attempt to follow the line of the Wall on this first stage, opting instead for a gentle riparian stroll through the very heart of the city. (Incidentally, note that, through all of Newcastle, the trail is called **Hadrian's Way** and this is what you'll see on the signs.)

It's an interesting first stage, one where you often follow railway when you're not following river. The disused train line that you walk along for several miles was once an extension of the Blyth and Tyne Railway, and by the side of the trail are the abutments of old bridges and the ironmongery of various parts of the railway, now finding secondary employment as makeshift stools and benches.

Having returned to the Tyne to amble through a pleasant countryside park, you'll find that it's a bit of an exhausting schlep to the top of the hill but **Heddon-on-the-Wall** (see p180), with its pubs, accommodation and, best of all, a decent strip of Hadrian's Wall, is a worthy reward at the end of a long but interesting first day. You'll notice over the next few days that the Wall turns up in the unlikeliest of places, and it's no different here: lying parallel to the busy B6528, this portion is, at over 100m, the longest section of *broad* Wall remaining. As you'll see on the next stage, the Romans soon reduced their building ambitions, for although they still had the foundations for a broad Wall, west of here they built a narrow Wall on top of them. The flat circular platform that's incorporated into the Wall is a kiln that post-dates the Roman era.

[*Next route overview p178*]

City guide

The perfect venue for a post-trek knees-up (or a fittingly grand location to begin an epic walk), Newcastle is a large, buzzing city with plenty of history, a thriving food-and-drink scene and a pleasantly attractive riverside waterfront.

If you're arriving here by train at the start of your trek, the first thing you'll see as you cross the Tyne is an eclectic mix of river bridges, followed by an untidy jumble of roofs; an interesting but somewhat messy skyline that belies the uniform elegance of much of the city centre with its stylish Classical 19th-century façades interspersed here and there with the latest in cutting-edge municipal designs. Yet Newcastle is like that; a city that is forever defying those who dismiss it as merely a home for brown ale, football and fun-runs. As the starting point for a major trek it's ideal: functional, convenient, with great amenities and plenty to keep you occupied round-the-clock. The Great North Museum: Hancock, is also the perfect introduction to the Wall (and like just about every other museum and gallery in the city, it's free), while if you are coming to the end of your Hadrian's Wall odyssey and Newcastle is your last stop, there couldn't be a better place to celebrate than the revamped Quayside, home to numerous cafés, bistros and bars.

ARRIVAL & DEPARTURE

Most visitors will first set foot on Newcastle ground at its rather grand **Central Station**. Built in 1850, the station stands in the heart of a metropolis that will forever be associated with George Stephenson (see box p181), the 'Father of the Railways' who was born in nearby Wylam. The terminus, lying just to the north of the River Tyne, has cafés, ATMs and its own Metro station. The **National Express coach station** stands a five-minute walk to the west on St James Boulevard; note, however, that **the ticket office here is now closed.**

DFDS **ferry terminal** (Port of Tyne International Passenger Terminal) is 7 miles (11km) east of the city centre. The DFDS Seaways Bus (💻 dfds.com/en/passenger-ferries then search 'bus transfers') waits for disembarking passengers outside the ferry terminal before conveying them to Bewick St in front of Central Station.

Going the other way, the bus departs from Bewick St at 2.45 and 3.45pm. The price is currently £6 each way and the journey time is 20-30 minutes.

The **airport** lies 25 minutes away from the city centre by Metro; the best way into the city. However, if you prefer the bus, Stagecoach's X78 (Mon-Sat 2/hr, Sun 1/hr) stops on the road outside the airport on its way to and from Eldon Square Bus Station.

TRANSPORT

Within the city

Newcastle, or at least its centre, is a fairly compact place and the chances are you'll be walking most of the time. The main local **bus** station (Eldon Square) can be accessed through Eldon Square Shopping Centre, which fronts Eldon Square itself. A second, Haymarket, is 100 metres to the north. There are lots of bus services from Newcastle to places on or near the Path. Most go as far as Hexham (Go North East's Nos 10, 74 & 684), but Arriva's/Stagecoach's No 685 goes all the way to Carlisle. See pp48-51 for further information.

There is also a pretty efficient **Metro** (underground) service connecting most parts of the city, which runs daily from approximately 5am to midnight. A Metro map can be found in most brochures and, of course, in the stations themselves.

Shields Ferry costs £2.10 one-way (day ticket £3.40) and runs daily (Mon-Sat from about 6.45am to 8pm but until 10-11pm on Thur-Sat; Sun from about 10.30am to 6pm; 2/hr; approx 7 mins).

❏ **WILLIAM ARMSTRONG –**
THE FORGOTTEN MAN OF THE INDUSTRIAL REVOLUTION

Though something of a local hero, William Armstrong's star has faded when compared to the lustre of his near contemporary, George Stephenson (see box p181). Yet the impact of both men on the history of Newcastle, Britain, and the wider world was equally enormous.

However high we climb in the pursuit of knowledge we shall still see heights above us, and the more we extend our view, the more conscious we shall be of the immensity which lies beyond.
William Armstrong

Born in 1810 in Pleasant Row, in the Shieldfield area of Newcastle, William George Armstrong's first calling was as a solicitor, a vocation in which he showed enough talent and ambition to become a partner in a legal practice in the city. Yet throughout this time Armstrong's first love was not the law of man but the immutable laws of science and, in particular, engineering. Indeed, he used to give lectures at Newcastle's Lit and Phil Society on this very subject, and it wasn't long before he was turning his hand to constructing the machines he talked about.

His first major project was a hydro-electric generator, which he unveiled to the world in 1842. Switching from hydro-electrics to hydraulics, just four years later Armstrong was persuading a number of wealthy local businessmen to back his plans to develop hydraulic cranes, which would be powered with the assistance of the Whittle Dene Water Company, a firm that he himself had helped to set up a few years previously. (Whittle Dene Reservoir is on the trail, see Map 26, p177). The result of

For the **Metro**, fares (£2.30-3.90 single) depend on the distance travelled. Alternatively, you may wish to buy a **Metro Day Ticket** (£3.60-5.70, depending on the number of zones covered), which enables unlimited travel on the Metro and the Shields Ferry. Or there's the **Network One Day Rover** (£7.80), which allows unlimited one-day access on all Metro, ferry and bus lines.

General information about all public transport in and around Newcastle can be found on **Nexus** (🖳 www.nexus.org.uk), the organisation responsible for all public transport in Tyne and Wear.

If the trial (started in 2021) has been extended or the scheme made permanent, you may also see orange **e-scooters** pootling around the city. There's a safety helmet attached to the scooter that's released electronically at the start of your journey. The e-scooter has two gears, a top-speed of 15mph, and stops working once you go beyond the city centre. At the time of writing, the cost was £1 to unlock the e-scooter and 18 pence per minute after that; it's 30p cheaper if you park in one of the designated scooter parking zones. A driving licence is required and the usual drink-driving rules apply.

SERVICES

Tourist information
Somewhat surprisingly for a city of this size, there isn't a tourist information centre, but you can get comprehensive tourist information online at 🖳 new castlegateshead.com.

---

all this endeavour was the Newcastle Cranage company, based at Elswick, which later became known as Armstrong's Factory – as mentioned in the song *Blaydon Races*. The manufacture of cranes became the cornerstone both of his industrial empire and of the Industrial Revolution itself; Isambard Kingdom Brunel was just one of his regular customers.

Yet Armstrong wasn't finished yet; with the advent of the Crimean War he became involved in the development of arms, manufacturing an 18lb breach-loading gun that was sold all over the world. Indeed, such was the popularity of his weapons that *both* sides in the American Civil War were armed with Armstrong's artillery. He also developed an interest in bridges, constructing Newcastle's Swing Bridge and much of London's Tower Bridge.

There were, of course, considerable financial benefits to his success. By 1850 over 300 men were employed in Armstrong's Elswick factory, bringing unprecedented prosperity to the area. (The modern incarnation of his company, Vickers, formerly Vickers Armstrong, still operates in the area and lies just off the path; see Map 30, p185.) The country at large also benefited, with Armstrong gifting his patents to the British government, an ostensibly selfless act which was nevertheless rewarded with a knighthood. His success also enabled him to own most of Jesmond Dene, as well as a magnificent mansion at Cragside. But as was typical of the man, despite the riches, he continued to invent, even though he became less involved in the company that he founded. It comes as no surprise, therefore, to find that Cragside has a place in history as the first house in the world to be lit by hydro-electric power.

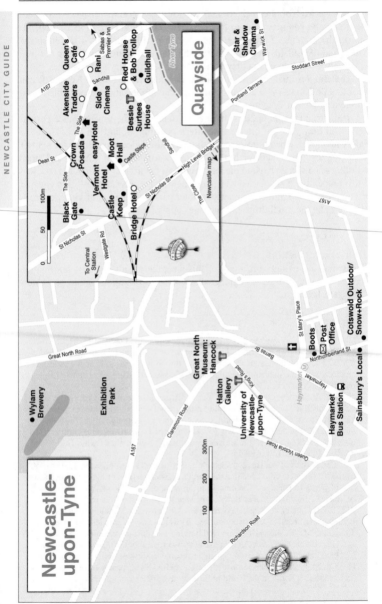

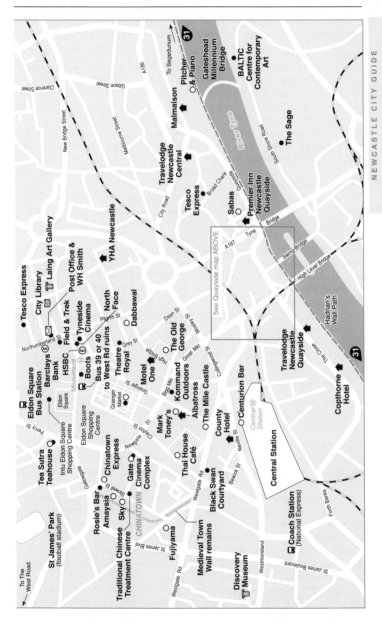

You'll also find leaflets at information points and kiosks dotted around the city, including at some bus stations and the railway station.

Other services

You'll have no trouble finding a **bank/ATM** in the city centre: they're everywhere. There are also plenty of **post office** branches including one in WH Smith on Northumberland St (Mon-Sat 9am-5.30pm, Sun 11am-3pm) and a second, slightly further north on the same street, with extended opening hours (Mon-Sat 6am-7pm, Sun 6.30am-5.15pm).

For self-catering or sandwich supplies, either head to one of the numerous **supermarkets** dotted around town – there's a Sainsbury's Local (daily 7am-10pm) on Northumberland St, a Tesco Express just off the Path on Broad Chare and another on Saville Row, off Northumberland St (both daily 7am-11pm), and a Waitrose (Mon-Sat 8am-8pm, Sun 11am-5pm) inside Eldon Square Shopping Centre. Alternatively, visit the fabulous **Grainger Market** (Mon-Sat 9am-5.30pm), a traditional covered market with cafés, delicatessens, fishmongers, bakers, fruit-and-veg stalls, and even a Chinese dumplings bar. It also boasts one of the original M&S Penny Bazaar stalls.

There are several **outdoor/camping/trekking shops** in town, including, on Northumberland St, both Field & Trek (which is inside Sports Direct; Mon-Sat 9am-7pm, Sun 11am-5pm), and a large branch of Cotswold (Mon-Wed, Fri & Sat 9am-7pm, Thur to 8pm, Sun 11am-5pm). Round the corner on Blackett St there's a North Face (Mon-Fri 9.30am-6.30pm, Sat 9am-6pm, Sun 11am-5pm). There's also a military-gear camping shop called Kommand Outdoors (Mon-Sat 9-4pm) on Bigg Mkt.

For **chemists** there's Boots, with branches all over the city, including near Monument and Haymarket Metro stations.

WHERE TO STAY   [see map pp200-1]

Some places do not accept one-night bookings on a Saturday night, though the hostels and budget hotels do. Note that rates are very variable, depending on the day of the week or the time of year, especially in the budget hotels.

Hostels

Remember that if you book well in advance you may be able to get a room in a hotel chain such as Travelodge for about the same price as you would pay to stay in a hostel dormitory.

The more central of Newcastle's two hostels is the 176-bed **Albatross** (☎ 0191-233 1330, 🖳 albatrossnewcastle.co.uk; 2- to 12-bed dorms), on Grainger St, with free tea and coffee, kitchen, and a satellite TV and pool table in the comfy lounge. It's housed inside the 150-year-old building of a former bank so has some character, although the rooms themselves are spartan to say the least. The cost of a bed (£17-27.90pp) depends on when you stay (Fri & Sat nights are more expensive) and the size of the dorm.

The other option, also pretty central, is the **Newcastle YHA** (☎ 0191-8141878, 0345-260 2583; 🖳 yha.org.uk/hostel/yha-newcastle-central; 238 beds in 52 rooms, shared dorms sleep 4-8; private rooms sleep 1-14, all en suite) at 17 Carliol Square. It's a pleasant place but note **there is no kitchen**. There are laundry facilities, however, and the good-value Carliol Square Café attached to the hostel. It's possible to get beds for as little as £10 here (or £14.50pp in a twin) but on a Friday the cheapest is nearer £20, and on Saturday £30.

Hotels You can call them charmless, you can criticise the uniform styling and soulless rooms – but you can't argue with the fact that the nationwide chains offer the best-value accommodation near the trail, at least if you book far enough in advance.

There are two very convenient branches of the Travelodge chain, with the *Newcastle Quayside Travelodge* (☎ 0871-9846 524, 🖳 travelodge.co.uk; 203D or Tr, all en suite, 🍷; wi-fi £3 for 24hrs; 🐾), on the Quayside, slightly closer to the Path (and slightly more expensive too, with room rates from £30.99) than the *Newcastle Central Travelodge* (☎ 0871-984 6164; from £24.99) branch, even though the latter is only a two-minute walk from the riverfront. Breakfast at either place costs £8.75.

Between the two Travelodges, by the foot of the Tyne Bridge on Lombard St, is a branch of Travelodge's near rival: *Premier Inn Newcastle Quayside* (see inset map; ☎ 0333-321 1347 or premium rate 0871-527 8804, 🖳 premierinn .com; 133D/19T, all en suite; 🍷) is central and offers early booking deals from £35 for a double, although rack rates are more like £60-85 for a room.

Another cheap option is *Easy Hotel* (see inset map; ☎ 0843-902 7007, 🖳 easyhotel.com; 104D or T, all en suite), which has a branch in the heart of the Quayside action, close to the best pub in town (Crown Posada; see Where to eat). The rooms are small and basic but it's still good value when you consider you can sometimes pay as little as £19.99 per room, though note that the cheapest ones are interior rooms without windows. Breakfast is not available here.

Right by the Path is *Copthorne Hotel* (☎ 0191-222 0333, 🖳 millennium hotels.com; 156D or T, all en suite, 🍷) which sits in a great location on The Close, right on the Tyne and just a couple of minutes west of the fun at the Quayside. Ugly as sin on one side, the side facing the water is better and the interior is decent, with rooms (all overlooking the water) equipped with everything you'd expect from a hotel of this standard. There's also a gym and a restaurant. Rates start at £37.50pp (sgl occ full room rate). Breakfast is extra.

Perhaps at the top of the pile of these waterfront properties, is sophisticated *Malmaison* (☎ 0191-389 8627, 🖳 malmaison.com/locations/newcastle;

📋 **WHERE TO STAY: THE DETAILS**

Unless specified, B&B-style accommodation is either en suite or has private facilities; 🍷 means at least one room has a bath; Ⓛ means a packed lunch can be prepared if arranged in advance; 🐾 signifies that dogs are welcome in at least one room but also subject to prior arrangement, an additional charge may also be payable; **fb** indicates a Facebook page. See also p86.

122D or T, all en suite, ⬤; 🐾) housed in the old Co-operative building on the Quayside overlooking the Millennium Bridge. Facilities are top-notch. Weekday/weekend rack rates start at £42.50/75pp (sgl occ full room rate).

The classy-looking *Vermont Hotel* (see inset map; ☎ 0191-233 1010, 🖥 vermont-hotel.com; 73D/27T, all en suite; ⬤), up by Castle Keep, is in a central yet quiet location beside the castle. The rooms are very smart and well equipped; the hotel offers 24-hour room service, has a restaurant, a couple of bars and a fitness centre. Rates change daily, but expect to pay at least £32.50pp (sgl occ full room rate), though the normal room rate is more likely to be double that, and breakfast is extra.

Moving to the town centre, funky and slick *Motel One* (☎ 0191-211 1090, 🖥 motel-one.com/en/hotels/newcastle; 222D, all en suite; 🐾) is a centrally located boutique-type hotel in a quiet lane off Bigg Mkt. Rates start at £34.50pp (sgl occ from £69). The continental breakfast buffet costs £9.50pp extra; the cocktails in the lounge bar get rave reviews.

Boasting 'Victorian grandeur & style', *County Hotel* (☎ 0191-731 6670, 🖥 countyhotel.co.uk; 13S/94D/7D or T/14T all en suite, ⬤), on Neville St opposite the Central Station entrance, resides in a 19th-century building. Their tariff is variable and can be as low as £36pp (sgl/sgl occ £63), but rates tend to start at around £50pp. Breakfast costs £10pp.

WHERE TO EAT AND DRINK

Food and drink choices are excellent in Newcastle, as you'd expect from a city of this size. There are plenty of cafés and pubs, as well as some decent restaurants, and even a small Chinatown. You can also eat at the wonderful **Grainger Market** (see p202).

Cafés & teahouses

Underneath the shadow of iconic Tyne Bridge, *Queen's* (see inset map; Mon, Wed, Fri 6.30am-3pm, Sat from 7am, Sun from 7.30am; 🐾) is housed on the ground floor of a delightful, wedge-shaped heritage building that's squeezed tightly underneath the northern approach of the bridge, on a quiet street corner at No 1 Queen St. It's a traditional no-frills but somehow stylish café that's been serving its astonishingly good-value breakfasts (from £2.95) to hungry punters for years. Walkers who like to make an early start will appreciate that they open at 6.30am most days.

Tea Sutra Teahouse (🖥 sutratea.com, **fb**; Mon-Sat noon-5pm) is a tea specialist which promises 'no coffee, no tea bags, no wi-fi', instead preferring to focus on quality loose-leaf teas (£3-4pp per pot) and good old-fashioned conversation (free). They also serve health-conscious salads, soups and sandwich wraps, plus homemade dairy-free cakes.

For a more straightforward coffee and sandwich, try *Mark Toney* (☎ 0191-232 7794, 🖥 marktoney.co.uk, **fb**; Mon-Sat 8am-6pm, Sun 10am-6pm), next to Albatross Hostel on Grainger St. They serve all-day breakfast including tea or coffee for £6.30, and are particularly well known for their range of ice-creams, which is how they first started way back in 1892. You can also get great-value lunches here (sausage, egg and chips £5.50).

Pubs

Those who love traditional British pubs and quality cask ale should do their best to pay a visit to the wonderfully unassuming *Crown Posada* (see inset map; 🖥 crownposada.co.uk; Sun-Thur 11am-midnight, Fri & Sat to 2am), a narrow slip of a pub that's been in business since 1880. With wood-panelled walls, 19th century stained-glass windows and music played exclusively on a 1941 record player, this place oozes character. They don't serve food, and although they do stock lagers and a variety of other beers, around seven out of every ten pints they pour come from one of their six cask-ale taps. Ale drinkers rejoice!

Up by Castle Keep, the 100-year-old *Bridge Hotel* (see inset map; ☎ 0191-232 6400, 🖥 sjf.co.uk/our-pubs/bridge-hotel, **fb**; food Tue-Sun noon-3pm) also has a decent selection of cask ales, and serves good-value pub grub too. They also have stained-glass windows, although not quite as old or impressive as the ones found in the Posada.

The Red House/Bob Trollop (see inset map; ☎ 0191-261 1037, **fb**; food served daily noon-9pm) is a very popular pub close to Tyne Bridge. Again, there are plenty of real ales on tap, but they also have an unusual food menu, which includes nothing but pie, mash and peas (£9.95), albeit with numerous types of each. The pies are homemade, and rightly lauded. They have some road-side seating out the front too. *Akenside Traders* (see inset map; ☎ 0191-260 3175, **fb**; food Mon-Thur 11am-9pm, Fri-Sun 10am-9pm) does standard pub grub as well as drinks and has live sport on TV.

The city centre also has some excellent drinking establishments. Claiming the title of oldest pub in Newcastle is *The Old George* (☎ 0191-260 3035, 🖥 craft-pubs.co.uk/oldgeorgeinnnewcastle, **fb**; food Mon-Sat 11am-9pm, Sun to 8pm), established in 1582 and hidden down a narrow back-alley off High Bridge, which in turn is off Bigg Market. Another real-ale specialist with bags of character, but no food, is *Rosie's Bar* just on the edge of Chinatown.

For something more mainstream, the smart chain gastro-pub *Pitcher & Piano* (🖥 pitcherandpiano.com; 108 Quayside; Mon-Fri 11am-11pm, Sat & Sun from 10am) has a great location overlooking the river by the Millennium Bridge. They have an extensive menu with mains such as chorizo mac & cheese from £12.75.

Finally, if the lack of Hadrian's Wall in the city is getting you down, drown your sorrows with a consoling pint from the Wetherspoons-owned *Mile Castle* (☎ 0191-211 1160, 🖥 jdwetherspoon.com; Sun-Thur 8am-midnight, Fri & Sat to 2am) on the corner of Westgate Road and Grainger St, serving the usual wonderful-value food. It, together with *The Centurion Bar* (☎ 0191-261 6611, **fb**) at the Central Station, are two of the few places that celebrate the Wall that once passed through the city. The latter has a café attached but it's the opulent, high-ceilinged, exquisite bar (formerly the First Class waiting room) that is the real draw; indeed, it's almost a tourist attraction in its own right. If you're waiting for your train there's no better place to kill time.

NEWCASTLE CITY GUIDE

Restaurants

Sometimes, walking through the centre of Newcastle, it can feel like every second shop is an eatery or bar. Most of them, to be honest, are aiming to attract the hordes of local twenty- and thirty-somethings on a night out, rather than scruffy, limping hikers with rustling waterproof trousers and flecks of cow pat adorning their boots. But Newcastle is an international city, and there are some great restaurants serving food from round the world, too.

Quayside (see inset map, p200) is one of the nicest places to come for an evening meal. *Sabas* (☎ 0191-261 4415, 🖳 sabas.co.uk, **fb**; Sun & Thur noon-8.30pm, Fri & Sat to 9pm) is an 'Italian tapas', serving pasta for as little as £7, pizza from £10. There are several Indian restaurants too, with one of the more established being *Rani* (☎ 0191-260 2801, 🖳 ranirestaurant.co.uk, **fb**; daily 5.30-11.30pm), right under the Tyne Bridge. The menu contains few surprises but it's a welcoming place and the food is done well.

Moving to the centre of town at 69-75 High Bridge, off Grey St, you'll find *Dabbawal* (☎ 0191-232 5133, 🖳 dabbawal.com, **fb**; Mon-Thur noon-2.30pm & 5-10.30pm, Fri & Sat noon-11pm, Sun noon-10.30pm), an award-winning Indian restaurant which specialises in Indian street food such as delicious *masala dosas* (south-Indian savoury crêpes; £12.95), as well as more familiar Indian-restaurant curries.

Thai House Café (☎ 0191-261 5717, **fb**; Wed-Mon noon-3pm & 5-9pm) at 93 Clayton St is an excellent place serving refreshingly large portions of all your Thai favourites including seafood tom yum (noodle soup; £10.95).

If you have a hankering for food from even further east, you need to head to the western part of the city centre and **Chinatown**. Less of a 'town' than a single street (Stowell St, to be precise), Chinatown, which runs alongside the best-preserved stretch of Newcastle's **medieval Town Wall**, is nevertheless chock full of restaurants; some sit-down, some takeaway, and a couple with enticing all-you-can-eat deals that are perfect for that end-of-trek blowout.

Starting by the elaborate decorative Chinese archway at the northern end of Stowell St, the first place you reach is *China Town Express* (Sun-Thur 11.30am-10.30pm, Fri & Sat noon-midnight), a no-nonsense Chinese takeaway joint (there are one or two tables too) that offers Express Meal Deals with selected mains and soup for £8, and is often crammed with Chinese university students – always a good sign.

Further south, *Amaysia* (☎ 0191-242 2330, 🖳 amaysia.com; daily 11.30am-10pm) works to a typically vast Chinese menu although with an excellent selection of vegetarian options encompassing a range of tofu dishes (from £8.50). On the same side, *Sky* (☎ 0191-230 3288; daily 11.30am-11pm) is a Cantonese restaurant that's well regarded amongst the local Chinese population and includes some decent three-course set lunches (£12).

Just beyond Chinatown, opposite the south end of the street on Bath Lane, *Fujiyama* (☎ 0191-233 0189, 🖳 fujiyama.restaurant; Mon-Fri noon-2pm & 6-11pm, Sat noon-11pm, Sun noon-3pm & 6-11pm) is a Japanese teppanyaki restaurant with sushi from £3.80 and set menus for £23.90.

ENTERTAINMENT

Opened in 1837, the Grade I listed **Theatre Royal** (☎ 0191-232 7010, 🖳 theatre royal.co.uk; see map p201) is Newcastle's premier theatre. Productions include ballet, contemporary dance, drama, musicals and opera, and the Royal Shakespeare Company visits annually. Further south, across the river, **The Sage** (🖳 sagegateshead.com; see map p201) is an international music venue.

For the latest Hollywood blockbusters, head to **Gate Cinema** (☎ 0871 200 2000, 🖳 thegatenewcastle.co.uk/venues/cineworld; see map p201) in the city centre. For something more thought-provoking, seek out one of the city's independent cinemas: **Side Cinema** (☎ 0191-232 2208, 🖳 amber-online.com/side-cinema; see map p200), by the Quayside; the 1930s Art Deco **Tyneside Cinema** (☎ 0191-227 5500, 🖳 tynesidecinema.co.uk), near Monument; or the volunteer-run **Star & Shadow** (☎ 07938 257663, 🖳 starandshadow.org .uk) on Warwick St, just south of Jesmond.

Football fans wanting to take in a game at Newcastle United's iconic 52,000-seater stadium, **St James' Park** (see map p201), should check the club website (🖳 nufc.co.uk) for fixture details. Walk-in tickets are sometimes available from the matchday box office.

WHAT TO SEE AND DO

There's so much to see and do in Newcastle; the following is a brief overview of the city's major highlights, with a bias towards those with a Roman or Wall

---

❏ **THE TYNE BRIDGES** [see Map 31, p191]

Where once there was just one bridge across the Tyne in the place we now call Newcastle – the Roman Pons Aelius that remained until 1248 – today there are seven bridges within reasonable distance of each other in the city centre.

The most eye-catching is also the one furthest east, **Gateshead Millennium Bridge**, which, despite the name, was formally opened in May 2002 by the Queen. One of the smallest (126m long and just 50m above water) this footbridge, also known as the 'Winking Eye', is one of the most revolutionary and even has its own cleaning mechanism: when the bridge is raised the rubbish collects in special receptacles which are then emptied. It's worth seeing it lifting or, more accurately, tilting (contact ☎ 0191-433 2986 for times).

Heading west, the next bridge is the iconic **Tyne Bridge**, opened in 1928 by George V and looking for all the world like its contemporary, Sydney Harbour Bridge. After that you come to the comparatively small **Swing Bridge**, built on the site of the Roman Pons Aelius in 1876. As its name might suggest, it rotates through 90° to allow ships to pass through. Next there's the oldest and arguably most impressive of Newcastle's seven crossings, **High Level Bridge**, built by Robert Stephenson, the son of George, and opened by Queen Victoria in 1849. **Queen Elizabeth II Bridge**, which carries the Metro, comes next, followed by **King Edward VII Bridge**, built in nearby Middlesbrough and another railway bridge. Finally, **Redheugh Bridge** (pronounced 'Red-yuff') was built on the site of two previous bridges and was opened in 1983 by the late Diana, Princess of Wales.

connection. All these and more are stops on Go North East's **Toon Tour** (🖥 gonortheast.co.uk/toontour; late May to early Sept daily 10.05am-4.05pm, Apr to late May & late Sept weekends only, 2/hr; £12.50). The hop-on, hop-off tours visit all the major sites in a one-hour loop, starting and finishing at Central Station.

Great North Museum: Hancock   [see map p200]

The first place any self-respecting Wall-walker should head to is the rather clumsily titled Great North Museum: Hancock (☎ 0191-208 6765, 🖥 greatnorth museum.org.uk; Mon-Fri 10am-5pm, Sat to 4pm, Sun 11am-4pm; free) which houses the collections that were once scattered across various museums in the city, including the Museum of Antiquities and the Shefton Museum.

Occupying centre stage both on the ground floor and in Wall walkers' imaginations is the interactive model of Hadrian's Wall. Characters from Roman Britain discuss various topics such as construction, religion and defence of the Wall at the press of a button, while surrounding the model are various treasures dug up near the Wall and its accompanying forts. A highlight is an ivory folding knife in the shape of a gladiator found at South Shields.

Perhaps the most impressive items are the various pieces of jewellery. They include the gold Aemilia finger ring from Corbridge, dating back to between the

---

❏ THE WEST ROAD – THE REAL WALL ROUTE

Most people know that Hadrian's Wall did not follow the river, as the trail does, but originally ran through the heart of Newcastle. However, you'd struggle to find much in the way of evidence to back this up. On Westgate Rd, in the small **Black Swan courtyard** by a pottery, you'll find some stone foundations unearthed in 1985 by the potter himself, David Fry, that have been interpreted as belonging to a milecastle (though it must be pointed out that it doesn't actually lie where the milecastle around here would have been). It's marked on the map on p201 and in the courtyard you can read an account of its discovery. However, apart from this, and some of the stones of Castle Keep which were once part of the Wall's fabric, Hadrian's Wall is virtually invisible in Newcastle.

However, if you travel up West Rd, which follows the line of the Wall through the western half of the city, you will find a few more sights with Roman connections. Modest to say the least, they are, nevertheless, worth seeking out if you have an interest in obscure historical remains, and there's something charming about finding links to Hadrian's Wall in the otherwise ordinary residential suburbs of a modern city.

Your chariot for this West Rd side trip should be Stagecoach North East bus No 10, 11, 39 or 40; buy one of the Day Rover passes (see p198) as you'll be hopping on and off several times to view the sites. The bus leaves frequently from in front of Eldon Square (currently from Stand B; check it's heading to Denton, not Wallsend) and goes past St James' Park football stadium and on to the A186 (West Rd).

After 10 minutes or so, and having passed the hospital, look out on your right for Weidner Rd (which is beside the bus stop), before taking the first right onto Westholme Gdns, then the first left onto Broombridge Ave. Right beside the first house on the left are the remains of **Benwell Roman Temple**, complete with a platform on which a statue of the god Antenociticus once stood, flanked by a couple of

2nd and 4th centuries AD, which is believed to be one of the oldest Christian artefacts ever found on British soil. There's also a beautiful 3rd-century cameo of a bear on sardonyx, found in 1877, and a whole jewellery 'set' including brooch, necklace, bracelet and rings – all of which you would believe could have been made yesterday, such is their condition. Other highlights of the museum include the model of the skeleton of *Tyrannosaurus rex* at the rear of the museum on the ground floor and the giant Japanese spider crab near the entrance.

Castle Keep (New Castle)   [see Quayside map, p200]

Perhaps better and more precisely known as the **Castle Keep** (🖳 newcastle castle.co.uk; daily 10am-5pm, £9.25; tickets from Castle Keep or Black Gate, or online), these are the most visible remains of the New Castle built during the reign of Henry II (1168-78). This New Castle was established on the foundations of Castle Garth, built in 1080 by William the Conqueror's eldest son Robert Curthose – the edifice that gave the city its name.

Though impressive, the Keep itself, and the **Black Gate** (daily 10am-4.30pm) that was part of the same fortifications, are perhaps of limited interest to the average, Roman-obsessed Wall walker. However, one case in the Keep's museum section does have a few Roman artefacts. There are also details of the

---

replica altars (as with most treasures, the real altars, along with the head and limbs of the statue that were found, are now in Newcastle's Great North Museum: Hancock). Antenociticus himself was probably worshipped by the Vangiones from the upper Rhineland region who lived in the nearby Benwell Fort; as is usual, the soldiers built their temples away from the fort, considering the latter no place for holy sites. The current residents of Broombridge Ave do not, it is believed, still worship at this site.

The next site – a **Vallum crossing** that would have led to the entrance to **Benwell Fort**, of which this is the only bit left above ground – is within easy walking distance; from the main road, take the next left after Weidner Rd, then walk to the bottom end of the noose-shaped cul-de-sac known as Denhill Park. As with all the sites on this road, the Vallum crossing is owned by English Heritage, who provide a fair artist's impression of how it must have looked in its heyday. You can walk around the ruins.

Jump back on a bus and about a mile (1.5km) further west, just before the main intersection with the A1, is a fairly broad and impressive piece of **Wall** lying serenely beyond the pavement to the left of the road. Halfway along its length is a foundation that gives the whole ruin its name: **Denton Hall Turret**. As is usual with all turrets along the Wall, this one would have been manned by around ten men. An inscription recovered from the site suggested that it was built by the First Cohort of the Second Legion of Augusta. Presumably, the soldiers who manned it would have walked back to their abode at Benwell Fort. But by good fortune there's a bus stop on the other side of the road to take you back into town.

To get to these sights from Hadrian's Wall Path, walk north up Denton Rd (the A191; see Map 30, p188), then turn left at the second roundabout to reach Denton Hall Turret (half a mile/1km), or turn right to reach Denhill Park (1½ miles/2.5km; for Benwell Fort), or Weidner Rd (1½ miles/2.6km; for Benwell Roman Temple).

extent of the original Roman fort which was built to guard the bridge nearby. This bridge was **Pons Aelius** (*Pons* being Latin for 'bridge', Aelius being Hadrian's family name), which stretched across the Tyne in approximately the same location as the small Swing Bridge that you see today. It was from this bridge that the Roman fort took its name; a bridge that would have been about 700ft long (210m) and 18ft (5.4m) wide and the most impressive of the three main bridges the Romans built to cross the Tyne (the others were at Corbridge and Chollerford). In the 19th century, two altars were found in the water near the site of the bridge, though there's nothing left there today. Having noted the extent of the Roman fort, pop upstairs to the roof to get a better idea of its size and layout, and for good rooftop views of the city, its river and bridges.

The South Bank   [see map p201]
The regeneration of Newcastle's city centre is a thing of wonder. From a run-down and slightly sleazy area, the waterfront is now the most photographed part of the metropolis; its dilapidated, crumbling constructions spruced up and given a new lease of life or replaced by some breathtaking works of modern architecture. From being the shame of the city, the waterfront is now a place to be celebrated. And nor has the work finished. Between the two institutions below further development is taking place to build an arena, conference and exhibition centre, to be ready in 2024.

Until then, perhaps the most impressive manifestation of this regeneration is **BALTIC Centre for Contemporary Art** (☎ 0191-478 1810, 🖥 baltic.art; Wed-Sun 10am-6pm), once a disused grain warehouse, now a world-class centre for contemporary art. It's a delight and, like most of the museums and galleries, is free, though there is a charge for some of the special exhibitions and you probably won't find it easy resisting the temptation to eat in one of the cafés, including the rooftop restaurant, or to buy something from the BALTIC's gift shop. Nearby is the strikingly surreal **Sage** building, an international music venue designed by architect Norman Foster that's been variously described as a glass wave, a blister and a giant slug.

Other museums & galleries
Bessie Surtees House (see map p200; 🖥 historicengland.org.uk; currently closed but usually open Mon-Fri 10am-4pm, closed bank hols; free) sits in the heart of Quayside at 41-44 Sandhill. The name is not strictly correct, for there are in fact *two* merchants' houses here dating back to the 16th and 17th centuries, one of which is a rare example of Jacobean domestic architecture. The name comes from one of the inhabitants, who eloped with John Scott, who later became Lord Chancellor of England. There's not much to see inside, just three rooms, the main one empty save for a few photos of the house in days gone by. The main attraction is, perhaps, the giant fireplace, the exquisitely carved over-mantel bearing a date of 1657. Note that the house is currently closed to the public, but it's due to open again soon.

Laing Art Gallery (☎ 0191-278 1611, 🖥 laingartgallery.org.uk, see map p201; Mon-Sat 10am-4.30pm; free but donations appreciated and charges made for some exhibitions), on New Bridge St, is the city's oldest gallery, having welcomed visitors for well over a hundred years. The collection includes both contemporary works and paintings from the 18th and 19th centuries.

Discovery Museum (☎ 0191-232 6789, 🖥 discoverymuseum.org.uk; see map p201; Mon-Fri 10am-4pm, Sat & Sun 11am-4pm; free) is the region's biggest free museum, housing a wealth of scientific and technological material as well as displays on social history, regimental militaria and costumes. The museum is also home to the Tyne & Wear Archives (🖥 twarchives.org.uk; Tue-Fri 10am-4pm).

Newcastle University's highly regarded **Hatton Gallery** (☎ 0191-277 8877, 🖥 hattongallery.org.uk; Mon-Sat 10am-5pm; see map p200), reopened after a multi-million pound redevelopment, lies conveniently near the Hancock Museum.

ARBEIA

(☎ 0191-277 1410, 🖳 arbeiaromanfort.org.uk; Apr-Sep Mon-Fri 10am-5pm, Sat 11am-4pm, Sun 1-4pm; Oct-Mar closed; free but £5 donation suggested)

Though not strictly a Wall fort, being on the other side of the Tyne and four miles further east of the end of the Wall at Segedunum, Arbeia was, nevertheless, an important part of the whole military set-up in Britain and anyone with a taste for all things Roman should seriously consider a visit.

The name *Arbeia* means 'Place of Arabs' after the soldiers from Tigris, in what is now modern-day Iraq, who were garrisoned here in the 4th century. The history of the fort goes back further than this, however, having been built around AD163 under Emperor Marcus Aurelius to keep an eye on the sea and river. That changed in AD208 when Emperor Septimius Severus converted it into a granary and supply base for his troops campaigning in Scotland (see p62). Though Severus was killed in York just three years later and his Scottish assault ended soon after, the fort continued to supply the troops along the Wall for up to two centuries afterwards.

Because of its purpose as a storeroom, granary and unloading bay for imports arriving up the Tyne from overseas, Arbeia doesn't follow the classic playing-card layout of your average Roman fort (about which, see box p155). Nevertheless, some great finds have been dug up by archaeologists, who are still painstakingly excavating the site today. Many of these finds can be seen in the reception, including some incredible carved ringstones. The inhumation (burial) room opposite is also enlightening, showing how the Romans interred their dead.

Outside, two Roman buildings have been reconstructed. **West Gate** provides great views over the site, though in all honesty it is probably not an exact replica of how the gate would have looked. Nevertheless, it is perhaps the most impressive reconstruction of any fort, beating even that at Vindolanda, and contains some useful information on the history of the site.

Of more interest, however, are the **barracks** at the south-eastern corner that offer a telling glimpse into the rudimentary living conditions of the average soldier in South Shields at the time. Walk around the back of the barracks and you'll find the bright murals of the unfairly large **Commanding Officer's House**, with the designs authentically Roman.

Though on the map Arbeia seems a long way from the centre of Newcastle, it's fairly straightforward to get to, and there are several ways to do it. For those who want to travel **from the city centre**, take the Metro to the new interchange at South Shields. Step outside, turn right, pass the bus station and take a left at the end of the road to head towards the Can Can Show-bar. A right here brings you onto the A183, aka Ocean Road; take the first left along here up Baring St passing, as you reach the brow of the hill, Vespasian St, Trajan St, Claudius Court and Arbeia Hair Studio. The fort lies opposite Hadrian Primary School (note the great use of Roman names round here). While for those coming **from Segedunum and Wallsend**, take the Metro eastwards and alight at North Shields. A ten-minute walk will bring you to the passenger ferry across to South Shields, from where it's a five-minute walk to Ocean Road, keep on following it as it passes through the town centre all the way to Baring St, where you can follow the instructions above to get to the fort.

APPENDIX A: THE ACOMB–HEXHAM–CORBRIDGE ALTERNATIVE ROUTE

THE ACOMB–HEXHAM–CORBRIDGE ALTERNATIVE
[Maps: 23 p170; 23a p214; 23b p215; 23c p217; 23d p219; 23e p222; & 24 p173]

This alternative trail (**12 miles/19.5km**; **4½-4¾hrs**; between St Oswald's Hill Head (p170) and Halton Chesters Roman Fort (p173), via Acomb, Hexham and Corbridge, has a bit of everything; magnificent stretches of woodland, a riparian stroll along the banks of the Tyne and even a few hills, which, if you've been walking westwards from Newcastle, will be a rare treat.

The market town of Hexham, with its ancient abbey overlooking the market place, is an unqualified delight, as is the compact town of Corbridge, home to a 17th-century bridge, a pele tower by the church that's made of Roman Wall stones and more pubs than you can shake a Roman spear at.

And then, of course, there's the main object of this Hadrian's Wall Path diversion: the excavated ruins of Corbridge Roman Town (see p223), just 15 minutes west of Corbridge near the banks of the Tyne.

ACOMB   [Map 23a, p214]
Acomb is a friendly, attractive place; a string of stone terrace cottages inhabited by unassuming locals and with the **pant** (fountain) at the top of the village's Main St. There's little to delay those who aren't staying here, save for three pubs, two of which offer **accommodation** but only limited **food** options.

The first is *The Sun Inn* (☎ 01434-602934, **fb**; 1T/1D shared facilities, 1T/1D en suite; ✆; 🐾; ⓛ) which charges from £32.50pp (sgl occ £40-55). Foodwise, they have a 'light lunch' menu of filled jacket potatoes and hot or cold sandwiches (Wed-Sat noon-3pm) and they also do a roast lunch on Sundays.

Down the hill, *The Queen's Arms* (☎ 01434-607857, 🖥 thequeensarms hotelacomb.co.uk, **fb**; 2S/2D/1Tr, all en suite; ✆; 🐾; ⓛ) offers bed and continental breakfast (from £40pp, sgl £45-55). The double and twin can be combined to provide a family room. The pub has also taken on the role of village **shop**, following the closure of the post office next door (Mon-Fri 10.30am-2pm, 4pm-approx 10pm, Sat & Sun noon-approx 10pm). They also serve food (same hours), and you can always pick up sandwiches and pies from the shop and eat them in the pub too.

Back at the top of the hill by the pant, *Miner's Arms* (☎ 01434-603909, **fb**; Mon-Fri 5pm-midnight, Sat & Sun noon-midnight; 🐾) is a quintessential Northumbrian pub where great local beers are served every night.

Other options for food include the long-standing takeaway **chippy** behind The Queen's Arms, called *Sea Chef* (☎ 01434-609721, **fb**; Thur 4.30-7.30pm, Fri 11.30am-1.30pm & 4.30-8.30pm, Sat 11.30am-1.30pm & 4.30-8pm); and *Acomb Tandoori* (☎ 01434-609990; Mon-Sat 5.30-11pm, Sat to 10pm), which is on a nearby industrial estate but does deliver for a nominal charge.

Public transport-wise, the AD122 **bus** stops here (though this is a request stop only), as does Go North East's No 680 bus service (see pp48-51 for further local transport details).

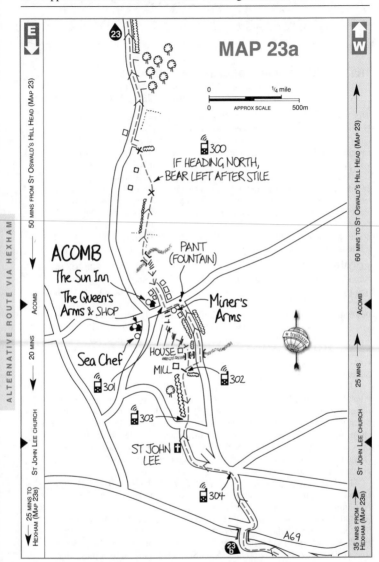

ALTERNATIVE ROUTE VIA HEXHAM

MAP 23b

ALTERNATIVE ROUTE VIA HEXHAM

□ **IMPORTANT NOTE – WALKING TIMES**
Unless otherwise specified, **all times in this book refer only to the time spent walking**. You will need to add 20-30% to allow for rests, photography, checking the map, drinking water etc. When planning the day's hike count on 5-7 hours' actual walking.

HEXHAM

The main market town for the district is a quaint and compact little place, the modern façades of shops and cafés detracting from, but not obliterating, the medieval character of the town centre.

Pride of place in the heart of town goes to the glorious **Hexham Abbey** (⌨ hexhamabbey.org.uk; Mon-Sat 10am-5pm, Sun 11am-5pm, services permitting; free but donations welcome). The first abbey was built here in AD672, though much of today's construction dates from the 12th century when it was refounded as an Augustinian priory. Following the Dissolution of the Monasteries in 1537 it became the Parish Church of St Andrew, which it still is today. Take your time to explore the Abbey's impressive interior and look out for the large Flavinus's Tombstone at the bottom of the Night Stair, which commemorates a 25-year-old Roman standard bearer from the 1st century AD; it's the original stone carving of which you'll see several casts in various museums, including Chesters and Newcastle's Great North Museum: Hancock. The crypt is also well worth seeing and the abbey has a good **café** (Mon-Sat 9.30am-3.30pm, Sun 11am-3pm).

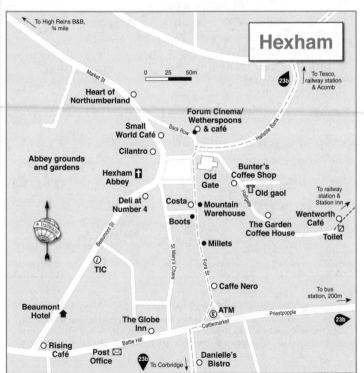

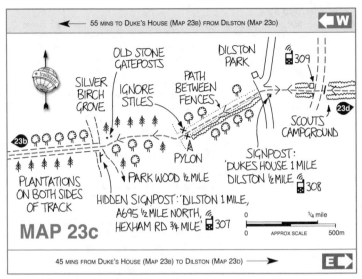

OLD STONE GATEPOSTS

DILSTON PARK

📱309

SILVER BIRCH GROVE

IGNORE STILES

PATH BETWEEN FENCES

SCOUTS CAMPGROUND

23d

23b

PYLON

PARK WOOD ½ MILE

SIGNPOST: 'DUKES HOUSE 1 MILE DILSTON ½ MILE. 📱308

PLANTATIONS ON BOTH SIDES OF TRACK

HIDDEN SIGNPOST: 'DILSTON 1 MILE, A695 ½ MILE NORTH, HEXHAM RD ¾ MILE' 📱307

MAP 23c

0   ¼ mile

0   APPROX SCALE   500m

45 MINS FROM DUKE'S HOUSE (MAP 23B) TO DILSTON (MAP 23D)

ALTERNATIVE ROUTE VIA HEXHAM

Across the square from the Abbey, **Old Gaol** (🖳 museumsnorthumber land.org.uk; Apr-Sep Wed-Sun, Oct Sat & Sun, daily in school holidays, 10am-4pm, winter closed; £5) is England's oldest purpose-built prison, built around 1330.

Services
The **tourist information centre** (☎ 01670-620450, 🖳 visitnorthumberland .com; Mon & Fri 9am-6pm, Tue-Thur 9am-5pm, Sat 9.30am-5pm) is in Queen's Hall on Beaumont St. It is in the same building as the library.

Fore St is very useful for walkers; you'll find **banks/ATMs**, a Boots the **chemist** (Mon & Fri 9am-5.30pm, Sat 8.30am-5pm), and branches of the **trekking shops** Mountain Warehouse (Mon-Sat 9am-5.30pm, Sun 10am-4.30pm) and Millets (Mon-Sat 9am-5.30pm, Sun 11am-4pm). Just round the corner on Battle Hill is the **post office** (Mon-Fri 9am-5.30pm, Sat 9am-2.30pm). Near the railway station are two large **supermarkets** – Tesco Extra (Mon-Sat 6am-midnight, Sun 10am-4pm) and Waitrose (Mon-Sat 8am-8pm, Sun 10am-4pm) – opposite each other (see Map 23b for both).

Transport
[See pp48-51] There are plenty of **buses** to and from Hexham. The AD122 bus calls at the bus and railway stations (see Map 23b). Arriva's/Stagecoach's No 685 & Go North East's X85, 10, 74, 680 & 684 also pass through.

From the nearby **railway station** (see Map 23b, p215) there is a frequent service to both Carlisle (approx 50-60 mins) and to Newcastle (35-40 mins).

If you need a **taxi** contact Advanced Taxis (☎ 01434-606565, 🖳 advanced taxis.com/hadrians-wall-service).

Where to stay

One mile north-west of the town centre, on Leazes Park, is *High Reins* (☎ 01434-603590, 💻 highreins.uk; 3S/1T/2D, all en suite; 🐾), a well-established B&B in a large country house and charging from £42pp (sgl £60).

The Station Inn (Map 23b; ☎ 01434-603155, 💻 stationinnhexham.co.uk; 4S/1D/6T/1Tr/1Qd, all en suite; 🐾; Ⓛ) is a very friendly pub close to the railway station that has a selection of smart but simple rooms (from £37.50pp, sgl £45, sgl occ £55); book in advance for cheaper rates. Their food's good too.

If you prefer a **hotel**, the family-run *Beaumont Hotel* (☎ 01434-602331, 💻 thebeaumonthexham.co.uk; 22D/11T, all en suite; 🐾; Ⓛ), has a very convenient location opposite Abbey Gardens and charges from £57.50pp (sgl occ full room rate), with breakfast an extra £15, but check their website for the best rates. Some rooms can have extra beds for children.

Where to eat and drink

Cafés and tea rooms There are more cafés and tearooms in Hexham than you can shake a cinnamon stick at.

Opposite the Abbey is the excellent *Deli at Number 4* (☎ 01434-608091, 💻 deliatnumber4.co.uk, **fb**; Mon-Sat 8am-4pm, Sun 10am-3pm), with much of its food locally sourced. Nearby is *Small World Café* (☎ 01434-606200, 💻 thesmallworldcafe.com, **fb**; Mon-Sat 9am-4pm), a bright, modern, health-conscious café with quality coffee and teas.

Through the Old Gate, and opposite the Old Gaol, is the cute, dog friendly tearoom known as *Bunter's Coffee Shop* (**fb**; 🐾; Mon-Sat 9am-4.30pm, Sun 11am-4pm), while slightly further down the hill, past the Old Gaol, you'll find *The Garden Coffee House* (Mon-Sat 9am-4pm; 🐾), with homemade soups and scones, and a back garden that welcomes dogs.

Walk a little further down the hill and you'll eventually reach the good-value, no-frills *Wentworth Café* (**fb**; Tue-Sat 8.30am-4pm, Sun 9.30am-4pm), overlooking the car park leading to Waitrose supermarket. There's a café at the southern end of Beaumont St that we *have* to mention. *Rising Café* (☎ 01434-394242, 💻 risingcafe.co.uk; Mon-Sat 10am-5pm) is aptly named, for the staff is made up of previously homeless and substance-addicted men and women and is the latest in a chain of similar cafés, with other branches in Birmingham and Lincoln. The style of the café and its menu are both deliberately designed to evoke the 1940s, with their 'Churchilli' just £2.95 and their 'Union Jacket spuds' the same price. Not only is it great value, but 100% of proceeds go directly towards funding their recovery, and that of many others around the country, in the charity work of Betel UK (💻 betel.uk).

Finally, for more mainstream cafés, there are branches of both *Costa* (Mon-Fri 7.30am-6pm, Sat & Sun 9am-5pm) and dog-friendly *Caffe Nero* (Mon-Fri 8am-5.30pm, Sat to 6pm, Sun 8am-5pm) on Fore St.

Pubs On Battle Hill, *The Globe Inn* (☎ 01434-603742, 💻 globehexham .co.uk) has a good choice of real ales. You can also watch sport on TV here. On the other side of the town centre, *The Forum* is an Art Deco **cinema** (💻 forumhexham.com) and a Wetherspoon's pub (daily 8am-midnight) serving breakfasts as well as good-value meal deals. Down the road, *Heart of Northumberland* (☎ 01434-608013, 💻 thehearthexham.com, **fb**; food Mon & Wed-Sat noon-9pm, Tue 4-9pm, Sun to 8pm) is a classy and friendly place

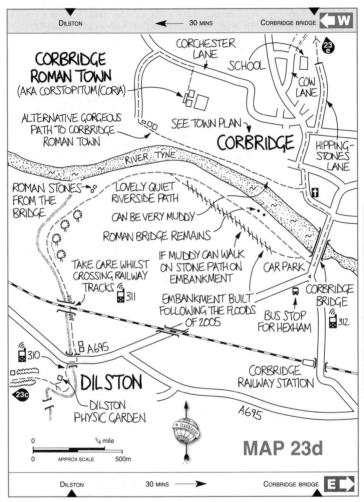

DILSTON ← 30 MINS CORBRIDGE BRIDGE ◄W

CORCHESTER LANE

SCHOOL

CORBRIDGE ROMAN TOWN
(AKA CORSTOPITUM (CORIA))

COW LANE

ALTERNATIVE GORGEOUS PATH TO CORBRIDGE ROMAN TOWN

SEE TOWN PLAN

CORBRIDGE

HIPPING-STONES LANE

RIVER TYNE

ROMAN STONES FROM THE BRIDGE

LOVELY QUIET RIVERSIDE PATH

CAN BE VERY MUDDY

ROMAN BRIDGE REMAINS

IF MUDDY CAN WALK ON STONE PATH ON EMBANKMENT

CAR PARK

TAKE CARE WHILST CROSSING RAILWAY TRACKS 311

EMBANKMENT BUILT FOLLOWING THE FLOODS OF 2005

CORBRIDGE BRIDGE 312

BUS STOP FOR HEXHAM

A695

310

23c

DILSTON

DILSTON PHYSIC GARDEN

CORBRIDGE RAILWAY STATION

A695

0 ¼ mile

0 APPROX SCALE 500m

MAP 23d

DILSTON 30 MINS → CORBRIDGE BRIDGE ►

ALTERNATIVE ROUTE VIA HEXHAM

serving very high quality pub fare, starting at the vegetarian option of red pepper halloumi burger with sweet chilli and fries (£12.50).

Restaurants For something more substantial, *Danielle's Bistro* (☎ 01434-601122, 🖥 danielles-bistro.co.uk, **fb**; Tue-Fri noon-1.30pm & 5.30-8.30pm, Sat 5.30-9pm) is on the way into town from Corbridge; it serves hearty English and Mediterranean dishes and charges around £19 for a two-course dinner. There's also a highly unusual Indian/tapas hybrid restaurant, *Cilantro* (☎

01434-601234, 🖥 cilantrotapas.com; Tue-Sun 5-10pm), right next to the abbey. Tapas options include keema nachos and chicken tikka quesadillas (£7).

CORBRIDGE

In many ways Corbridge is a typical little English market town; smart, quaint, with a largely medieval centre and plenty of teashops and pubs to keep the floods of visitors that come every summer refreshed. Some find the place a bit twee – every second shop seems to describe itself using the adjectives 'artisan' or 'designer' – but you can't deny that it's pretty and has just about everything a walker could wish for. In addition to the wonderful Roman Town (see p223) and the reconstructed remains of the Roman bridge abutment across the river (See Map 23d), in the centre of Corbridge is Northumberland's finest Anglo-Saxon church, **St Andrew's**, built around AD786. In the churchyard there's a **pele tower** built using Roman stones, while a Roman gateway, which presumably originally stood at Corbridge Roman Town, separates the baptistry from the rest of the church. Outside the church on the pavement is the site of the **King's Oven**, the main oven of the village in the 14th century.

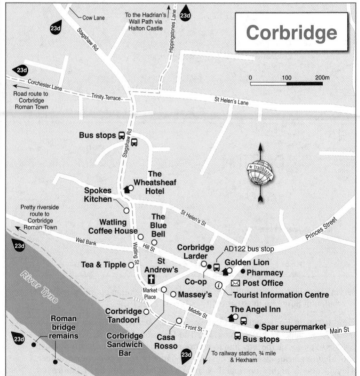

Services

The centre of Corbridge is compact. In the main square you'll find the **post office** (Mon-Sat 8am-5.30pm, Sun to 12.30pm), **tourist information centre** (☎ 01434-632815, 🖳 visitnorthumberland.com/corbridge; Wed, Fri & Sat 10am-3pm) and **pharmacy** (Mon-Fri 9am-6pm, Sun 9am-4pm). You'll also find a **Co-op supermarket** (daily 7am-10pm) and a small **Spar supermarket** (Mon-Sat 7am-9pm, Sun 7.30am-8pm); the Co-op has an **ATM**.

Transport

[See pp48-51] Arriva/Stagecoach's No 685, Go North East's Nos X85, 10 & 684 all stop here. **Train**-wise, there are services to Hexham – with some continuing on to Carlisle – and to Newcastle. The **railway station** is about half a mile south of the river (see Map 23d).

Where to stay

Near Market Place, ***The Wheatsheaf Hotel*** (☎ 01434-409588, 🖳 vixenpubs.co.uk/wheatsheaf-pub-corbridge; 1D/5T, all en suite; ☞; Ⓛ) is a smart pub that does B&B (from £42.50pp, sgl from £85, sgl occ room rate). In a similar style, though more down-to-earth, ***Golden Lion*** (☎ 01434-634507, 🖳 goldenlioncorbridge.co.uk; 5D/1T all en suite; ☞; Ⓛ) is a surprisingly vast place with a warm welcome. B&B costs around £40-45pp, (sgl occ £59.95-69.95) with the higher prices at weekends.

Down near the bridge, ***The Angel Inn*** (☎ 01434-632119, 🖳 theangelof corbridge.com; 3S/2T/3D/1D or T/1D with bunk beds/apartment with 2D, all en suite; ☞; 🐾; Ⓛ), a former coaching inn dating back to 1726, is the smartest place to stay. B&B costs around £67.50pp (sgl occ from £95; apartment £200). All three pubs also serve **food** (see Where to eat).

Where to eat and drink

Watling Coffee House (☎ 01434-634425, **fb**; Mon-Sat 9-4pm, Sun 9.30am-4pm) is one of the smartest of the many **coffee shops** in Corbridge. Across the road is a new place, ***Spokes Kitchen*** (☎ 01434-394180, 🖳 spokeskitchen.com, **fb**; Mon-Sat 9am-4pm, Sun 10am-4pm). As the name hints, this is a bicycle-themed café with various cycling memorabilia hanging from the walls and, of course, a bike rack outside. The place is smart and surprisingly spacious, with a pleasant outdoor seating area behind. Food includes 'avo on sourdough' (£6.25) and, for the truly ravenous, a stacked ciabatta (containing sausage, bacon, black pudding and egg; £9.25).

A little way south, ***Tea & Tipple*** (Mon-Wed & Fri-Sat 9am-5pm, Sun 10.30am-3pm) serves scones, sandwiches and light meals. Also around Market Place is the takeaway-only ***Corbridge Sandwich Bar*** (**fb**; Mon-Tue 10.30am-3pm, Wed-Sat 9am-4pm), and the very friendly ***Massey's*** (☎ 01434-633130, 🖳 masseystearoom.co.uk, **fb**; Mon-Fri 10am-4pm, Sat from 9.30am, Sun from 10.30am), with its great choice of breakfasts (£6-9.25) and sandwiches (£6.75). Close by, the popular ***Corbridge Larder*** (☎ 01434-632948, 🖳 cor bridgelarder.co.uk; Mon-Fri 9.30am-4pm, Sat 9am-5pm, Sun 10am-4pm; 🐾) is a good-quality ground-floor deli with a health-conscious café upstairs.

Restaurants include the Italian ***Casa Rosso*** (☎ 01434-634214, 🖳 casa rosso.co.uk; **fb**; Mon-Thur noon-9pm, Fri & Sat to 10pm Sun to 8pm) on Front St, with a big menu of familiar pasta and pizza dishes.

For decent **pub grub** head to one of the three pubs offering B&B (see Where to stay). At *The Angel Inn* (breakfast Mon-Fri 7.30-9.30am, Sat & Sun 8-10am; lunch Mon-Sat noon-3pm, Sun noon-5pm; dinner Mon-Thur 5-8pm, Fr & Sat to 8.30pm, Sun 6-8pm) the menu is varied with lunches such as Bloody Mary prawn roll (£8) and mains including summer vegetable risotto (£15). Also good is *Golden Lion* (daily noon-9pm) with mains starting from £7.95, and *The Wheatsheaf Hotel* ((Mon-Sat noon-8pm, Sun noon-4pm) including pie of the day from £11.99.

Food is served at *The Blue Bell* (☎ 01434-634748, **fb**; daily noon-3pm), which is also your best bet for quality cask ale. For Indian grub, the *Corbridge Tandoori* (☎ 01434-633676, 🖥 corbridgetandoori.com; daily 5-11.30pm) is still going strong.

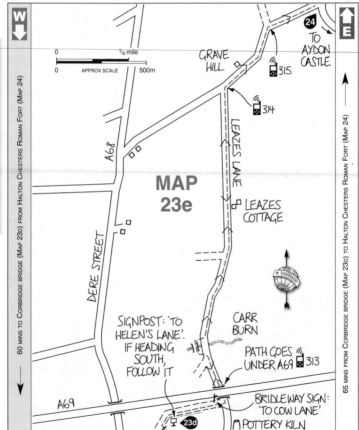

60 MINS TO CORBRIDGE BRIDGE (MAP 23d) FROM HALTON CHESTERS ROMAN FORT (MAP 24)

65 MINS FROM CORBRIDGE BRIDGE (MAP 23d) TO HALTON CHESTERS ROMAN FORT (MAP 24)

ALTERNATIVE ROUTE VIA HEXHAM

W · E

0   ¼ mile
0   APPROX SCALE   500m

GRAVE HILL

TO AYDON CASTLE

24

315

314

LEAZES LANE

MAP 23e

LEAZES COTTAGE

A68

DERE STREET

SIGNPOST: 'TO HELEN'S LANE'. IF HEADING SOUTH, FOLLOW IT

CARR BURN

PATH GOES UNDER A69   313

A69

BRIDLEWAY SIGN: 'TO COW LANE'

POTTERY KILN

23d

CORBRIDGE ROMAN TOWN   [Map 23d, p219]

(☎ 01434-632349, 🖳 english-heritage.org.uk; Apr-Sep daily 10am-5pm, Nov-Mar Sat & Sun 10am-5pm (winter days/hours subject to change, check in advance); £9)

It is, perhaps, a measure of how much we still have to learn about the Romans in Britain that when the first edition of this book was published, in 2006, this site was known as 'Corstopitum' after what everybody believed was the Roman name for the fortress that originally stood here. However, doubt has since been cast as to whether this was true, with many experts now believing that the fortress, built to guard what was, at ten piers wide, Britain's largest stone bridge in Roman times, was actually called 'Coria' by the Romans. Proponents of this latter theory point to the Vindolanda tablets (see p149) to back up their assertions. On one of the tablets, commanding officer Julius Verecundus reports that there were 337 soldiers at 'Coris', and this is just one of nine definite references to Coria/Coris on the Vindolanda tablets. But while it is generally accepted now that Coria was the most likely name for this site, it is not universally so, with a dwindling band of archaeologists still preferring the name Corstopitum (even though there is only one contemporary occurrence of this name, in a document known as the *Antonine Itinerary*). As such, English Heritage now officially calls the site Corbridge Roman Town.

Regardless of what the original name was, the site's current name is probably more informative. For whilst its origins were undoubtedly as a Roman fortress – indeed it was, for many years, the nerve centre of Roman operations in northern England – the site was rebuilt time and again over the years, each time with modifications to suit its changing function. Consequently it is one of the most important sites near the Wall, for archaeologists have been able to peel back each of these different stages, like layers on an onion, to discover the history of the fort; and bits of each of those layers are visible to the visitor today.

That history is a long and complex one. The first fort, built around AD85 under the governor Agricola, was situated about half a mile west of here and lasted only about 20 years before it was burnt down, to be replaced by a second, made of turf and built on this site the following year. This, too, lasted fewer than 20 years before being abandoned, as Hadrian began to build his Wall and troops were moved north to new fortresses such as Halton Chesters

---

❏ THE WORLD'S FIRST ARCHAEOLOGICAL DIG?

The history of the Roman site at Corbridge didn't abruptly come to an end when the Romans retreated to the Mediterranean. A few Saxon relics have been found to suggest that there was life here after the 5th century. Perhaps the most intriguing part of the fort's history, however, occurred in 1201 when King John undertook an excavation of the ruins in search of treasure. Though he found nothing except 'stones marked with bronze and iron and lead', his hunch was a good one: in 1911, more than 700 years later, 160 coins were found in a bronze jug; one of the largest hoards of Roman coins ever found in Britain. The find now resides in the British Museum. It may have been a fruitless search for John, but it earned him a prize of sorts: his excavation is seen by some as the first recorded archaeological dig in British history.

(Onnum; see p174) that lay along its length. Corbridge was revived again, however, around AD140 under Emperor Antoninus, when it became a supply base for the soldiers fighting his Scottish campaign. Soon after this, in about AD180, its function seemed to change again and in place of its strictly military role the fort began to take on the appearance of a town. By the 3rd century it was home to a largely civilian population, though still with a military core, and remained like this until the Romans departed in the 5th century. Thus, while this site probably once had the typical 'playing-card' layout so familiar from the fortresses along the Wall – and, indeed, in many parts still does – there are also ruins from its days as a largely civilian settlement. And it is these that make this place unique amongst today's Wall remains.

The proof of the importance of this fortress to the Romans can be seen merely by looking at a Roman road atlas. Running from the fortress to the north is **Dere Street**, the road the Romans built and would eventually use to launch their campaigns north into what is now Scotland; to the south, across the bridge, the same road continued to York; while running away to the west from here all the way to Carlisle was the **Stanegate**. As such, Corbridge was the transport hub of the region and a major supply town for forts along the Wall.

The Stanegate is still the main thoroughfare through the fort, though now it's at a higher level than the rest of the site thanks to all the resurfacing that went on during its lifetime. A stroll along here will take you past the **granaries** with their underfloor channels, built around AD180 when this site was metamorphosing from a regular fort into a supply base for troops on the Wall; the **fountain** next door which would once have been the centrepiece of the entire site; and the remains of various civilian buildings to the south of the Stanegate.

The original fortress that lay half a mile (1km) west of here (the one that was built under the reign of Agricola and burnt down), was rediscovered only in 1974 during the construction of the Corbridge bypass. You can see some of the things the archaeologists dug up there, as well as the best of their excavations here, in the museum adjacent to reception. Most famously of all, the so-called **Corbridge Hoard** – the contents of an iron-bound leather-covered wooden chest found on-site in 1964 – are now on display; dating from around AD138, it comprises armour, tools, weaponry, wax writing tablets and papyrus – the essential possessions, one assumes, of your average Roman soldier. You can also see a replica of the famous **Corbridge Lanx** (the original is in the British Museum, London), a silver salver discovered in the 1730s near the riverbank by a young girl out walking.

From the fort, the quickest way back into town is to turn right and head east along Corchester Lane and Trinity Terrace. A far more pleasant route, however, is to turn left and, after a short distance, left again. This leads alongside a tributary down to the North Tyne, from where it's a pleasant stroll to the impressive bridge that gave the town its name. Built in 1674, this bridge replaced an Anglo-Saxon one on the same spot that became derelict in the 17th century.

APPENDIX B: GLOSSARY

Antonine Wall Turf wall built to the north of Hadrian's construction by his successor, Antoninus Pius. There is a strong case to be made that this wall, and not Hadrian's, was actually the northern edge of the Roman Empire, and not Limestone Corner (see p164); but while it is undoubtedly to the north of Hadrian's Wall, it was never very secure.

Bastle house A fortified house built during the Middle Ages in the border region to protect the owner and his family from bandits

Brigantes The main tribe whose land was crossed by the Wall

Caledones The collective name for the tribes living north of the Wall

> ❑ **NORSE WORDS**
> Squashed between the Saxons and the Scots, the area of the Borders and the Lake District has kept many Norse words that you'll find today in the local place names. Amongst them:
>
> | Norse | Meaning |
> |---|---|
> | fell | upper slope of hill |
> | beck/burn | stream |
> | haugh | flat land beside river |
> | holm | island in river |
> | hope | sheltered valley |
> | moss | peat bog |

Gask Frontier The first border separating the conquered lands in the south from the 'Barbarians' in the north. Established by Domitian (AD81-96), it was also built to watch over the glens but moved further south when troops were required elsewhere in the empire

Milecastle A series of 'mini-castles' spaced 1000 paces apart (or one Roman mile) along the entire length of the Wall. Built to house troops, each could hold an estimated 32 men

Military Road Now the B6318, the Military Road was an 18th-century thoroughfare built on the orders of General Wade to thwart further attacks from Bonnie Prince Charlie

Military Way A Roman thoroughfare built around AD160 between the Stanegate and the Wall, often along the northern earthwork of the Vallum (which had by then been largely decommissioned)

Pele tower A square defensive tower built by wealthier families in the 16th century in the border counties of England and Scotland to defend themselves against the trepidations of reivers. The layout would typically follow the same design, with a storeroom on the ground floor, from which a staircase would lead upstairs to the living quarters. On the roof the family would light a beacon to summon help during a raid

Reivers Bandits and cattle rustlers during the Middle Ages

Stanegate The east–west road that ran between the Roman settlements of Carlisle and Corbridge which was one of the major reasons for the construction of the Wall

Trig points Small concrete pillars erected in the 1930s to aid surveying

Turret Observation posts constructed along the Wall, 161 in total, to watch the surrounding land. They were placed equidistantly along the Wall, with two turrets between every milecastle (though there is an extra one, Peel Tower, see p151, near the middle of the Wall at Steel Rigg).

Vallum Roman earthwork, consisting of a deep ditch running between two high mud or earth walls, that ran to the south of and parallel to the Wall. The exact purpose of the Vallum remains uncertain.

APPENDIX C: GPS WAYPOINTS

Each GPS waypoint listed was taken on the route at the reference number marked on the map as below. This list of GPS waypoints as well as instructions on how to interpret a way-point reference can be found on the Trailblazer website: 🖳 trailblazer-guides.com (click on GPS waypoints).

MAP	WAYPOINT	LAT/LONG COORDINATE	DESCRIPTION
1	001	N54 57.240 W3 12.773	Small shelter on Banks Promenade marking the western end of the path
1	002	N54 56.983 W3 11.317	Port Carlisle; path junction with main road to Bowness-on-Solway
1	003	N54 56.397 W3 10.708	Entry to Glendale Holiday Park
2	004	N54 56.052 W3 10.045	Junction by former Highland Laddie Inn
2	005	N54 55.932 W3 10.198	Path junction with road at Glasson
2	006	N54 55.346 W3 09.452	Gate across track
2	007	N54 55.639 W3 08.904	Crossroads in Drumburgh
3	008	N54 55.351 W3 05.013	Gate and cattle grid at Dykesfield
4	009	N54 55.301 W3 03.413	Greyhound Inn
4	010	N54 55.287 W3 02.522	Gate off/onto road
4	011	N54 55.491 W3 01.121	Black and white house
4	012	N54 54.806 W2 59.883	Cross Sourmilk Footbridge
5	013	N54 54.752 W2 59.179	Path joins/leaves road at Grinsdale
6	014	N54 53.946 W2 57.775	Go under disused rail bridge over Eden
6	015	N54 54.007 W2 56.091	Sands Sports Centre
6	016	N54 54.273 W2 55.208	Bridge and kissing gate
7	017	N54 54.395 W2 54.431	Path onto/off road by The Beeches
7	018	N54 55.194 W2 52.922	Join/leave River Eden embankment
8	019	N54 55.452 W2 52.510	Bridge over stream
8	020	N54 55.755 W2 51.169	Leave/join road through Crosby-on-Eden
8	021	N54 55.901 W2 51.053	Stile and gate onto/off Sandy Lane bridleway
8	022	N54 56.334 W2 51.308	Leave/join Sandy Lane
9	023	N54 56.805 W2 48.853	Gate by bus stop at Oldwall
9	024	N54 57.219 W2 47.361	Kissing gate by end house in Newton
10	025	N54 57.812 W2 46.431	Bridge over a stream
10	026	N54 58.118 W2 45.651	Gate before/after Swainsteads Farm
11	027	N54 58.146 W2 45.362	Gate at edge of woods
11	028	N54 58.296 W2 44.435	Abutment just west of bridge
12	029	N54 58.392 W2 41.942	Haytongate Farm
12	030	N54 58.462 W2 40.952	High chunk of wall with faint 'SPP' carved on northern side
12	031	N54 58.468 W2 40.171	Cross stile off/onto road
12	032	N54 58.604 W2 39.602	Join/leave road at stile near Pike Hill Signal Tower
13	033	N54 58.845 W2 38.486	Leave/join track to Coombe Crag
13	034	N54 59.007 W2 37.901	Gate off/onto farm track
13	035	N54 59.375 W2 36.245	Gate at Birdoswald
14	036	N54 59.375 W2 34.720	Cross cattle grid near Turret 48A

MAP	WAYPOINT	LAT/LONG COORDINATE	DESCRIPTION
14	037	N54 59.368 W2 34.156	Through gate off/onto road leading to Samson Inn
14	038	N54 59.325 W2 33.365	Cross track at stile
14	039	N54 59.281 W2 32.353	Cross stile to join/leave road
14	040	N54 59.301 W2 32.050	Gate opposite Thirlwall Castle
15	041	N54 59.268 W2 31.223	Join/leave road to the north of the Roman ditch
15	042	N54 59.205 W2 31.163	Walltown Visitor Centre
15	043	N54 59.598 W2 30.057	Stile by track to Walltown Farm
16	044	N54 59.585 W2 27.117	Stile by bridge over Haltwhistle Burn
16	045	N54 59.629 W2 26.819	Hole Gap

Walking to and from Haltwhistle

MAP	WAYPOINT	LAT/LONG COORDINATE	DESCRIPTION
16	*200*	*N54 59.179 W2 27.516*	*Cross B6318*
16	*201*	*N54 58.769 W2 27.746*	*Gate across Willia Rd*
16	*202*	*N54 58.645 W2 27.501*	*Bridge by Old Brickworks*
16	*203*	*N54 59.232 W2 27.119*	*Gate onto/off B6318*
16	*204*	*N54 59.262 W2 26.959*	*Gate off/onto B6318*
16	*205*	*N54 59.585 W2 27.117*	*Gate off/onto road by bridge over Haltwhistle Burn*

Main route

MAP	WAYPOINT	LAT/LONG COORDINATE	DESCRIPTION
17	046	N54 59.809 W2 25.522	Bogle Hole
17	047	N55 00.099 W2 24.433	Path to Winshields Farm
17	048	N55 00.120 W2 24.282	Green Slack (trig point)
17	049	N55 00.092 W2 23.281	Gates by shortcut to Once Brewed
18	050	N55 00.229 W2 22.528	Milecastle 39 (Castle Nick)
19	051	N55 00.731 W2 20.258	Milecastle 37
19	052	N55 00.880 W2 19.715	Knag Burn Gate
19	053	N55 01.474 W2 18.844	Trig point
19	054	N55 01.540 W2 18.395	Milecastle 35
20	055	N55 01.685 W2 17.660	Grindon Turret 34a
20	056	N55 01.861 W2 15.978	Milecastle 33
21	057	N55 02.122 W2 13.624	Cross road
21	058	N55 02.034 W2 13.366	Mithras Temple
21	059	N55 02.183 W2 12.857	Stone stile from/to Brocolitia
21	060	N55 02.301 W2 11.558	Trig point
21	061	N55 02.182 W2 11.043	Cross track to/from Green Carts Farm
22	062	N55 01.946 W2 09.159	Join/leave road at stile; enter farm
22	063	N55 01.763 W2 09.203	Junction with road to Walwick
22	064	N55 01.723 W2 08.297	Chesters entrance
22	065	N55 01.564 W2 07.459	Road junction by water wheel
22	066	N55 01.420 W2 07.605	Path to Brunton Turret
22	067	N55 01.335 W2 07.151	Leave/join road at start/end of wood
23	068	N55 01.259 W2 06.669	Cross road by track to quarry
23	069	N55 01.155 W2 06.050	Path to Acomb
23	070	N55 01.153 W2 05.742	Cross road
23	071	N55 01.161 W2 04.591	Cross stile before/after crossing track
23	072	N55 01.091 W2 03.854	Stile and steps

MAP	WAYPOINT	LAT/LONG COORDINATE	DESCRIPTION
Acomb–Hexham–Corbridge alternative			
23a	300	N54 59.939 W2 06.515	Stile
23a	301	N54 59.582 W2 06.452	Acomb (by The Sun Inn)
23a	302	N54 59.369 W2 06.350	Gate by mill
23a	303	N54 59.230 W2 06.327	Join/leave road
23a	304	N54 59.103 W2 06.098	Junction of roads south of Acomb
23b	305	N54 57.911 W2 05.273	Signpost to Duke's House ¾ mile
23b	306	N54 57.730 W2 04.803	Signpost to Hexham and Dilston
23c	307	N54 57.785 W2 03.897	Signpost to Dilston, A695 & Hexham Rd
23c	308	N54 57.940 W2 03.090	Signpost to Duke's House & Dilston
23c	309	N54 57.952 W2 02.657	Cross track
23d	310	N54 58.001 W2 02.422	Path onto/off A695 near bridge
23d	311	N54 58.141 W2 02.416	Cross railway tracks by bridge; take care
23d	312	N54 58.276 W2 01.174	Leave/join path by River Tyne
23e	313	N54 59.023 W2 00.885	Path goes under A69
23e	314	N54 59.882 W2 00.870	Leave/join Leazes Lane
23e	315	N55 00.050 W2 00.647	Stay on road
24	316	N55 00.122 W2 00.375	Road fork

Main route

MAP	WAYPOINT	LAT/LONG COORDINATE	DESCRIPTION
24	073	N55 00.767 W2 01.232	Port Gate
24	074	N55 00.642 W2 00.355	Path to/from Corbridge
25	075	N55 00.670 W1 59.764	Stile by B6318
25	076	N55 00.745 W1 59.128	Join/leave road by wall
25	077	N55 00.692 W1 56.977	Cross B6318
25	078	N55 00.680 W1 56.604	Gate leads out of/into Roman ditch
26	079	N55 00.590 W1 55.415	Robin Hood Inn
27	080	N55 00.468 W1 52.160	Cross road to Albemarle Barracks
27	081	N55 00.284 W1 50.989	Cross B6318; steps either side of road
27	082	N55 00.217 W1 50.375	Leave/join B6318 by Two Hoots
27	083	N55 00.094 W1 49.482	Cross road by Rudchester
28	084	N55 00.005 W1 48.629	Path joins/leaves road at gate
28	085	N54 59.815 W1 47.322	Last (or first) major piece of Roman wall on the trail
28	086	N54 59.463 W1 48.213	Bend in path
28	087	N54 59.273 W1 48.207	Path and track junction by stone wall
28	088	N54 59.067 W1 47.485	Western end of Wylam waggonway
28	089	N54 59.013 W1 45.985	Eastern end of Wylam waggonway
29	090	N54 58.884 W1 45.938	Gate at Ryton Island
29	091	N54 58.900 W1 44.649	Newburn Bridge
29	092	N54 58.807 W1 43.962	Over A6085 at Newburn
29	093	N54 58.613 W1 42.902	Path goes under bridge
30	094	N54 58.459 W1 42.143	Eastern end of Ottringham Close
30	095	N54 58.611 W1 41.886	Bridge across A1
30	096	N54 58.364 W1 41.571	Path joins/leaves road by Denton Dene
30	097	N54 58.130 W1 41.204	Milepost
30	098	N54 57.927 W1 39.866	Cross A695
30	099	N54 57.831 W1 39.372	Riverside path leaves/joins road

MAP	WAYPOINT	LAT/LONG COORDINATE	DESCRIPTION
31	100	N54 57.731 W1 39.035	Car park
31	101	N54 57.965 W1 36.755	Copthorne Hotel
31	102	N54 58.215 W1 35.993	Gateshead Millennium Bridge
32	103	N54 58.280 W1 35.370	Bridge over Ouseburn
32	104	N54 58.017 W1 34.658	St Lawrence Rd
32	105	N54 57.722 W1 32.737	Snaking path
33	106	N54 58.431 W1 32.376	Wincomblee Bridge
33	107	N54 59.313 W1 31.846	Segedunum

APPENDIX D: TAKING A DOG

As noted on p29, the Hadrian's Wall Path is not that dog-friendly. Much of the land through which the path passes is grazed by livestock and dogs must be kept on a lead. However, if you're sure your dog can cope with (and will enjoy) walking 12 miles or more a day for several days in a row, you need to start preparing accordingly. The best starting point is to study the village and town facilities table on pp32-3 and the advice below.

Looking after your dog

To begin with, you need to make sure that your own dog is fully **inoculated** against the usual doggy illnesses, and also up to date with regard to **worm pills** (eg Drontal) and **flea preventatives** such as Frontline – they are, after all, following in the pawprints of many a dog before them, some of whom may well have left fleas or other parasites on the trail that now lie in wait for their next meal to arrive. **Pet insurance** is also a very good idea; if you've already got insurance, do check that it will cover a trip such as this. On the subject of looking after your dog's health, perhaps the most important implement you can take with you is the **plastic tick remover**, available from vets for a couple of quid. These help you to remove the tick safely (ie without leaving its head behind buried under the dog's skin).

Being in unfamiliar territory also makes it more likely that you and your dog could become separated. For this reason, make sure your dog has a **tag with your contact details on it** (a mobile phone number would be best if you are carrying one with you).

When to keep your dog on a lead

- **Near the crags** It's a sad fact that more than one dog has perished after falling over the edge of the crags. Keep them on a lead through the central part of the walk.
- **When crossing farmland**, particularly in the lambing season (around May) when your dog can scare the sheep, causing them to lose their young. Farmers are allowed by law to shoot at and kill any dogs that they consider are worrying their sheep. During lambing, most farmers would prefer it if you didn't bring your dog at all. It is also **compulsory to keep your dog on a lead through National Trust land**. The exception to the dogs on leads rule is if your dog is being attacked by cows. A few years ago there were three deaths in the UK caused by walkers being trampled as they tried to rescue their dogs from the attentions of cattle. The advice in this instance is to let go of the lead, head speedily to a position of safety (usually the other side of the field gate or stile) and call your dog to you.
- **Around ground-nesting birds** It's important to keep your dog under control when crossing an area where certain species of birds nest on the ground. Most dogs love foraging around in the woods but make sure you have permission to do so; some woods are used as 'nurseries' for game birds and dogs are only allowed through them if they are on a lead.

What to pack

• **Food/water bowl** Foldable cloth bowls are popular with trekkers as they're light and take up little room in the rucksack. You can also get a water-bottle-and-bowl combination, where the bottle folds into a 'trough' from which the dog can drink.

• **Lead and collar** An extendable one is probably preferable for this sort of trip. Make sure both lead and collar are in good condition – you don't want either to snap on the trail, or you may end up carrying your dog through sheep fields until a replacement can be found.

• **Medication** You'll know if you need to bring any lotions or potions.

• **Bedding** A simple blanket may suffice, or more if you aren't carrying your own luggage.

• **A favourite toy** Helps prevent your dog from pining for the entire trek.

• **Food/water** Remember to bring treats as well as regular food to keep up mutt morale.

• **Corkscrew stake** Available from camping or pet shops, this will help you to keep your dog secure in one place while you set up camp/doze.

• **Poo bags** Essential.

• **Hygiene wipes** For cleaning your dog after it's rolled in stuff.

• **Tick remover** See opposite.

• **Raingear** It can rain a lot!

• **Old towels** For drying your dog after the deluge.

When it comes to packing, it's a good idea to leave an exterior pocket of your rucksack devoted to your dog's kit. Some dogs even sport their own 'doggy rucksack', so they can carry their own food, water, poo etc – which certainly reduces the burden on their owner.

Cleaning up after your dog

Dog excrement should be cleaned up to ensure it is not left to decorate the boots of others. In towns, villages and particularly in fields where animals graze or which will be cut for silage, hay etc, you must pick up and bag the excrement.

Staying with your dog

In this guide we have used the symbol 🐕 to denote where a hotel, pub or B&B welcomes dogs. However, this always needs to be arranged in advance and some places make an additional charge while others may require a deposit which is refundable if the dog doesn't make a mess. Hostels do not permit them unless they are an assistance (guide) dog; smaller campsites tend to accept them, but some of the larger holiday parks do not. In some cases dogs need to sleep in a separate building. When it comes to eating, most landlords allow dogs in at least a section of their pubs, though few restaurants do. Always ask first and ensure your dog doesn't run around the pub but is secured to your table or a radiator. Note that some establishments accept only small dogs, or only one dog at a time. Make sure you are clear about their rules before turning up!

INDEX

Page references in bold red type refer to maps

Map key

♠	Where to stay	📖	Library/bookstore	●	Other	
○	Where to eat and drink	@	Internet	CP	Car park	
Δ	Campsite	🏛	Museum/gallery	🚌	Bus station/stop	
⊠	Post Office	✝	Church/cathedral		Rail line & station	
©	Bank/ATM	☏	Telephone		Park	
ⓘ	Tourist Information	☒	Public toilet	082	GPS waypoint	
		☐	Building			

Walking Track		Gate		Stream	
Minor Track		Bridge		River	
4WD Track		Fence		Forest / Wood	
Road		Stone Wall		Boggy Ground	
Steps		Hedge		Hadrian's Wall	
Slope		Water		Vallum	
Steep Slope		Sand		Ditch	
Stile		Stones		Map Continuation	

238 Other walking guides from Trailblazer (for full list see opposite)

Peru's Cordilleras Blanca & Huayhuash
The Hiking & Biking Guide *Neil & Harriet Pike,* 2nd edn, £17.99
ISBN 978-1-912716-17-3, 242pp, 50 maps, 40 colour photos
This region, in northern Peru, boasts some of the most spectacular scenery in the Andes, and most accessible high mountain trekking and biking in the world. This practical guide contains 60 detailed route maps and descriptions covering 20 hiking trails and more than 30 days of paved and dirt road cycling.

Tour du Mont Blanc *Jim Manthorpe,* 3rd edn, £16.99
ISBN 978-1-912716-15-9, 256pp, 60 maps, 50 colour photos
At 4807m (15,771ft), Mont Blanc is the highest mountain in western Europe. The trail (105 miles, 168km) that circumnavigates the massif, passing through France, Italy and Switzerland, is the most popular long-distance walk in Europe. Includes day walks. Plus – Climbing guide to Mont Blanc

Kilimanjaro – the trekking guide *Henry Stedman,* 5th edn, £14.99
ISBN 978-1-905864-95-9, 368pp, 40 maps, 50 colour photos
At 5895m (19,340ft) Kilimanjaro is the world's tallest freestanding mountain and one of the most popular destinations for hikers visiting Africa. Route guides & maps – the 6 major routes. City guides – Nairobi, Dar-es-Salaam, Arusha, Moshi & Marangu.

Moroccan Atlas – the trekking guide
Alan Palmer, 2nd edn, £14.99
ISBN 978-1-905864-59-1, 420pp, 86 maps, 40 colour photos
The High Atlas in central Morocco is the most dramatic and beautiful section of the entire Atlas range. Towering peaks, deep gorges and huddled Berber villages enchant all who visit. With 73 detailed maps, 13 town and village guides including Marrakech.

Iceland Hiking with Reykjavik city guide
Jim Manthorpe, 1st edn, £15.99
ISBN 978-1-912716-15-1, 204pp, 41maps, 50 colour photos
Iceland offers a world of hiking opportunities like no other place on earth. The famous 55km Laugavegur trek takes you past glaciers, volcanoes, steaming fumaroles and hot springs all set in a landscape of yellow rhyolite and black ash. This guide gives you plenty of other options from hiking below the largest ice-cap in Europe at Skaftafell, to Reykjavik day hikes.

The Inca Trail, Cusco & Machu Picchu
Alex Stewart & Henry Stedman, 6th edn, £14.99
ISBN 978-1-905864-88-1, 370pp, 70 maps, 30 colour photos
The Inca Trail from Cusco to Machu Picchu is South America's most popular trek. This guide includes hiking options from two days to three weeks. Plus plans of Inca sites, guides to Lima, Cusco and Machu Picchu. Includes the High Inca Trail, Salkantay Trek and the Choquequirao Trail. Plus two Sacred Valley treks: Lares Trail and Ausangate Circuit.

Trekking in the Everest Region *Jamie McGuinness* 6th edn, £15.99
ISBN 978-1-905864-81-2, 320pp, 95 maps, 30 colour photos
Sixth edition of this popular guide to the world's most famous trekking region. Covers not only the classic treks but also the wild routes. Written by a Nepal-based trek and mountaineering leader. Includes: 27 detailed route maps and 52 village plans. Plus: Kathmandu city guide

TRAILBLAZER TITLE LIST

Adventure Cycle-Touring Handbook
Adventure Motorcycling Handbook
Australia by Rail
Cleveland Way (British Walking Guide)
Coast to Coast (British Walking Guide)
Cornwall Coast Path (British Walking Guide)
Cotswold Way (British Walking Guide)
The Cyclist's Anthology
Dales Way (British Walking Guide)
Dorset & Sth Devon Coast Path (British Walking Gde)
Exmoor & Nth Devon Coast Path (British Walking Gde)
Glyndŵr's Way (British Walking Guide)
Great Glen Way (British Walking Guide)
Hadrian's Wall Path (British Walking Guide)
Himalaya by Bike – a route and planning guide
Iceland Hiking – with Reykjavik City Guide
Inca Trail, Cusco & Machu Picchu
Japan by Rail
Kilimanjaro – the trekking guide (includes Mt Meru)
London Loop (British Walking Guide)
London to Walsingham Camino
Madeira Walks – 37 selected day walks
Moroccan Atlas – The Trekking Guide
Morocco Overland (4x4/motorcycle/mountainbike)
Nepal Trekking & The Great Himalaya Trail
Norfolk Coast Path & Peddars Way (British Walking Gde)
North Downs Way (British Walking Guide)
Offa's Dyke Path (British Walking Guide)
Overlanders' Handbook – worldwide driving guide
Pembrokeshire Coast Path (British Walking Guide)
Pennine Way (British Walking Guide)
Peru's Cordilleras Blanca & Huayhuash – Hiking/Biking
Pilgrim Pathways: 1-2 day walks on Britain's sacred ways
The Railway Anthology
The Ridgeway (British Walking Guide)
Scottish Highlands – Hillwalking Guide
Siberian BAM Guide – rail, rivers & road
The Silk Roads – a route and planning guide
Sinai – the trekking guide
South Downs Way (British Walking Guide)
Thames Path (British Walking Guide)
Tour du Mont Blanc
Trans-Canada Rail Guide
Trans-Siberian Handbook
Trekking in the Everest Region
The Walker's Anthology
The Walker's Anthology – further tales
West Highland Way (British Walking Guide)

For more information about Trailblazer and our
expanding range of guides, for guidebook updates or
for credit card mail order sales visit our website:

www.trailblazer-guides.com

TRAILBLAZER'S BRITISH WALKING GUIDES

We've applied to destinations which are closer to home Trailblazer's proven formula for publishing definitive practical route guides for adventurous travellers. Britain's network of long-distance trails enables the walker to explore some of the finest landscapes in the country's best walking areas. These are guides that are user-friendly, practical, informative and environmentally sensitive.

● **Unique mapping features** In many walking guidebooks the reader has to read a route description then try to relate it to the map. Our guides are much easier to use because walking directions, tricky junctions, places to stay and eat, points of interest and walking times are all written onto the maps themselves in the places to which they apply. With their uncluttered clarity, these are not general-purpose maps but fully edited maps drawn by walkers for walkers.

'The same attention to detail that distinguishes its other guides has been brought to bear here'.
THE SUNDAY TIMES

● **Largest-scale walking maps** At a scale of just under 1:20,000 (8cm or 3¹/₈ inches to one mile) the maps in these guides are bigger than even the most detailed British walking maps currently available in the shops.

● **Not just a trail guide – includes where to stay, where to eat and public transport** Our guidebooks cover the complete walking experience, not just the route. Accommodation options for all budgets are provided (pubs, hotels, B&Bs, campsites, bunkhouses, hostels) as well as places to eat. Detailed public transport information for all access points to each trail means that there are itineraries for all walkers, for hiking the entire route as well as for day or weekend walks.

Cleveland Way *Henry Stedman,* 1st edn, ISBN 978-1-905864-91-1, 240pp, 98 maps

Coast to Coast *Henry Stedman,* 10th edn, ISBN 978-1-912716-25-8, 268pp, 109 maps

Cornwall Coast Path (SW Coast Path Pt 2) *Stedman & Newton,* 7th edn,
  ISBN 978-1-912716-26-5, 352pp, 142 maps

Cotswold Way *Tricia & Bob Hayne,* 4th edn, ISBN 978-1-912716-04-3, 204pp, 53 maps

Dales Way *Henry Stedman,* 2nd edn, ISBN 978-1-912716-30-2, 192pp, 50 maps

Dorset & South Devon (SW Coast Path Pt 3) *Stedman & Newton,* 3rd edn,
  ISBN 978-1-912716-34-0, 340pp, 97 maps

Exmoor & North Devon (SW Coast Path Pt I) *Stedman & Newton,* 3rd edn,
  ISBN 978-1-9912716-24-1, 224pp, 68 maps

Glyndŵr's Way *Chris Scott,* 1st edn, ISBN 978-1-912716-32-6, 220pp, 70 maps (**mid 2023**)

Great Glen Way *Jim Manthorpe,* 2nd edn, ISBN 978-1-912716-10-4, 184pp, 50 maps

Hadrian's Wall Path *Henry Stedman,* 7th edn, ISBN 978-1-912716-37-1, 250pp, 60 maps

London LOOP *Henry Stedman,* 1st edn, ISBN 978-1-912716-21-0, 236pp, 60 maps

Norfolk Coast Path & Peddars Way *Alexander Stewart,* 1st edn,
  ISBN 978-1-905864-98-0, 224pp, 75 maps

North Downs Way *Henry Stedman,* 2nd edn, ISBN 978-1-905864-90-4, 240pp, 98 maps

Offa's Dyke Path *Keith Carter,* 5th edn, ISBN 978-1-912716-03-6, 268pp, 98 maps

Pembrokeshire Coast Path *Jim Manthorpe,* 6th edn, 978-1-912716-13-5, 236pp, 96 maps

Pennine Way *Stuart Greig,* 6th edn, ISBN 978-1-912716-33-3, 272pp, 138 maps

The Ridgeway *Nick Hill,* 5th edn, ISBN 978-1-912716-20-3, 208pp, 53 maps

South Downs Way *Jim Manthorpe,* 7th edn, ISBN 978-1-912716-23-4, 204pp, 60 maps

Thames Path *Joel Newton,* 3rd edn, ISBN 978-1-912716-27-2, 256pp, 99 maps

West Highland Way *Charlie Loram,* 8th edn, ISBN 978-1-912716-29-6, 224pp, 60 maps

'The Trailblazer series stands head, shoulders, waist and ankles above the rest.
They are particularly strong on mapping ...'
THE SUNDAY TIMES

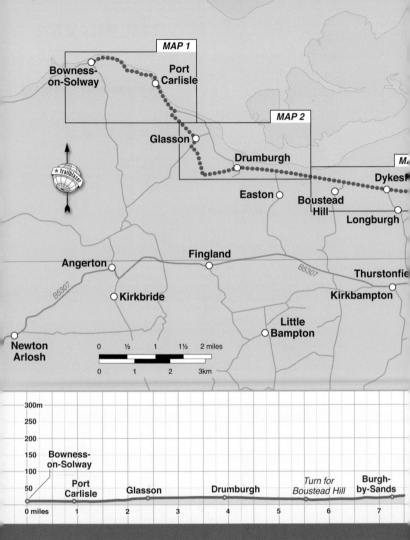

MAP 1

Bowness-
on-Solway

Port
Carlisle

Glasson

MAP 2

Drumburgh

Easton

Boustead
Hill

Dykest

Longburgh

Fingland

Angerton

B5307

Kirkbride

Little
Bampton

Thurstonfie

Kirkbampton

Newton
Arlosh

| 0 | ½ | 1 | 1½ | 2 miles |

| 0 | 1 | 2 | 3km |

300m
250
200
150
100
50

Bowness-
on-Solway

Port
Carlisle

Glasson

Drumburgh

*Turn for
Boustead Hill*

Burgh-
by-Sands

0 miles   1   2   3   4   5   6   7

E▷ Maps 1-6, Bowness-on-Solway to Carlisle
14 miles/22.5km – 5¼hrs

◁W Maps 6-1, Carlisle to Bowness-on-Solway
14 miles/22.5km – 5¼hrs

NOTE: Add 20-30% to these times to allow for stops

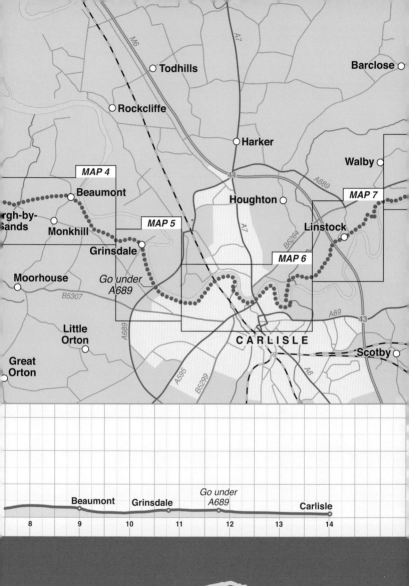

Todhills

Barclose

Rockcliffe

Harker

Walby

MAP 4

Beaumont

rgh-by-
ands

MAP 7

Monkhill

Houghton

MAP 5

Linstock

Grinsdale

MAP 6

Moorhouse

Go under
A689

**Little
Orton**

CARLISLE

Scotby

**Great
Orton**

Beaumont	Grinsdale	Go under A689	Carlisle
8	9	10	11	12	13	14

**Bowness-
on-Solway**

Wallsend

Carlisle

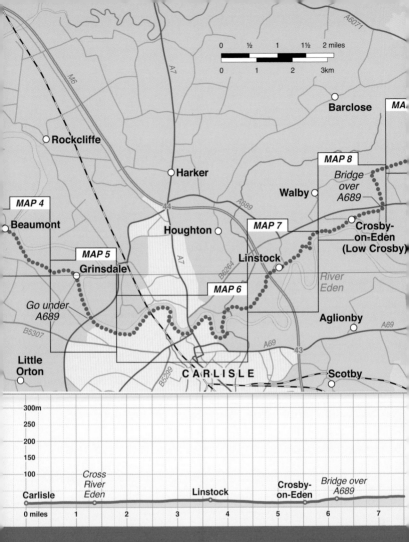

Maps 6-11, Carlisle to Walton
11½ miles/18.5km – 4hrs

Maps 11-6, Walton to Carlisle
11½ miles/18.5km – 4hrs

NOTE: Add 20-30% to these times to allow for stops

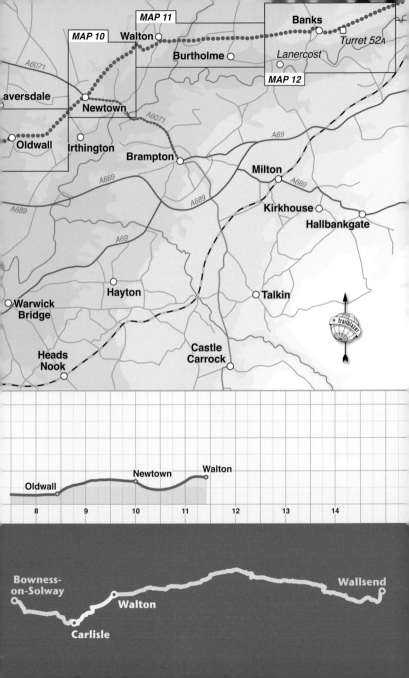

MAP 11

Banks

MAP 10

Walton

Turret 52A

Bartholme

Lanercost

aversdale

A6071

Newtown

A6071

MAP 12

Oldwall

Irthington

Brampton

Milton

A69

Kirkhouse

A69

Hallbankgate

A689

A689

A69

Warwick
Bridge

Hayton

Talkin

Heads
Nook

Castle
Carrock

★ trailblazer

Oldwall

Newtown

Walton

8   9   10   11   12   13   14

Bowness-
on-Solway

Walton

Wallsend

Carlisle

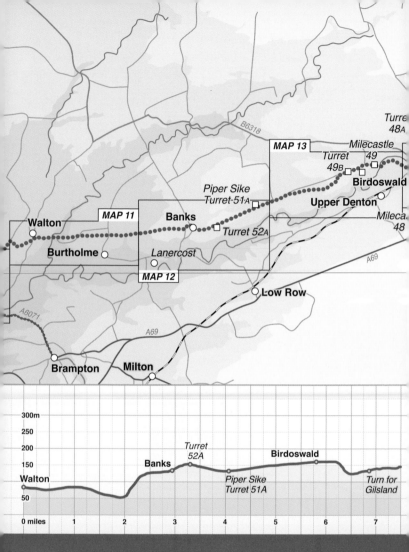

Maps 11-17, Walton to Steel Rigg
15 miles/24.2km – 6hrs 40 mins

Maps 17-11, Steel Rigg to Walton
15 miles/24.2km – 6hrs 40 mins

NOTE: Add 20-30% to these times to allow for stops

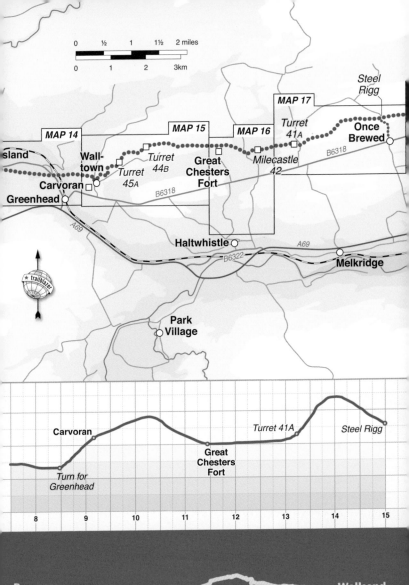

0   ½   1   1½   2 miles
0   1   2   3km

Steel Rigg

MAP 17

MAP 14

Wall-town

Turret 41A

Once Brewed

Carvoran

Turret 45A

Turret 44B

MAP 15

Great Chesters Fort

MAP 16

Milecastle 42

B6318

Greenhead

A69

B6318

Haltwhistle

A69

B6322

Melkridge

trailblazer

Park Village

Carvoran

Turret 41A

Steel Rigg

Great Chesters Fort

Turn for Greenhead

8   9   10   11   12   13   14   15

Bowness-on-Solway   Walton   Steel Rigg   Wallsend

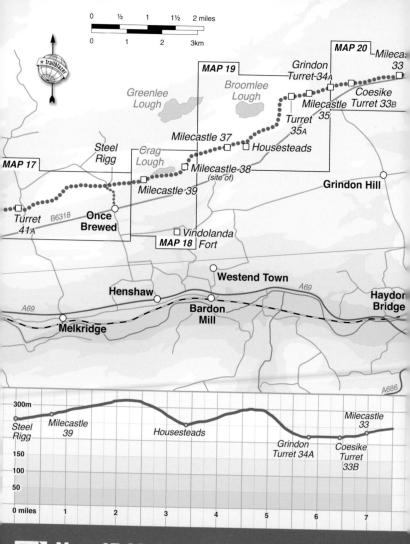

E▶ Maps 17-22, Steel Rigg to Chollerford
13 miles/21km – 5hrs 15 mins

◀W Maps 22-17, Chollerford to Steel Rigg
13 miles/21km – 5hrs 25 mins

NOTE: Add 20-30% to these times to allow for stops

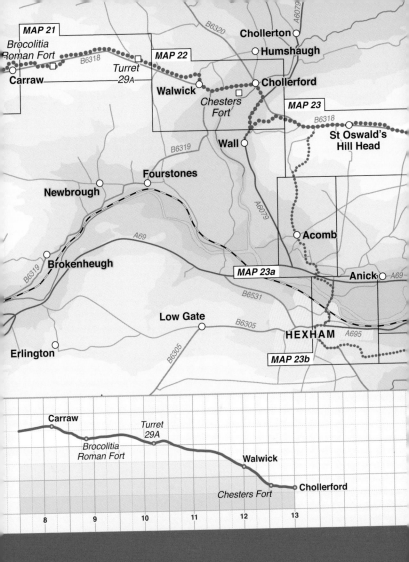

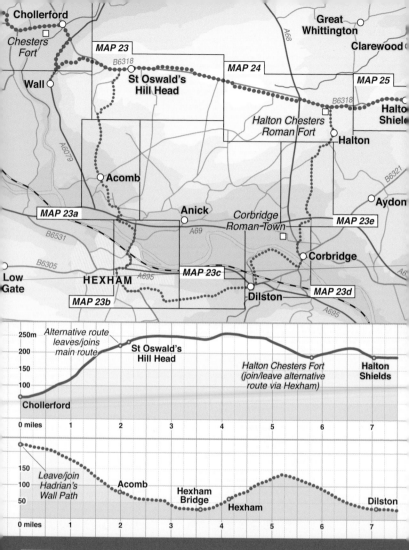

Map labels (top map):
Chollerford
Chesters Fort
MAP 23
Great Whittington
Clarewood
Wall
B6318
St Oswald's Hill Head
MAP 24
MAP 25
Halton Chesters Roman Fort
B6318
Halton Shields
A68
A6079
Acomb
MAP 23a
Anick
A69
Corbridge Roman-Town
MAP 23e
Aydon
B6321
B6531
B6305
Low Gate
HEXHAM
A695
MAP 23c
MAP 23b
Dilston
MAP 23d
Corbridge
A695

Elevation profile (upper):
250m
200
150
100
Alternative route leaves/joins main route
St Oswald's Hill Head
Halton Chesters Fort (join/leave alternative route via Hexham)
Halton Shields
Chollerford
0 miles   1   2   3   4   5   6   7

Elevation profile (lower):
150
100
50
Leave/join Hadrian's Wall Path
Acomb
Hexham Bridge
Hexham
Dilston
0 miles   1   2   3   4   5   6   7

E▶ Maps 22-28, Chollerford to Heddon-o/t-Wall
15 miles/24.2km – 7hrs

◀W Maps 28-22, Heddon-on-the-Wall to Ch'ford
15 miles/24.2km – 7hrs

Corbridge-Hexham-Acomb alternative route (Maps 23a-e)
12 miles/19.5km – E▶4hrs 30mins / ◀W4hrs 50mins

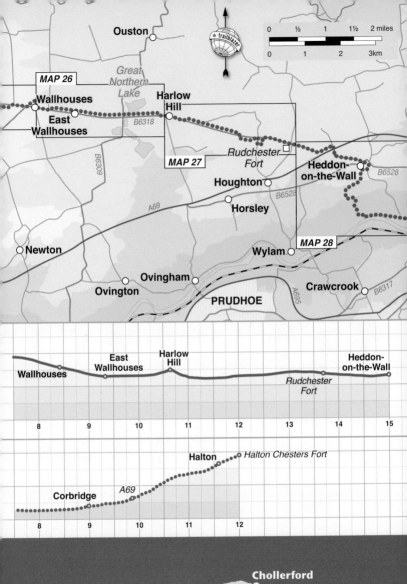

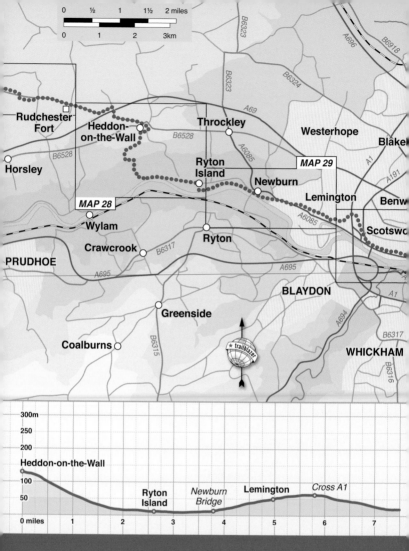

Heddon-on-the-Wall

300m
250
200
150
100
50
0 miles   1   2   3   4   5   6   7

Ryton Island   Newburn Bridge   Lemington   Cross A1

E▷ Maps 28-33, Heddon-on-the-Wall to Wallsend
15 miles/24.2km – 5hrs

◁W Maps 33-28, Wallsend to Heddon-on-the-Wall
15 miles/24.2km – 5hrs 10mins

NOTE: Add 20-30% to these times to allow for stops

B1505

Forest
Hall

A189

A191

A19

wdon

A1

B1318

A189

LONGBENTON

Gosforth

A191

Battle
Hill

Howdon

A1058

A193

A186

A1058

A188

WALLSEND

NEWCASTLE
UPON TYNE

Jesmond

A1058

Heaton

MAP 33

Segedunum

B1297

A167

B1318

A1058

A193

Walker

HEBBURN

enham

A189

A187

City
Centre

A186

B1516

30

69

Redheugh
Bridge

Byker

Monkton

A185

ers

aradise

A595

Elswick

Millennium
Bridge

GATESHEAD

A184

MAP 32

A194

MAP 31

B1426

B1426

Wardley

A184

Dunston
Hill

A184

A167

Mount
Pleasant

Felling

A195

A692

A1

Team
Valley

B1296

Leam
Lane

B1288

A194(M)

Vickers

Redheugh
Bridge

Millennium
Bridge

Byker

Segedunum

8   9   10   11   12   13   14   15

Bowness-
on-Solway

Heddon-
on-the-Wall

Wallsend

Distance chart (miles in upright, kilometres in *italic*)

	Wallsend (Newcastle)	Newburn	Heddon	East Wallhouses	Port Gate	Wall	Chollerford	Housesteads	Steel Rigg	Carvoran	Gilsland
Newburn	11										
	17.6										
Heddon-on-the-Wall	15	4									
	24	*6.4*									
E Wallhouses	21	10	6								
	33.6	*16*	*9.5*								
Port Gate	25	14	10	4							
	39.9	*22.4*	*16*	*6.4*							
Wall	29	18	14	8	4						
	46.3	*28.8*	*22.4*	*12.8*	*6.4*						
Chollerford	30	19	15	9	5	1					
	47.9	*30.4*	*24*	*14.4*	*8*	*1.6*					
Housesteads	39	28	24	18	14	10	9				
	62.4	*44.8*	*38.4*	*28.8*	*22.4*	*16*	*14.4*				
Steel Rigg	43	32	28	22	18	14	13	4			
	68.8	*51.2*	*44.8*	*35.2*	*28.8*	*22.4*	*20.8*	*6.4*			
Carvoran	48.5	37.5	33.5	27.5	23.5	19.5	18.5	9.5	5.5		
	77.6	*60*	*53.6*	*44*	*37.6*	*31.2*	*29.6*	*15.2*	*8.8*		
Gilsland	51	40	36	30	26	22	21	12	8	2.5	
	81.6	*64*	*57.6*	*48*	*41.6*	*35.2*	*33.6*	*19.2*	*12.8*	*4*	
Birdoswald	53	42	38	32	28	24	23	14	10	4.5	2
	84.8	*67.2*	*60.8*	*51.2*	*44.8*	*38.4*	*36.8*	*22.4*	*16*	*7.2*	*3.2*
Banks	55.5	44.5	40.5	34.5	30	26.5	25.5	16.5	12.5	7	4.5
	88.8	*71.2*	*64.8*	*55.2*	*48*	*42.2*	*40.8*	*26.4*	*20*	*11.2*	*7.2*
Walton	58	47	43	37	33	29	28	19	15	9.5	7
	92.8	*75.2*	*68.8*	*59.2*	*52.8*	*46.4*	*44.8*	*30.4*	*24*	*15.2*	*11.2*
Newtown	60	49	45	39	35	31	30	21	17	11.5	9
	96	*78.4*	*72*	*62.4*	*56*	*49.6*	*48*	*33.6*	*27.2*	*18.4*	*14.4*
Crosby-on-Eden	65	54	50	44	40	36	35	26	22	16.5	14
	104	*86.4*	*80*	*70.4*	*64*	*57.6*	*56*	*41.6*	*35.2*	*26.4*	*22.4*
Carlisle	70	59	55	49	45	41	40	31	27	21.5	19
	112	*94.4*	*88*	*78.4*	*72*	*65.6*	*64*	*49.6*	*43.2*	*34.4*	*30.4*
Grinsdale	73.5	62.5	58.5	52.5	48.5	44.5	43.5	34.5	30.5	25	22.5
	117.6	*100*	*93.6*	*84*	*77.6*	*71.2*	*69.6*	*55.2*	*48.8*	*40*	*36*
Burgh-by-Sands	77	66	62	56	52	48	47	38	34	28.5	26
	123.2	*105.6*	*99.2*	*89.6*	*83.2*	*76.8*	*75.2*	*60.8*	*54.4*	*45.6*	*41.6*
Drumburgh	79.5	68.5	64.5	58.5	54.5	50.5	49.5	40.5	36.5	31	28.5
	127.2	*109.6*	*103.2*	*93.6*	*87.2*	*80.8*	*79.2*	*64.8*	*58.4*	*49.6*	*45.6*
Glasson	80.5	69.5	65.5	59.5	55.5	51.5	50.5	41.5	37.5	32	29.5
	128.8	*111.2*	*104.8*	*95.2*	*88.8*	*82.4*	*80.8*	*66.4*	*60*	*51.2*	*47.2*
Port Carlisle	83	72	68	62	58	54	53	44	40	34.5	32
	132.8	*115.2*	*108.8*	*99.2*	*92.8*	*86.4*	*84.8*	*70.4*	*64*	*55.2*	*51.2*
Bowness-on-Solway	84	73	69	63	59	55	54	45	41	35.5	33
	134.4	*116.8*	*110.4*	*100.8*	*94.4*	*88*	*86.4*	*72*	*65.6*	*56.8*	*52.8*